I'LL LOVE YOU IF...

I'LL LOVE YOU IF...

Matthew Huggins

Psychology News Press
London

First published in 2009
by Psychology News Press
9a Artillery Passage
London E1 7LN

dcpsychologynews@googlemail.com

Set in Palatino
by Keyboard Services, Luton
keyboardserv@sky.com

Printed in Great Britain by
the MPG Books Group, Bodmin and King's Lynn

Distributed by Melia Publishing Services
Godalming
Telephone 01483 869839
melia@melia.co.uk

ISBN 978-0-907633-18-1

Contents

Foreword

The onion memory, as the poet Craig Raine puts it.

It has become common for memoirs to include verbatim conversations. *I Love You If...* includes many of these but they fall into two very different categories. The author's memories of what happened to him as a child and a teenager, recollections of family life and events in care, are emotionally accurate and reflect reality. But since he doesn't have total recall they are not necessarily accurate word for word. As a psychologist I have written a good deal about the frailties of human memory.

But the accounts of conversations in the chapter on the politics of Barking and Dagenham Council are totally accurate because there are either witnesses or transcripts of some of the key encounters that took place. These can be found on our website, details of which are on page iv.

Matthew Huggins' experiences are a timely reminder of what children in care often have to go through.

David Cohen

1

Aged Ten – Going Into Care

It was the night before Mother's Day and Mum was back at work. I lay awake in my bed, anxious and in despair. I got up and climbed the stairs into the lounge where Kevin, my stepdad, lay sleeping on the sofa in front of the gas fire. A cigarette burned in the ashtray, and a beer can lay crushed on the floor. The room smelt stale with beer, smoke and ash. I hated that smell: *his* smell.

I sat watching him, a thin man with an ugly mole on his face. He was snoring and dribbling. I couldn't stop hearing his vicious words in my head and they connected with the pit of my stomach. It was a strange feeling, like just before you go over the peak of a rollercoaster. My body could feel his drunken beatings all over again, each sharp pain a reminder that I didn't belong here.

I walked around the room. I didn't know what I was going to do next, I just knew I had to do something with this feeling, expel it somehow; open the lid of the shaken coke bottle. Over on the sideboard I could see two homemade Mother's Day cards. My brothers must have made them. By then she had as much chance of getting a Mother's Day card from me as I had of playing for Manchester United. I took one of the cards and sat watching the fire: my mum's words rang through my head *'You do what you have to do Matthew, but he is staying.'*

I placed the card in the fire and let it burn slowly at the edges, tempting the flames to do what I dared not. In seconds it was alight; I took the burning card to the sofa and placed it underneath. Within seconds the sofa was burning. My heart was pounding as I raced down the stairs back to my bedroom. I could smell the smoke, I could hear the roaring flames – but I couldn't hear Kevin. Was he dead? My brothers! I didn't think about my brothers. What could I do now? If I moved he'd know it was me. The smoke alarm drowned out my thoughts and soon I heard loud coughing and wheezing. A few minutes later I heard the loud thumping of someone running down the stairs. I kept my head down and closed my eyes pretending to be asleep; I could feel Kevin looking in the room. He was coughing, but didn't say anything. He just walked back up the stairs.

I hadn't planned to set the sofa alight. I didn't want to hurt my brothers and was relieved they were safe. But as I drifted off to sleep, exhausted, I couldn't help but feel a little disappointed that Kevin was still alive.

'What the fuck do you think you were doing?' I woke up, startled, yet immediately aware it was Mum.

'Did you think about your brothers? You could have killed someone.'

It took a few minutes for me to realise what she was talking about. Then it sunk in; last night, the fire, the sofa, the smoke. Then it really sunk in. *'You could have killed someone.'* Despite my hatred of Kevin I felt guilty, even ashamed. I hadn't planned on starting a fire. How could things ever get better now? I had to leave and it had to be that day. I got myself dressed. I knew where I was going – Southend, where my real Dad lived.

The road was lit by multi-coloured lights, the magical

sound of alluring tunes and money hitting metal from below. People milled in and out of the arcades holding hands, eating candy floss, smiling. I could smell the fish and chips, taste the vinegar; it was ice-cold, yet the stars were clear; I remember the stars from that night well. I looked up at them as I hung from the side of the bridge, my feet resting on the narrow ledge, and wondering where I would be tomorrow. I held on to the railing behind me as I leaned out over the drop. Across the road was the entrance to the pier; the longest in the world, a full mile in length. I had never walked it, though I'd always wanted to. My heart was thumping as I glanced down at the road from on top of the bridge. It seemed so far down, and only my grip on the cold railing kept me from falling.

I don't know where the police officers came from; two just suddenly appeared, one down on the road below me and one on the bridge behind, both calm.

'Hello son. I'm David,' the one behind me said. His voice was soothing. How could he be so calm with me hanging off the side of a bridge?

'What are you doing up here then?'

'Stay there. I'm not going home'. I shivered, and my voice shook as I spoke. I was scared he would grab me. I started to cry from fear: the fear that I would slip and fall, and the fear of what would happen if I climbed back onto solid ground. Where would they take me?

'That's okay, we are not here to take you home. What's your name?'

'I'm not telling you. Just stay away from me.'

'I'm not moving from here. I just want to know who I am talking to. You know my name, don't you?'

They couldn't tell much from my name, could they? I didn't want to make him angry.

3

'Matthew.'

'Matthew. I have a son called Matthew. I would be very scared to see him on a bridge like this', he said.

I was crying loudly now. More people were watching and I could hear sirens in the background. I didn't want to be on this ledge any more. I didn't want to fall.

'My Mum wouldn't care.'

'I'm sure that's not true, Matthew. You seem like a lovely kid. I bet she is at home now wondering where you are. What are you doing out here?'

'I'm not coming down. Not until you promise me I don't have to go home. I am not going home. I'll jump, I will'. I didn't want to jump. I wasn't going to jump.

'Calm down, Matthew. Let's talk about this. Nobody is going to make you go home. You don't have to go anywhere tonight if you don't want to. But I can't let you stay that side of the bridge, it's not safe. Why don't you come this side and we can talk about it? You can tell me why you don't want to go home.'

'Do you promise I don't have to go home?'

'You don't have to go home tonight. Come this side and we'll talk about the rest of it.'

That was enough for me; I couldn't stand any more of this, with all those people watching, with my hands going numb as they gripped the cold railing. I was terrified that my feet would slip. I didn't come here to die. I just didn't see any other way to make them listen.

I let them take me down.

I didn't stay calm for long. At the police station they put me in a cell, shutting the thick steel door behind them. There was a loud thud as it hit the doorframe, and then the lock clicked, caging me. The room was small and white with a grey floor. There was a round metal toilet in the

4

corner and a big blue mat next to the wall. I couldn't breathe. I didn't understand what I had done wrong; why was I locked up? Did Mum and Kevin plan this? Did they know about the fire? I screamed for them to let me out.

I banged my small fists hard on the steel door, barely making a sound. I noticed a button next to the door and pressed it repeatedly; it made a loud beeping noise. A few times policemen looked through the hole in the top of the door, but when they saw I was okay, they left me again.

I kept pressing the buzzer until it stopped making any more sound. I started hitting my head against the wall shouting loudly that I was killing myself. I picked up the side of the mat and let it drop so it made a loud bang. When they came to check on me again I tried to put my fingers in the plug socket. Suddenly lots of police rushed in and pushed me down to the floor, holding me tight. I kicked and punched, trying to bite my way out of their grip. Soon enough, I couldn't move. I could see that some of the officers were distressed. They hadn't become coppers to manhandle little kids. It's not the kind of night on the job you boast of to your wife or mates.

Somebody talked to me, soothing words, soft soap. They were trying to calm me down. I screamed myself hoarse and cried myself dry. In time, they loosened their grip and said that I could come out and wait with them if I promised to be calm. Five minutes later, I sat sipping my warm, sugary tea. Someone waited with me, talking quietly, in a soothing tone. I don't know what they were talking about, but I started to feel safe again.

Eventually a woman in normal clothes arrived; she talked to the officers briefly, and then sat in a quiet room, some paper on her knee, facing me. She was from Social Services, she said. Her job was to help me. She had been told what had happened but she wanted to hear it from me. It was important I told her the truth. There was something about the way she said it, the way she looked me straight in my eyes, and the way she sat waiting for me to talk, that made me believe her. I told her everything. I didn't want to live at home any more and if they took me back, I'd kill myself. I remember so clearly her face when she kept contact with my eyes, held my hands and told me she believed me. The minute she said those words I started to cry. I knew I wasn't going home, for now at least.

A few hours later

I couldn't understand what Mum had to be so upset about. This was all her fault. For years home had been an unhappy place. She was always working and my stepdad did the 'caring'. When he was sober he didn't seem to like me much. But he really couldn't stand me when drunk. I knew this from the bruises his beatings left on my skin, and the way he would always put me down when mum wasn't around. I didn't like him much either. He was lanky, skinny and weak; the mole above his lip was ugly – a reflection, I thought, of his inner ugliness. It hadn't always been like this with him, though.

I remember the first day I met Kevin. My two younger brothers and I went on a picnic with Mum while Dad was at work. It was a scorching day and we ate under a giant green tree; but the rest of the details remain a blur, except for seeing Mum and Kevin together. I felt how attracted they were to each other almost immediately. Brief, intimate touches of the hand, sly glances when they spoke about each other to us, as if they knew something we didn't.

Mum used a soft voice when she spoke to him, a gentle tone that I knew well, as she'd sometimes used it to lull me to sleep. At the time I didn't understand exactly what all this meant. But I knew what it felt like: wrong, all wrong, a betrayal; at the age of only seven I can't have known they were having an affair, but children can sense danger.

Later that day Mum delicately approached the subject of what I thought about 'Mum's new friend.'

'I don't know. He seems nice'. I really didn't know. He was nice. What more could a seven-year-old say about someone after an afternoon's picnic?

'You see, he is a very special friend to me,' she said.

I was right, there was something more to this than the word 'friend' suggested.

'And me and your Dad haven't been getting on very well for a long time now,' she went on. 'He's always at work and when he is here he is always asleep'. Dad was always away. He worked with big mainframe computers although I never really understood what he did. I would hear him leave and return on his giant roaring motorbike, but I didn't see him until the weekends. Then he would be sleeping; he slept all the time, it seemed. And when he was awake he didn't seem to like being with me.

'Do you like living with your Dad?' She knew the answer. She used that soft voice again, as if she were convincing me to eat my vegetables or tidy my room. When she was in a good mood she would speak like this and I liked it. It made me feel loved and I knew if I did what she wanted me to do I'd get a hug; *'I'm really pleased with you Matthew.'* But she had a harsh voice too.

'I don't know. It's not much fun with Daddy. I don't think I make him very happy.'

7

'I was thinking your Dad could move out of the house for a while. Let us have some time together, just the four of us'. That sounded good! He often shouted and ordered. I always felt uncomfortable around the house; a strange feeling that I wasn't welcome, that I was somehow different to my brothers. Dad was the one who made me feel that way.

'What do you think? Do you want your Dad to move out for a while?'

I said yes, so did my brothers; although at three Danny was too young to understand. The idea didn't seem all that bad. We could have our Mum all to ourselves for while. It felt exciting, like we were about to have a massive adventure.

I didn't expect Dad to leave so soon. I don't remember him saying goodbye, but maybe he did. In my mind he was there in the morning and gone by night. Mum told us the news. I didn't feel even a little bit sad; it may seem strange when I say that. But we had never been that close. He seemed to like my brothers more, particularly John, who was just a few years younger than me. I felt guilty, though, because it was my decision for him to go. Looking back now, it seems strange that Mum seemed to need me to say I wanted him to go from the house; I couldn't work out why until almost twenty years later. At the time I just thought it was because I was the oldest.

The next day my guilt turned to anger and a feeling of betrayal. 'Mum's special friend' was in the kitchen making us breakfast with a big smile on his face. They explained that Kevin was moving in and that we would be a family together.

'Kevin's a nice man and makes me happy. He will make you happy, too. Things are going to be different, son.'

8

There had been something in those gooey glances. That's what the picnic had been about. It all happened so quickly. It was like I had been tricked and manipulated. I'd sensed there was something 'romantic' up under the giant tree, but Kevin being here, in our house, was a shock. This wasn't part of the deal I'd signed up to. I wasn't the only one surprised. My Granddad remembers popping into see us on a Sunday soon after Dad left, only to be greeted at the door by a skinny, bony, man wearing only boxer shorts, who blew smoke in his face.

My memories of that time – and this book is all about memory – are happier than many others of my childhood. Our loveless home suddenly blossomed like a dying plant given new light and life by a burst of sunshine. The sunshine was Kevin, and Mum was much happier. We did things together as a family. On the weekends we drove to Canvey Island and spent the day on a special patch of beach, eating cockles and toying with the tuppenny fruit machines. Mum had friends come round for drinks and parties. Most of them had children so we'd play kids' games while the adults partied in the lounge, drinking their wine, laughing and chatting.

Mum even started working at something she enjoyed. For a few years she had been doing a Saturday job at Argos; that was where she met Kevin, who was her boss. But she loved to cook. She'd bake sweets and cakes on a Friday night and sell them at the Church market on Saturday mornings. We'd get to eat the leftover rock cakes, coconut ices, fudge and more besides. I can still taste the buttery, sugary icing on the fairy cakes. They were heaven on a stick for a kid.

The heaven for Mum was independence and making her own money, however little. She was also becoming something of an 'entrepreneur', though I didn't know the word, of course. She wanted to free herself from her lack of education and make her way in the world. We'd wait outside in Kevin's car while Mum finished her agency catering jobs, waitressing at manor hall weddings. She eventually got a full-time job at an American-style restaurant. Our sugar almonds were replaced by burgers, fries and two or three hours of madly frantic play at Al's Adventure world.

Mum's start-up spirit flourished with help from that seductive charm I'd seen her use on Kevin. In no time she was a 'duty manager'. What this meant to me was my Mum wore nice black clothes to work instead of the red and white striped costume the waitresses wore. She had a big walkie-talkie which would crackle into life every now and then; Mum would talk back, suddenly looking very important. As we entered the building the giant men at the door with things in their ears would nod at her and she would smile back; except for one big black man who would kiss my Mum on both cheeks affectionately and laugh and joke then place his hand over mine, like a father clasping his baby's little finger, and ask me how I was. I felt enormous pride at these times. My Mum was the boss. I didn't know what that meant exactly, but it involved nods, free food and a huge walkie-talkie – to a nine-year-old, it was all very impressive.

Mum put all her new-found energy for life into her career. As time went by our family weekends away came to an end. She'd work until the early hours of the morning, sleeping by day. Soon her career outshone Kevin's.

After a few odd jobs delivering *The Yellow Pages* Kevin became a milkman. He'd start work as dawn broke and mum finished hers. He would be back by the time we left for school; we were now old enough to send ourselves off. I would get Danny dressed so Mum could rest in the morning. She had definitely changed; she was grumpier. She had always been temperamental, to the point I was never quite sure what mood she would be in when I got home from school. But when she flew off the handle, she would soon make it better with a hug and a kind word. Now she didn't seem to bother. It would be our fault; we were arguing too much, in trouble at school too much, not appreciating her work enough.

'I work hard for this family' she'd say, as if we had foisted some unbearable weight onto her shoulders. I felt lost. I just seemed to get things wrong all the time; 'Why do you always start arguments with your brother, Matthew?' she'd ask. 'Why is it always you who gets bullied at school and not the others?' 'I work hard for this family and all you do is cause me trouble.'

Her relationship wasn't going well either. The cuddles and kisses with Kevin had been replaced by violent arguments. I remember arguments about how much Mum worked and Mum would fight back. She earned more and put food on the table. The fights went on for what seemed like hours; crying, shouting and swearing at each other as if they were two gladiators bludgeoning each other with accusations. Mum had blossomed at work and now resented the shackles of a young family and the burden of a deadbeat partner.

Kevin couldn't deal with it all, and hit the bottle. I remember violent punch-ups at his family's place on Christmas day. His brother-in-law knocked out his father; Kevin screamed that he was going to find a shovel to bury him. My grandparents didn't drink and I don't remember Dad drinking that much. Exposure to drunkenness was a new experience for me, and a frightening one.

When Mum was off work Kevin would go down to the

local pub; when she was at work he would go to her restaurant while we played in the adventure playground. By the time he picked us up I could smell stale beer on his breath; he'd speed home in his white van with us in the back, driving so erratically our bodies shook with the vibrations of the vehicle in sync with his screaming. He was like a crazed monster on a suicide mission. He thought it was funny. The more I got scared, the more I cried, the more he'd laugh and call me a wimp. He sometimes put his face inches from mine so I could smell his breath, a weird mixture of cigarettes and beer that made me feel sick. The final insult was that he'd spit at me.

It was when Kevin was in these moods that he started to beat me.

He'd hit me hard, without any care for the pain he inflicted, then leave me alone. My brothers would be curled up on the sofa watching a film with him while I was crying in my room. When Mum called home to let him know what time she was leaving work I'd scream and shout for her, desperate to be rescued. But I usually wasn't allowed to speak to her.

Like many abusive men (as I now know) Kevin would calm me down, apologise and rationalise that if I'd just 'behaved' it wouldn't have come to this. He'd put his arm around me as if nothing had happened and I would be consoled. We would snuggle with my brothers watching the film. My brothers always seemed to escape this treatment. Some people have asked me since, why me? Why did I get punished and not my brothers? I didn't know the reasons for my being singled out and how could I have known? I was nine years old. Kevin had no children of his own, and didn't really know how to deal with us. Perhaps it was just that I became the focus of his frustrations about life, love and money. I will never know why and it is not really for me to answer. I was the child; he was the adult.

I might have been beaten up but I wasn't beaten down. I started to fantasise about leaving home and then my fantasy became a plan. I was sick of feeling like a bad child all the time, a failure in my mother's eyes. I didn't get on with John and Danny was too young. I hated my life. I knew there was another option. There was a boy at school who lived in a children's home. If I ran away I'd get some refuge from all this; I could leave it all behind and start again. I wouldn't need to worry about getting things wrong or Kevin's drunken violence. So I ran away. The first time I didn't plan where I'd go or what I'd do. I just found myself doing it.

One day on my way to school I took a detour. Just like that! I didn't know how far I was going. I started across some large fields with crops double the size of my body. It was silent and scary. It reminded me of the jungle and I tried to put the thoughts of snakes and spiders out of my head. The crop fields seem to go on forever and I kept thinking that they must already be trying to find me. As I got the other end of the fields I got on a bus. I went straight to the top of the bus, and kept my head down. I had no idea where the bus was going. I just wanted to get far away. Several minutes later the bus stopped and I saw police cars blocking the road.

Two big burly policemen came on the bus and one of them picked me up, screaming and crying, threw me over his shoulders and shouted, 'got him.'

My great escape had lasted all of four hours. I was home by lunch-time; my Mum was distressed, Kevin angry. I don't remember much from that afternoon, except going straight to sleep, exhausted.

That first time, Mum asked why I was so unhappy at home. When I told her about how Kevin treated me when she wasn't around, she asked him to leave. That night she stayed up with me watching telly, hugging me and showering me with love. I was safe and warm in her arms and she wouldn't let him hurt me again. Happiness didn't last long. The next day he was back and, it seemed, back to stay. They took me to McDonalds to 'talk'. Kevin said he was sorry and sometimes he got angry with things I did, but he promised he wouldn't lose his temper any more. I didn't believe him. It felt like those times when, after one of Mum's calls, he'd make his peace with me before she came back from work.

We got back home and I told her I didn't want him to stay. There are those moments in life when you can describe exactly what was said and how you felt and will never forget a bit of it. I knew this was one of those moments the minute it happened. We were standing at the top of the stairs.

'Is *he* staying?' I asked. I already knew the answer by the way she looked down at the floor. She paused a moment, then raised her head and looked straight at me.

'Yes, he is staying.'

'If he's staying then I'm leaving.'

'Matthew, you do what you have to do, but he is staying.'

At that exact moment I knew I was leaving and never coming back. I knew I had lost my Mum, and that things were never going to be the same between us again.

In the weeks that followed the pressure got worse. I had tantrums, on a scale that scared Mum so much she would call Grandad over to calm me. As my desperation with life at home grew so did my temper; even Grandad, who I loved so much, couldn't calm me. Once I punched him in the face. I loved him and didn't know how I would face him again. It just made me want to leave all the more. I thought I could go and live with my Dad. I forgot in my confusion that he hadn't shown me much love or affection. Instead I forged a dream that life with him would be good. Just the two of us, a fresh start. I wouldn't feel guilty all the time and I could start again at school and make new friends.

But I had to get in touch with him. At first they wouldn't give me the number. Mum said he didn't need to be worried by this. But I would sit there with the *Yellow Pages* and dial every James I could find in the Southend area. Eventually they gave it to me; but it just rang and rang and I cried and cried, uncontrollably until I slept. Kevin had stopped hitting me after I ran away, perhaps just because Mum was taking time off work to look after me. She didn't know what to do and was visibly distressed. It didn't hurt me seeing her this way; it just made me angry. How could *she* be upset, I thought.

I'm not sure what happened the second time I ran away. I know it lasted longer and I know I ended up being caught by the police in Southend. That made sense; my Dad lived there. I didn't know exactly where though and I didn't find him. He didn't come to collect me either.

The next day we went to an old stone building that looked like a little castle; it was surrounded by large tower blocks, council houses and flats. Mum explained that it was a social service office and that we were there to see a social worker. Grandad waited outside with me as Mum and Kevin went in to talk to the social worker alone. I sat there wondering what they were talking about, angry that I didn't get to talk to them first. I wanted to tell someone how I felt and what Kevin was doing to me. They were getting their chance first. The social worker commented in his report how happy they seemed together. They said my Dad never gave me any affection and I was happy with Kevin, choosing to call him Dad very soon after they got together. He had given me lots of love and affection, as had Mum, even more than my two younger brothers got. I needed it, they said, because I was a difficult child, a bit of a loner. They had tried so hard to understand me and meet my needs but were finding it harder as time went by.

Eventually I was called in. I could tell, from the looks on their faces and the way they were sitting grouped together, facing me, that it was all decided.

'Matthew, I've had the opportunity to talk with your Mum and Dad. They care about you a lot and are very worried about how you have been behaving recently.' I looked at them coldly.

'I just want to leave home.'

'Why?'

Because I don't fit in, I thought. Because Kevin treats me like an unwanted piece of meat, gets drunk and hits me. Because my Mum is never home.

'I just don't want to live there any more,' I just said.

'Well, that is not a reason,' the social worker said. 'We have to have a very good reason for taking you away from home. Your Mum and Dad want you home'. They were holding hands. It hurt me to see them so united, when I was so divided from them. Mum wouldn't believe me if I told her how he treated me when she wasn't there. How could I say it with him in the room?

'I just don't like it there any more.'

The social worker kept trying to get more out of me. I think Mum and Grandad said a few things, but by this time I had shut down completely. I didn't care what they said. I knew this man wasn't going to help me; I was going to have to go home.

'Matthew, I can't help if you don't tell me anything.' Silence. 'Okay. After assessing the situation I have to agree that home with your Mum and Dad is the best place for you.'

'You can't make me stay there. I'll just run away.'

'And you will be taken back.'

'I'll keep running away. I don't want to live there.'

'If you tell us what's wrong, maybe we can help you.'

I was desperate now.

'I'll only tell you if *he* goes.'

'Who? Your Dad?' The social worker asked.

'He's not my Dad. If he goes I'll come out and tell you what's wrong.'

There was an argument outside. Mum and Grandad asked Kevin to leave so they could talk to me: Kevin stormed out, slamming the door. I came out and sat down with them. With my Grandad's arm around me I broke down. I told them how Kevin would get drunk and hit me, how he would call me names and treat me badly. I hated living with him and didn't want to any more. That was the night Mum asked him to leave. But the next day he was back: and, as my Mum said at the top of the stairs, he was back to stay.

Once I knew he was staying, I was determined to go. I went downstairs with black bags and packed all my stuff into them. I placed them in the corridor ready to go. She said I could do what I wanted, but she had to go back to work, she had already taken enough time off. Over the week the tantrums were replaced by self-seclusion; I kept myself away from the family. I declined any sweets or treats; I stopped going to school. I was like a prisoner

17

protesting at his treatment through hunger strike; my hunger strike was the withdrawal of my love for Mum and the family. They would not let me leave, so I left in all ways but my physical presence.

Kevin hadn't hit me for a few months, since I had started having problems and running away, and we kept out of each other's way. The night before I left I got into an argument with him about something, I can't remember what; he was drunk and lost his temper. He raised his hand to me and I shouted to him to do it, hit me, then they will see what you are like. He stopped. Then he picked me up, wearing only my pants, and put me outside the front door. I screamed and cried.

'If you want to leave home, leave home. See what it's like outside in the cold for a while'. Then he slammed the door shut. I screamed and shouted for him to let me in, banging on the door.

Back at my grandparents' after the meeting I ran up to the bedroom and barricaded myself in. They banged on the door and shouted through to let them in, pleading with me.

Balgores 1992 – my first children's home

The car was silent, as if someone had just died. The air was thick with words unspoken and raw unexpressed emotion. It was day, but the sky was dark, and rain relentlessly beat down on the car. I sat behind the woman driving, my legs just touching the floor; I was skinny and pale white, drained of all hope. I didn't look ten; more like eight. My sea blue eyes and sandy blonde hair disguised a lost, washed-up boy.

'You'll be home soon.' Hearing the pain in my Mum's voice made me fidget.

'This is just for a little while; when you want to you can come home. I want you home Matthew.'

She was crying now. I felt squeezed; I couldn't expel this tension. She touched my hand; I flinched and whipped it away. She started to cry again.

I couldn't feel any love for her right at this time. I didn't know if I would ever again.

As the car pulled into the gravel drive of my new home I noticed just how big the place was. It had a red brick exterior with large white framed windows. The building had two floors with an indented flat roof. I noticed two heavy men outside, who looked as if they could squash me like a grape if they sat on me. Two children much older than me, fifteen, sixteen I thought, were up on the roof, swearing at the two men below. I started to feel scared.

Inside the walls were white but dirty. There was no carpet, just a mucky grey lino floor. I noticed a big fire hose reel that looked out of place in a home where children lived. Notices warned people of health and safety, whatever that meant, strip lights lit the corridor. There was a smell of bleach, yet everywhere looked unclean, bruised and battered.

'Hello. You must be Mrs James. I'm Irene, the house warden here at Balgores.' The very old woman addressed Mum, taking no notice of me.

'And I'm Maggie from Social Services.'

I had been wondering who the lady driver was. She had arrived at the police station with Mum saying she was taking me to a new place to stay. I had been too nervous to ask anything more and too relieved that I wasn't going back home to care. The old woman who introduced herself was big and wore an ugly flowery dress that was so short you could see her fat legs. They were hairy; I noticed her lip and that was hairy too, and her chin had a beard. I immediately didn't trust her.

Irene showed us around; the corridors seemed to go on forever. There was a huge dining room not unlike the one at school. In the lounge children much older than me were playing a computer game. The bearded woman said something to them but they didn't look away from their game. I was pleased about the computer though; we never had a computer at home. In the corner there was a pool table. This was even better news. This place was going to be fun.

The bedrooms were on the top floor – rows and rows of bedrooms. I wondered just how many other children lived here. Irene opened one door and announced this was my room. My face dropped. The walls were a muddied and shabby white like the rest of the building. There was a bedside cabinet, a wardrobe and a chest of drawers; two of them were broken. The floor felt hard and cold. Then I noticed there were two beds. I didn't know I had to share a room – would my roommate like me? Would I like them? I still wet the bed. Miraculously then, the woman said not to worry about the second bed as they already had too many rooms. I was so relieved I forgot about the shabbiness. I'd done so much to get away from home, no matter how bad it was I knew I couldn't go back now. *Kevin* was still there.

The bearded woman sat behind her desk facing us. Papers and brown files with tattered edges were piled high either side of the desk.

'We just need to go through the placement agreement.'

I had no idea what she was talking about. Luckily Mum didn't either.

20

'What's one of those?' Mum said. 'Matthew is only going to be here for a few days, I don't think we need any agreements.' She sounded forceful, even angry.

'It's just an agreement about the rules for Matthew while he's here, things like pocket money, any special food requirements and bed times, small things like that. He could be here for more than a few days but even if it is just that we still need an agreement.' And so the rules were agreed; bed by nine, £2.30 pocket money a week and no television in the bedroom. It all seemed so simple. A quick tour, a few rules, a signature on a paper and there I was in my new home, my new life. There wasn't any more conversation; it had been a long day for all of us. My Mum got ready to leave. I did not dare look her in the eye.

I'd felt like this only once before, on my first day at proper school where I would be away from my Mum all day. In those days she didn't work and we spent a lot of time together. She was my world and I loved every minute of being with her. She took me to the school gates and explained that I was going to have a great day. At the end, she would pick me up and cook me a special tea. I didn't believe her. As she left I cried; I missed her already. I was standing in the playground on my own when I realised she was gone. I didn't know where all the other children had disappeared to. I suddenly had a new feeling; a strange empty pain in my stomach and a lump in my throat. I hid behind a wall hoping nobody would find me. Eventually a teacher did find me and took me by the hand. It turned out from the look of every other child there that I didn't need to worry. They were all as new and scared as I was. On my little desk was my name in big colourful letters and some bright Lego to play with. This place would be fun after all. As promised, at the end of the day my Mum

21

was outside the gates to give me a big hug and cook my special tea.

Now in Balgores, Mum looked me in the eyes, wiping away her stream of tears. I turned away. I couldn't cry. Just like my first day at school, she took me by the hand and told me she would be back to pick me up soon. It took all I had to look at her straight in the face. I knew I was never going home. I think she did, too.

Soon after she had left I was taken to my room to settle down for bed. There was no Lego, no name in colourful letters and no children to share my fear. I felt as bruised and battered as the house that was my new home. As I lay in bed I wondered what was going to happen now. What had I done? And for the first time, I started to cry. I missed my Mum.

2

Early Experiences of Care

The stuffy room was packed with adults in suits. Mum and Kevin were dressed casually and looked out of place. Grandad was the only one looking smart, in a shirt and tie, as if he understood the significance of the meeting. The atmosphere was new to me; serious-looking people with pens and notepaper, a bit like teachers but with less obvious kindness. I sat next to the bearded lady opposite Mum and Kevin; I didn't dare look at them or anyone else. I kept my head to the floor, not sure of my place, what was going to happen or what was expected of me.

'Welcome to the placement meeting for Matthew. Can I just thank everyone for attending, particularly Matthew's School Headteacher, Mrs Hinchlin, and Matthew's mother and step-father, Kevin,' said the head grey man.

'This meeting is to decide on Matthew's short term future. First I would like to hear the duty social worker's report and then have a discussion as to the wishes of the family. Then, finally, we'll agree a plan for getting Matthew back home where he belongs.'

Back home? That isn't what I want, I thought, too scared to say it out loud. *Kevin* is not my family. Had nobody listened to what I said about how he treated me? I looked up briefly at Mum ; she was crying and holding Kevin's hand. I had lost her to this man.

The duty social worker read her report. She started with Southend.

There were a lot of reports about what had happened, the pier, the social worker who'd met Mum and Kevin that day, who talked about how devoted they seemed to me. My Head Teacher talked about my recent difficult behaviour at school. Eventually I was asked to leave the room.

Then something strange happened. When I stood up, Kevin came towards me and kissed me on the forehead.

'We still want you home Matthew. I love you,' he said.

I felt uncomfortable; I couldn't understand why they let him do that after everything I had said about him. The report later noted the significance of this incident; it said: *'Matthew's step-father kissed him affectionately as he left the room. Matthew seemed to welcome this.'* At the time I didn't know how to react. If I'd spat and punched Kevin it would have been taken as proof I was just a bad kid, a crazy kid, whose own wishes didn't matter.

Eventually I was called back in and it was explained to me that I would stay at my new home for another month. Mum was going to call every day to check on me and I would still see both of them, although not my brothers for the time being; the minutes of the meeting noted that I was known to be violent to my younger brothers, although they didn't mention anything about what Kevin had done to me. I was never asked whether the statement about my brothers was true. Reports would later expand upon this, inserting words so that it became *'very violent'* until the final insertion *'extremely violent'* – which stuck until I left care. It didn't matter that it wasn't true.

I was given a piece of paper with all the details about what had been decided; bed times, pocket money, special rules. I would return to school a few days later so as to keep as much of a normal routine as possible. My Mum signed the paper, then Kevin did. I was angry that he signed it. After everything I had said why was he allowed to be here? But I didn't say anything, still intimidated by the number of people in the room, and I just wanted to get away from my Mum as soon as possible. I couldn't stand her crying there in front of everyone, people feeling sorry for her. I was the bad boy and she was the good Mum. I signed it and left. I didn't kiss her and I didn't say goodbye. I wanted her to hurt as much as I did.

There is not much I remember about those first few days in the children's home. I was calm, at least for a short while, and happy to be away from home. I didn't think a lot about what had happened; no regrets, no guilt, no sadness – not even loss. I didn't meet many of the children. I just kept myself to myself, playing the computer games. I was hooked as soon as I touched the keyboard.

There was one boy though, Dennis, who I knew from school. He was famous at school, not just only as the boy from the children's home, but also as the boy who stank. I discovered that he didn't like to wash; it would take the staff ages to convince him he should do something about the smell. They banned him from the canteen till he did wash!

As I sat in the council mini-bus on the school run, I felt like it was my first day at school, the day my Mum dropped me off to my first full day all those years ago. But it wasn't just that I was nervous; I was anxious that I was somehow being tricked into going home. The school was a five minute walk from Mum's house and my brother also went there, two years below me. It would be the first time we saw each other since I'd left home; although, as they had agreed at the placement meeting, I wasn't allowed to talk to him.

As I went into the class I could hear whispers; people

were looking, some smiling, some with genuine concern on their face and some as if I had just walked into the room without any clothes on. The school was in the middle of a small council estate. It was a tightly-knit community and everyone knew what had happened, they all would have heard their parents' thoughts on the matter; whether I was abused at home or just a troublemaker, a bad boy. It wasn't as if they didn't have some ammunition for that view either.

I had never been an angel at school. At infant school, where most of my classmates had also been, I was regularly in the 'black book' – a list of naughty children the head teacher would read out in assembly each week. The thing that got me into regular trouble at junior school was my lateness. My class teacher, Mr Taylor, would make me sit at lunch and write lines to learn my lesson; 50, 100, 150 ... it would go up each time, he said, until I learnt to be on time. I cried and cried through the punishment; it hurt my hand writing the same thing over and over again. The other children would walk past me and laugh. Mr Taylor hated me and it was mutual; he thought I was an 'attention seeking, sneaky little troublemaker' and often told me so. He looked like the fat controller in *Thomas the Tank Engine*, and always talked about how much he liked sausages. When he got angry, he became furious, fast. If you upset him, he would turn beetroot red, with steam escaping from his ears until BANG! He would explode. Inches from your face he would scream *'who do you think you are, little boy?'*, and you would be too scared to wipe his spit from your face. If you dared answer back he would take you by the arm, sometimes the ear, and march you outside to the principal's office. But rarely did he do that because he knew the principal took a more reasonable approach. I never really knew how I wound My Taylor up so much.

I could be quite a charming little boy with my strawberry blond curly hair, blue eyes and cute looks. But most of the time I seemed to be in my own little world, a bit of a daydreamer. I didn't fit in with the boys; I couldn't play football and I was a wimp. If there was a fight I would just get on the floor and curl into a ball, not able to punch back. I was bullied, but I don't remember it ever being really bad except with Tony, who was a small version of Mr Taylor. I sometimes wondered if Tony could be Mr Taylor's secret son. He was fat and stupid; I could outwit him, but, at that age, fists are stronger than wit and the fists always won. I told Mr Taylor when Tony beat me up; sometimes he would get caught doing it, like once when Mr Taylor came into the toilets to find me curled up on the floor and Tony laying kicks into me. But Mr Taylor would blame me saying I wound people up; I liked 'playing the victim' he said. I hated parents' evenings because Mum would always come away disappointed. I misbehaved, did not concentrate, my work was poor and I answered back. No wonder I tried to throw myself off Southend pier.

I had three years of Mr Taylor as a form tutor, including that last year when I came into care. The third year, though, I had an amazing teacher. Ms Dennis was a young, beautiful bespectacled woman, sweet and soft, like a safe, warm quilt keeping you snug at night. She seemed to like me as much as Mr Taylor hated me. And she knew so much. We learnt lots about history, which I grew to love that year, and through her I learnt that I had a talent and passion for art and drama. She decided we were going to do a school play. She wrote a script and gave us all characters; I had a small, but important part, she said, the jester who would deliver a vital message to the Queen.

We rehearsed for months and when the time came Mum

was in the audience and I was determined to make her proud. I delivered my lines with great passion; just at the end, I ad-libbed something that I thought was funny, my heart pounding as I did so. Luckily, many people fell about laughing. I had a talent, people said, and Mum was convinced I could be a famous actor. I was chuffed with pride.

My school reports also improved and I actually looked forward to parents' evening, for once. Sadly Ms Dennis decided to leave after that one year. I was distraught when she left. The last day with her, when we said goodbye I remember her hugging me and crying just like I was. For about a year after that we would write to each other; I took a long time with my letters wanting to impress her with my handwriting, something I had never been good at, and I would be so excited and happy to receive one of hers. But eventually, she stopped replying and I was back with beetroot-face Taylor, the sausage-fancier.

Now, after everything that had happened in recent weeks, I didn't care about him any more. What could he do to hurt me? He couldn't shout in my face, I would just walk out. I had a worker from the children's home in the class with me on the first day and Mr Taylor was different, nicer even. Maybe he felt sorry for me. I wanted him to come up against me so this time, when I had nothing to lose, I could fight back. But nothing happened. The bell rang and it was time for break; the care worker followed me out into the playground.

The minute I got outside it was as if a swarm of bees were coming towards me, buzzing frantically. I was surrounded by what felt like hundreds of children all talking at once; 'what happened to you?', 'what is it like in a children's home?', 'why did you run away from home?' Buzz, buzz, buzzing in my ear. I couldn't stand it – I ran away and hid in a classroom until the break was over. At lunchtime, I saw my brother John; he glanced over at me and then looked away. I felt ashamed, but also angry that everything was alright for him. We had never been close and I imagined it suited him just fine that I was no longer at home competing for attention. I couldn't wait to leave that day.

The next day I pleaded with the care workers not to make me go to school, but I got on the mini-bus in the end. All morning I was restless, not listening to Mr Taylor. I was pushing him to notice; to make a scene so that I could leave the class and not come back. He didn't. At break-time I refused to leave the class. All the energy building up inside me started to spill over. I grabbed a pair of scissors and held them to my chest.

I warned him and the care worker to stay away – or I would kill myself. I was standing by the window on the second floor and tried to open it, saying I was going to jump out. I wasn't, and they knew I wasn't, but I just didn't want to be there any more. If I pushed too far, I thought I wouldn't have to come back. But he talked to me calmly and seemed genuinely concerned for me. It wasn't the man I'd known and hated all those years. In the end, I calmed down and agreed to try and stay for the rest of the day.

An hour later, I decided I didn't want to stay and didn't want to ever come back. I think it was still too close to what I had been so desperate to escape; with Mum living down the road and John going to school there.

It wasn't just that I seemed to annoy Mr Taylor all the time or get myself into trouble. From my first year of junior school, as far back as I can remember, there were times I would just feel sad and not know why. I'd stop daydreaming about the possibilities of life and start thinking about its limits and 'what ifs?' I didn't realise it then, but I was depressed for most of my childhood and these spells of depression would go up and down throughout the year. Of course there were some people in my life who didn't treat me well and that made it harder to understand my confusion. I had plenty of reasons to feel angry and betrayed, but beyond that, I also did get overwhelmed with feelings of paranoia.

In my second year of secondary school, I became more involved in the local church, going to Beavers and then Scouts, Wednesday Club and Sunday school. On Saturday I'd run the stall selling eggs from the local city farm and on Sunday mornings I'd help Rene, an old woman, who treated me as if I was her own grandson. Church became a second home for me; I helped to prepare and pack up the jumble sales and almost lived in the church during the Christmas fête. The local vicar, Roger, was a small man who looked a bit like a monk; he had a bald patch and he'd play with his beard when he was thinking. He rarely told me off, and when he did, I knew I probably deserved it. He showed me respect by giving me jobs to do and then praising me afterwards. He kept giving me the opportunities I needed to keep some sanity about me and some happiness in my life.

The church gave me a chance to be creative. Spurred on by Ms Dennis, I wrote a play to put on at the church. I held rehearsals with classmates as my actors; I was the writer, director and lead actor of course! I can't remember what the play was about but it had a Santa Claus character and the story involved the migration of swallows in winter. I sang the lead song, *Swallow oh Swallow*, and felt every inch the star I longed to be. My Grandad played the part of Santa, but because we couldn't find a Santa costume, we had to dress him up in a big furry jacket and a bear skin hat. He looked like a bear hunter from the icy wastes of Siberia. I wrote into the story that Santa was away on business in the North Pole, so his uncle, a hunter from Siberia, had to stand in.

These ventures allowed me to get through some of the low times because they won me praise and attention. I'm not sure I was conscious of that at the time, but after that first experience at school with Ms Dennis in the school play, when Mum was so proud and even Mr Taylor was pleased with me, I began to feel I should keep on doing such stuff. If they were happy with me, I wouldn't need to worry about whether I had done something wrong or not. But, as with a drug that requires ever-increasing doses to achieve the same effect, I had to find new ways of making people happy with me. At home it became more and more difficult to do that; as Mum worked longer hours, she became grumpier and often lashed out at the smallest things. It wasn't being shouted at that I minded so much. It was the way she would make me feel guilty for her having to work so hard, as if having to look after me and my brothers was eating her life away. As if I was a nuisance. As if her life would be better if I wasn't there.

I started to try other ways to deal with these feelings; I'd wake up as early as I could, sometimes at five or six, and clean the house from top to bottom so that Mum wouldn't have to do anything when she woke up. This made her happy and she would always treat me to sweets or give me fifty pence. She once said to me 'I hope you're not doing this for the money, Matthew'. It had nothing to do with the money: the real reward was her 'thank you', the hug and my relief that she couldn't be annoyed with me, for once.

But that, too, didn't work for that long. Over time, nothing seemed to please Mum, Kevin or Mr Taylor. I realise now it wasn't just because of the feelings of depression and paranoia but also because I suffered from a multitude of inconsistencies. Mr Taylor never gave me a real sense of how good, or bad, my behaviour was, or how well I was doing at school, because he simply said my that behaviour and marks were terrible most of the time, which I knew wasn't entirely true. And I didn't have the security of unconditional support and affirmation; I had it in bouts, but it depended on the moods of Mum or Kevin. My search for attention and adulation through all my sometimes frantic activities was really the start of a lifelong search for love. The kind of love only a mother can give; unconditional love. I didn't have that at home and I wasn't going to find it at school or church or anywhere else.

I gave up on that search for unconditional love, at home at least, when I set fire to the sofa while Kevin slept on top of it. There was no going back after that. After Ms Dennis left, I was in school again with a teacher who had made me feel worthless over the years.

One day I excused myself to go the toilet and left the classroom. But I didn't go to the toilet: I went to do something I now knew would make them listen.

I stepped over the railings on the stairwell and held on as if preparing to jump. As another child came up the stairs they screamed and I slipped; I managed to grab the railings and cling on. I began screaming for help. Mr Taylor opened the classroom door and walked calmly down the stairs, as if completely unsurprised to see a small boy hanging off the edge of a stairwell. He found a table, stood on it, picked me up and lifted me to the floor. Although his face was calm, his hands were sweaty and I realised he was just as scared as I was. At the end of that day, I left the school for good.

After a meeting of the school governors the head teacher wrote to Social Services to say they couldn't cope with my behaviour, as it was a risk to me and the children around me. I had the result I wanted. Another part of my life had been disposed of like a piece of rubbish, the school life that had never been much use to me anyway.

I didn't attend the second review meeting, an emergency meeting to discuss what to do with me now I wasn't at school. I wasn't invited, but I knew about it. The more I thought about it the more I felt angry that Kevin was there making decisions about me. He was the problem; if he wasn't there I would still be at home. Nobody asked me about him or how he treated me.

Years later, when I saw the minutes from the meeting, I found that the picture they had of me was that of a troubled, attention-seeking boy. My Mum would talk about me as if I was a violent thug, twisting every argument I'd ever had with my brothers. It was like a bad divorce, where the two warring parties portray every mistake the other party made as part of a pattern of crazy, bad, mad, cruel behaviour. At one point she even painted me as psychotic, demonic, with squinting eyes and foaming mouth. The social workers lapped it up, without question. I can't remember once being asked what happened in those early days. They were even apologetic to her, sympathising that it must be so hard for her, 'having to deal with all this without any explanation'. She responded 'I just want to help Matthew. If he tells us what's wrong we can help him'. Well I had told them what was wrong. They just hadn't listened. I had only two weapons, my love for my mother and my behaviour: if it remained bad enough, they couldn't make me go home. After that review meeting Mum tried to see me.

'I don't want to see her.'

'You don't have a choice, Matthew. It's her right to see you, we can't stop her. You are voluntarily cared for, that means she still has the right to see you whenever she wants.'

'You can't make me see her. I'm not seeing her.'

I walked towards the door. One of the staff in the room, a big guy, stood in front of me. The bearded lady called for reinforcements.

'Your mother wants to see you and you don't have a choice. She is still your mother, even though you're living here.'

I tried to push past the big man but he didn't budge. I went towards the window and he grabbed me from behind.

'I'm not fucking seeing her,' I screamed as loudly as I could, hoping she would hear me. I kicked Mr Big in the legs. Another man came into the room and helped push me to the ground on my front. I was now flattened, with one man sitting on my legs and the other pushing my arm as far across my back as it would go. It felt like it would snap if I moved. I tried to bite them but they managed to avoid my teeth.

'Tell that bitch to fuck off. I hate her. Did you hear me? I fucking hate you.' Mum heard me. I didn't see her that day or the next. Each time she tried, I refused to see her. Each time I knew she was coming, I'd run off. One of the only weapons I had was to withdraw my love for her.

As the weeks went by, my behaviour became crazier. I ran away often; sometimes for no reason at all other than I felt overwhelmingly anxious or angry. The home was near a railway station and I would threaten to jump on the tracks. Sometimes I'd walk along the tracks, tempting fate, until they turned the electricity off. I didn't realise I was delaying trains or messing up people's travel plans. The police got to know me well.

Once, when we went to the Dolphin swimming pool in Romford, Mum was in the entrance with my brothers. I said I wanted to go home but the staff said I couldn't spoil it for the other children on the trip. So I lost it and started running about the place screaming and shouting. Several of them restrained and carried me, kicking and screaming, to the car. I was shouting, 'Help, I'm being kidnapped'. They put me in a staff member's car – and later that night, the police turned up at his door, to investigate reports of a kidnapping. I was, I now realise, acting out, but it didn't help that nobody ever talked to me about the problems in my life. They focused on my bad behaviour – without ever asking where it came from. I was mad, bad, and dangerous to know – and they all assumed that was simply how *I was*, born bad, as if the adults in my life couldn't have had anything to do with it.

As my behaviour grew worse, the other children, who were mostly older than me, made me the whipping boy for their frustrations. After about a month, a group of them demanded that I leave the home; the bearded lady wrote to the team manager at Social Services several times, pleading with them to move me. I caused too much disruption, she said, and they couldn't cope. But her request was refused, every time. Eventually they moved me to an adjoining wing, which had been designed to accommodate a disabled resident. It was me and a staff member 24/7. Things started to improve – I still had my tantrums and ran off – but not as frequently.

I've said nobody talked me to me about my problems. Now finally, they took me to a psychologist who asked about the experiences my Mum had described. The psychologist had not just been told that I foamed at the mouth when angry, but also that I talked to myself as if hearing voices. Distressed children don't always take the first opportunity to stand up for themselves. I didn't talk much in the sessions with him. I was always aware of the camera hanging from the ceiling in the corner of the room, its red light indicating that everything I said would be taken down – and maybe used in evidence against me. I'd refuse to talk unless he turned it off, but he never did. There was a mirror that I assumed you could see through, like the ones on television crime shows. I found out later I was right; Mum was on the other side, sometimes with Kevin.

Eventually the psychologist recommended I be tested for *petit mal*, a form of epilepsy. I was sent for a brain scan and blood tests to help determine why I was behaving this way. It didn't occur to them I didn't need a brain scan or blood tests – just some intelligent affection.

Finally, I was moved to an expensive house in Essex run by a single woman, called Janette, and her housekeeper. I didn't realise the technical term for this was a 'special placement'. She had one son my age. It's unusual for children to be fostered by people of a different ethnicity, but I didn't care that Janette and her son were black. I was to share a room with him. Apparently, Janette had a high success rate turning troubled children into good kids.

The house was immaculately clean. I'd never known such luxury. The floors were soft as a duvet and the walls looked like they were laced with gold. Magnificent pots and ornaments were everywhere. This lady was rich. She immediately put me at ease by welcoming me to the family and making her intentions clear; she wasn't going to make me talk to my Mum. That was my choice, not hers, or anybody else's. I felt safe: finally someone was listening to me. Janette said she was expecting me to start school

36

in September and was going to get me into the best school in the area; all of her children did well she said. Finally, and the most exciting thing for me, she was going to take me on the family trip to New York later that year. New York! That meant flying on a plane. The furthest I had ever been was to Clacton. I'd never dreamed of going abroad, let alone to this magical place I only knew from movies.

But there was a catch. Janette wanted me to go on medication. If I didn't she couldn't help me. I couldn't understand why I needed pills. Janette told me she had worked with a number of children like me and the solution had been medication.

She didn't push the issue until several weeks later. I had an argument with her son about what we were watching on the TV. She took his side, saying it was his room and he was kind enough to let me stay there, so I should watch what he wanted. It made me feel like an intruder, just an inconvenience. I swore at her and ran; she tried to restrain me but I hit out, smashing one of her precious expensive vases. Then I stormed out of the house. I ran off, not knowing which way to go.

I had few options. I couldn't go back to Balgores and I wasn't going home. I saw a foot bridge over the dual carriageway, climbed over the barrier and looked down at the cars below. The cars zoomed by at such a speed I wondered what it would be like to fall on one moving that fast. The more I thought of jumping, the tighter I held on. Eventually one car stopped. Then a man came towards me on the footbridge.

'Stay away from me,' I said. He looked every bit as scared as I felt.

'I'm not coming any closer,' he said, 'I just want to see if you are okay. Help is coming.'

He was shaking and I could hear sirens. People were getting out of their cars and looking up. Police cars arrived and started to move people back, creating a wide gap. This was much bigger than the drop at Southend Pier. I would definitely die if I jumped. A policeman approached me on the footbridge and started with the same routine as I had, by now, gone through several times; *what's your name, son? Keep calm, I have a son your age...* It's strange how they all had a son my age. Things were more serious this time though; I had nowhere left to run to, and killing myself seemed to be my only way out. Now I had given up hope.

I felt completely alone and had nowhere and nobody to turn to. I was angry; angry with everyone, not just Mum and Kevin. Killing myself wouldn't just end all this for me – it would also punish them. I wanted to punish them so much. More police arrived; a van load now stood around either side of the footbridge. They had lit up the area with floodlights and closed the road off completely. I couldn't understand why so many people were needed for one person back then; but, of course, this wasn't just 'a person'. This was a vulnerable ten-year-old who seemed intent on killing himself, who might die by accident if he slipped.

Suddenly I was brought back to reality by another police offer speaking to me; a gentle man with a firmer voice than the others. He seemed to be in charge.

'There's a lot of people here very worried about you.'

'You can all fuck off. I don't want you here.'

'We can't do that; we care about you. And to be honest I can't deal with the amount of paperwork this would cause', he laughed trying to win me over with the same cheap joke I'd heard before in this situation.

'I'm going to jump. Don't come near me. Tell those officers to stay away.'

'No one is coming near you. Why don't you tell me your name?'

I didn't say anything.

'We can't even start to help you if you don't tell us your name.'

'Matthew.'

'Okay Matthew. Thank you. I'm James. Now why are you standing up here? What's been happening?' We spent the next twenty minutes going round in circles. By now two fire engines and an ambulance had joined the 999 circus.

'Now I need you to come down Matthew. I can see you are cold and you might fall.'

My legs were shaking. I could see several officers putting on their safety belts. I knew they were going to come and get me soon. I had to decide to either jump or come down.

'No one listens to me. He has been hitting me and no one cares. Why isn't he in prison? Why don't you arrest him?'

'Arrest who, Matthew? Who has been hitting you?'

'Kevin, my stepdad. Go arrest him and I'll come down.'

'Okay, Matthew. If someone has been hitting you then that's not right. Just tell us where he lives and we can arrest him.'

I believed him. He sounded serious. I gave him the address and he sent several officers off in a car. The sirens blared away as they sped off and it left me with some hope; enough hope not to jump.

'I'm not coming down until you bring him back and show me he is arrested.'

'Why don't you just come the other side so you're a bit safer?'

'No. I'm staying here. If those officers come anywhere near me I'll jump.'

But the more I thought about it, I wasn't so sure I could

jump. A big part of me wanted to, but I couldn't stand the thought of actually doing it. Still, for now, I wasn't giving up the only power I had – not when someone was finally listening to me. About ten minutes later, the firemen started to assemble something down below; it looked like a big round trampoline. The police car returned.

'Matthew we have done what you asked. We have arrested your step-dad.'

'I want to see him in handcuffs.'

'If you come down you can see him. I have kept my end of the deal, now you have to keep yours'. The firemen below circled around the trampoline. The officers on the footbridge were edging forward.

'I need you to come down Matthew. If you jump it will hurt but you won't die. Do you want to hurt yourself?'

I was trapped; if I jumped I'd be caught below. If I didn't, I'd be grabbed from above. I edged myself quickly from side to side trying to avoid the trampoline; I was psyching myself up to jump. The firemen followed my movements, running backwards and forwards, as if to catch someone jumping from a burning building. I didn't jump in time. Before I knew it I was yanked by several officers who grabbed me over the railings and held on tight. I could hear the collective sigh of relief around me; I screamed out loud in despair at my own weakness. I was too gutless to jump and too weird to live normally.

I sobbed on the floor held by the officer who had been talking to me.

'It's okay, son, it's all over now.' My only hope was that they had arrested Kevin. They took me quietly down to the police van where they said Kevin was been held. Peering inside I saw several officers surrounding a man who looked like Kevin in the back. It was too dark to see if it was really him. I asked them to turn the light on but they refused. I knew then it wasn't Kevin.

'You fucking lied to me', I screamed.

I tried to run off, but they held me to the floor. I was handcuffed behind my back and my wrists ached with the tightness of the metal around them. Three officers held me down as they drove me to the hospital. I became more hysterical as the journey went on; I had completely lost any sense of control, any sense for my own safety. If I'd been on that bridge right then, I wouldn't have hesitated: I would have jumped.

As I was taken into the hospital I could see my social worker and Janette. I don't know why but I was screaming out for my real Dad and crying uncontrollably.

They put me on a bed and held me down. IMy pants were pulled down. Then I felt a sharp pain in my bottom, like a bee sting.

'Ahhhh, you fucking bastards, you hurt me you fucking bastards ... you...'

My rant trailed off as I slowly lost consciousness. They had given me a sedative.

I woke up in the early hours alone in the hospital accident and emergency entrance, on a trolley. I could turn my head slightly, but it was hard to move the rest of my body. I was still lying face down and felt scared someone would inject me again. I tried to move but couldn't; I twisted and turned until I lost consciousness once more. I spent the next four days in hospital drifting in and out of a daze. I felt exhausted; my last bit of trust now spent. I woke up the next day to find Janette sitting next to me.

'You will be home with us soon and things are going to change for you. This is not your fault. We are going to help you. The medication will help.'

'What medication?'

'Just some pills. It has worked before. You need something to help you with this anger. It can't go on like this.'

'I don't want to talk any more. I'm not coming home with you and I'm not taking any pills.'

'Say what you want right now but you are going to do what I say.'

Several days later when, I left the hospital my social worker, Haniff, took me to meet Janette on neutral ground to discuss returning home with her. I was determined not to; I didn't fit in with any family and despite the lure of New York I didn't like her rules and the talk about pills. She was trying to control me and I didn't think I needed control; control and punishment meant the same thing to me and I saw no reason to be punished.

'I'm not going back there', I interrupted them, addressing Haniff and ignoring Janette.

'Matthew, you have two options. Either you come back with me or you go home with your mother. There are no other places for you to go.'

'I'm not going anywhere with you and I'm not going home.'

I looked at Haniff for some help; surely he wasn't part of this. He didn't say anything; just watched like he had nothing to do with it.

'You have no choice. No one else wants you. You either come back with me or we are sending you to your mother.'

'You can't do that.' I got up, picked up a chair and threw it against a wall. 'I'm not fucking going anywhere.'

'You see what I have to put up with,' Janette said.

'Why doesn't everybody calm down? I'm sure we can talk about this,' Haniff said, finally breaking his silence.

'I'm not going anywhere. If you make me I will run away now.'

'No one is going to make you go anywhere you don't want to,' Haniff said, looking worried at the thought of me running off.

'I don't have to put up with this,' Janette said. 'I am very well-respected. I am personally friends with the Mayor and if you don't come back with me I will write to the Mayor to tell him you are a very naughty boy and should be put in prison.'

I started to shout abuse at her and threw another chair onto the floor. Haniff looked more worried. This was not how he had planned his sensitive professional intervention.

'You can't make me go anywhere. I'll kill myself. Watch me kill myself.'

I started to run and banged my head against the wall. Out of his depth, Haniff called for help.

'I think you should leave now.' He took a strong tone. Janette looked up at him, shocked.

'I am not going anywhere unless he either comes with me or goes home to his mother'. I banged my head harder and screamed more.

'I am asking you to leave now,' Haniff sounded firmer this time.

'I am going to write to the Mayor. And you will be hearing from my solicitors.'

With that, Janette left. I stopped banging my head and just sat there crying. Haniff sat down. I thought I could see him shaking a little. He turned to me and I could see some guilt in his eyes as if he knew he had let me down.

'That shouldn't have happened. I'm sorry,' he said.

After a pause I looked up at him. I felt sorry for Haniff; he had been silent earlier not because he was against me but because he didn't know how to handle the situation.

Since coming into care only two months earlier, I had been surrounded by people who didn't know what to do with me. They all made me feel like a crazy child. This was the first time someone had said sorry. I wiped away my tears.

'That's okay,' I told him.

3

Aged Eleven – Woodstock

Woodstock was an assessment centre for children, its 'mission' was to explore how grave their problems were and work out what they – we – needed. That was the label on the tin. In reality, it was more like a holding pen, a place to contain the most difficult adolescents in care until they turned sixteen, and the authorities would no longer be responsible for them. Most of the chimps in the cage would never live with a family again and would probably spend the rest of their time in care moving from placement to placement. You did not get into Woodstock unless you were out of control, beyond unruly and dangerous.

It was a lot like a prison. You were asked 'what you in for then?' when you arrived, as if you were an inmate talking with fellow criminals, and you answered: 'drunken Dad' or 'Mum couldn't look after me'. It was smart to stick to cooler, less intense 'charges' – 'drunken father' was better than 'sexual abuse'. It didn't leave you so exposed.

My first day was intimidating, mainly because I was the youngest by far. All the other residents were aged between fourteen and sixteen. It was a mixed home with separate wings for the boys' and girls' bedrooms, and plenty of rules to prevent the sexes from mingling too much. Not that anyone obeyed the rules. The place was much larger than Balgores, with a games room that included a pool table, a large dining room and kitchen, a school and a suite of management offices. It had the same institutional features as any children's home; large fire hoses, corridors without carpets, dirty white walls, the smell of cleaning chemicals.

My room was in the boys' wing, shared with six other kids. I had a small single bed, a cupboard, chest of drawers and my own sink. The room was bare and cold. The showers reminded me of school changing rooms and the toilets were message boards of pain and hate.

The first day I arrived I was introduced to Ada, a middle aged woman, who was going to be with me most days; 'one to one' they called it. My Grandad came to see my new home and asked where my belongings were so I could unpack. One of the staff told him that my belongings had been transferred in bin bags and had accidentally been thrown away as rubbish. He couldn't believe they could be so stupid. He spoke with the manager who apologised and said they would get me some new clothes. But to them it didn't seem that important an issue.

The first day I was introduced to the home manager, Clive, who took me to my room and gave me a copy of the Bible. He said that I could find some hope in what was said there. I was not convinced. Another manager, called Grant, scared me quite a lot and whenever things kicked off he would be the one to be sent in to enforce the rules. He had lost one arm and had a metal hook for one 'hand'; he reminded me of Captain Hook in *Peter Pan*.

The question of going home came up soon in a conversation with the team manager, Pat.

'I'm never going home again,' I said

'I'm sorry Matthew, but at some time you will be going home. You cannot stay here forever, this is just an assessment centre. Once you've been here for twelve weeks you will go back home.'

'No, I won't,' my voice started to rise; I got a lump in my throat. 'You can't make me go home.'

'We can, Matthew, and you will. If your mother wants you home that's what is going to happen and you have to get used to that. You can have as many tantrums as you want but you can't always get your own way.'

'I'm not fucking going home. You can't make me, I'll just keep running away.'

'And we will just keep taking you back.'

'I'll fucking kill myself then. You can't make me do something I don't want to do.'

'We will take you home and make you stay. You won't kill yourself.'

I swore at her some more and cried until it ended with me being held down by her and Dennis, another staff member; he was built for this kind of work, as he had the physique of a rhino. My head was on the floor, tears were pouring down my face, snot out of my nose, and un-controllable bubbles from my mouth. I felt the full weight of Dennis sitting on my back pressing against my lungs, while Pat held my legs. But I was still trying to kick. I couldn't believe they could make me go home. Kevin was still there. I had refused to see my Mum for a few months now, and I didn't want to speak to her again. At the time I didn't have the insight – one of the effects of being in care is that you do learn psychobabble, therapy-speak – to realise I was still punishing her for forcing me to leave home like that, for choosing Kevin over me. But mostly I was punishing her for changing so much, for spending all those years making me feel guilty, for nearly leaving me for ever, back when I was only six years old.

Hospital memories

It was supposed to be a happy day. Every other birthday had been, but not this one. My brother John, Dad, my grandparents and I stood around Mum's hospital bed. Tubes were entering and exiting her body. That scared me, as did the fact that she looked white. She'd been in hospital for several months.

We had been sledging in the snow one day and, as she went down a hill, she collided with a car, breaking her arm. To make things worse, she was pregnant. There were complications with her blood and other traumas I wasn't told about as I was only six. Mum was only twenty-two years old. Looking at her, I didn't need anyone to tell me she might die. The whispers, the anxiety on people's faces in that room, said it all.

Mum held my hand and we all started to sing 'Happy Birthday' enthusiastically, although there was something fake about the enthusiasm. As we walked home, I asked Dad what was happening.

'Is Mum going to die?'

He didn't look shocked. 'She is very bad at the moment but we don't know what is going to happen.'

'Will she get better?'

'We don't know yet. The hospital is doing everything they can to help her.'

I stopped my questions. I didn't cry. I didn't feel like crying. I was scared more than anything; it was more selfish than you might think. I was scared that I was going to lose the one person who loved me. Leaving me with Dad would have been the worst thing she could do; I dreaded the idea of having to grow up with just him. We had spent the months Mum was in hospital being cared for by grandparents, who

48

took it in shifts. The longest I had ever been alone with Dad was a day. I spent the next weeks imagining, fearing the news of her death. It never came.

When we went to see my new baby brother, Danny, I remember the mixture of emotions I felt. As I looked at Mum holding him tenderly I felt angry; he was like a poison that had tried to kill her. Now he was the centre of everyone's attention. What had he done to deserve that? I didn't like my new brother for months; he took every bit of attention away from me. I felt unwanted and discarded. Then one day we were all walking down to the shops with Danny in his buggy. Mum stopped to talk to someone. I looked down at him and for the first time I didn't feel any bitterness or anger. He was wearing a big shell suit jacket covering his whole body, and his tiny, cute face poked out. Without thinking I leant down and hugged him tightly; what I felt then was intense love. The anger had melted away.

Soon after Danny was born and Mum was better, she began to change. She started going out to work more at weekends when Dad was home; she eventually got the job at Argus where she met Kevin. She now had three children and was completely dependent on Dad, a man she obviously didn't love. I think that near-death experience made her question her choices in life; whether she was right to have a child so young. Whatever conclusions she came to about that I will probably never know, and maybe I don't want to, but she made a decision that she was going to have a future beyond us children. I am sure she rationalised it as being about us, making a better home for us all. She had good intentions, but the road to Hell is paved with those. Unfortunately, she was too young to realise that we were still children, and not yet ready to lose our Mum.

These memories flooded back as Dennis the Rhino pinned

me to the floor. I knew I'd hate to return to Mum now. It would be worse than before; she wouldn't just remind me of the sacrifices she was making for 'us children' all the time, she would also remind me of what I had done to the family. Even if Kevin wasn't going to be there, I couldn't go 'home'. When they let go of me, I resigned myself to the fact that I had to leave Woodstock. But this time, I had to make sure they wouldn't find me.

I spent the next few days thinking about how I would make my escape. I would need supplies. I imagined myself as a wild crusader making my way into the hills, and living on the fruits of the forest. Nobody could touch me there.

My social worker came to visit me and check if I was okay. I explained to him what had happened and he told me it wasn't true that I'd be made to go home. They all wanted the best for me and they thought that meant going home, but they couldn't force me. I even told him I was planning on running away, but he assured me that I was going to stay at Woodstock.

The children soon tired of me getting so much attention from the staff. I felt scared without an adult present and they knew it; the 'children' scared the adults, too, and they kept out of each others' way. Every night something would flare up, a fight would break out, or kids would rampage across the building. Windows were smashed and fire alarms would ring. I would barricade my bed against the door before going to sleep – or trying too. Sometimes my fellow inmates would try to get into my room, bashing against the door. Other times they'd stick knives through the cracks in the doorframe, saying they would kill me when they got hold of me. I would curl up on the bed, terrified. I didn't dare go out to the toilet so I just urinated in the corner.

One night I woke up startled to a bottle of piss been tipped on me by two of the boys; they were standing over me and laughing. Another time, one of the girls helped me hide in a small toilet. A brick crashed through the window, almost hitting my head.

The staff didn't try to control the children and, in fact, couldn't. There would only ever be a maximum of two staff-members on duty by night, and sometimes just a night porter. If it really got out of control they would call in the police. The police sometimes came three times a week to break up riots.

At some point, I realised that to survive at Woodstock, I had to join them. I was no angel, anyway – but at first, I'd tried to make a clean break with the past by behaving myself, and I enjoyed the 'one to one' attention. But I felt I had to become part of the gang for my own safety.

One night Ada, was in my room chatting with me, and I punched her in the face without warning. At first, she fell back, shocked and then called for help. In a few minutes, I'd been restrained but I still had a leg free and I kicked out at her. She acted very professionally, called me a little bastard and came at me. But Ada wasn't expert at violence. As she lunged at me, she tripped and hit her back on the bed.

I was shocked. I never planned to hurt her, I didn't think before I hit her. An ambulance had to be called and she was taken to hospital. I never saw her again. I was now one of the gang but that did not make me safe. I was only treated better as long as I did what they wanted me to. I became the gang pet; the girls were protective but the boys would use me. When they needed Tipp-Ex to sniff I was the one who could fit through the window to the on-site school to steal it. There were always drugs around. A dealer used to come to the home, call up to the top window, climb up a ladder and sell what the older children wanted, usually speed or ecstasy tablets, which were the cheapest. If they didn't have drugs they'd sniff glue or Tipp-Ex. I tried it a couple of times, but it scared me too much.

Once, when I sat watching them at the end of the field getting high on drugs, I went to tell the staff. They told me I was just causing trouble and they were only messing about. I insisted I was right; so they took me out to the children and asked them to look after me saying I thought they were on drugs. 'He just wants some attention' the staff said, leaving me behind. The minute they had gone inside the kids surrounded me, their eyes wide like rabid dogs. I curled up on the ground ready for a kicking; but they subtly just leaned over my face and started dribbling spit all over me; it was warm and sticky and covered my face. I cried for them to stop but they carried on spitting into my face until I screamed so loud they ran off. I never told on them again.

The girls and boys were all fifteen or sixteen – hormonal adolescents. Most of them had paired up as boyfriend and girlfriend and some even swapped partners. There was a shed at the top of the field, which they used to go to have sex. Until then I didn't know what sex was; it sounds strange for a ten-year-old boy, but no one had ever sat me down and explained. I just thought kissing and cuddling was sex. My job was to stand guard from the inside and look through the hole in the door to check if any staff members were nearby. I refused the first time they asked, but a boy named Michael threatened to beat me with a golf club.

As I stood guard, couples would have sex. I would hear their grunting and pounding. Once they dared me to try one of the girls. I didn't want to, but, scared I would get hit, I got on top of one of them. She stuck her tongue in my mouth and it felt sloppy and disgusting. I didn't know what to do. Then she grabbed hold of my penis and it felt uncomfortable; she screamed and said it was tiny. They all fell about laughing and started calling me 'frigid', a word I didn't know at the time, but which says a lot about what you learn in children's homes – therapy-speak.

As I cried, they laughed harder. I decided then that sex was a bad thing and that I never wanted to do it.

The kids could be terrifying. When they got drunk or high I'd be their punching bag. Once, one of them came up to me and hit me right in the penis with a golf club. I screamed in pain and coiled up on the floor unable to move for several hours. The staff and some of the other children challenged him but he just thought it was funny. When I finally got up and looked at my penis, it was black from bruising. For days it hurt when I went to the toilet or sat down. Another time I sat in class, and one of the children ran in and punched me in the face, then ran out again. This time he was restrained by staff. When he was asked why he did it, he just said it was because I annoyed him.

The staff also thought that I was annoying. Often I probably was. The others were all teenagers who had been round the block and through the mill but I had mainly had a sheltered childhood. But, because I attracted such extreme aggression from the other children, staff put it down to me being a wind-up.

Rob Tomlinson, the service manager at the time, wrote in an internal report that 'Matthew's antagonistic behaviour attracts demonising aggression from his peers'. What antagonistic behaviour warrants being hit in the penis with a golf club or having piss tipped over your head? The staff didn't know how to cope with any of us. So the easiest thing to do was to lay it at me. And it made me hate them, as much as I did the children who victimised me.

My anger at everyone around me knew no bounds, but I was scared to show it to other children. It was an 'us and them' situation; us against the adults. But, within that group, I was the odd one out, the one who didn't fit. Not only because I was much younger, but because I came from a good family. I'd been sheltered from drugs and sex, things that the other children were used to. So I sat in between the adults and the children, firmly against the adults, but not really with the children. Being in no man's land is hard: both sides shoot at you.

I learned to test the limits of the adults' patience. In the endless riots, I'd try to go further than the others to try and impress them; once I was shut in a room with one of the staff who was trying to stop me jumping out of the window to join the chaos outside. I grabbed a fire extinguisher and let it off it in his face. He raised his hands to his eyes to stop the foam stinging and screamed in pain; I panicked and escaped through the window. I later found out the staff member had to be taken to hospital and was going to wear patches on his eyes for some time. I felt guilty afterwards, but that didn't matter at the time. The adrenaline took over. No one mattered. Rage was my only fuel.

Another time I was shut in a room with a male staff member whilst the others tried to control the rampaging children. He was a strong man but looked a bit like Wally from *Where's Wally?* I hit out at him. I was only wearing a T-shirt and shorts. He pounced on me pushing me to the floor. He kept muttering he was going to make me behave. For the first time with an adult at Woodstock I was scared of what they might do to me physically. I didn't expect what came next. The details remain a muddle in my head but what I remember clearly is ending up completely naked, with him sitting on top of me holding me down. He was fully clothed so I am sure he just restrained me. He was laughing, saying I couldn't get away now I was naked. As I looked up, I could see some of the other children looking through the big windows from the back garden, also laughing at me.

I still refused to see my Mum, much to the frustration of the staff. They were still determined to get me home; the review meetings from which I was excluded, discussed the plans for me to return home, as if my views on the matter had never been expressed. They still discussed me as if I was a child possessed, never addressing the reasons why I'd come into care in the first place, simply referring to my violent behaviour at home. My Mum would ask what they could do to help me. She would cry and they consoled her that none of this was her fault. Kevin sat with her, holding her hand as the supportive partner and loving stepfather. It made me sick to my stomach to see them arrive. They would always try to see me, but I would refuse, either running off or causing so much trouble I had to be restrained. Sometimes, I'd let off the big fire hose drenching the corridors and making it impossible for the staff to grab hold of me.

But the staff tried the carrot as well as the stick. The day before we were all due to take a day trip to Alton Towers theme park, Pat sat me down and explained my Mum wanted to see me. If I didn't, I would not be able to join the others on the trip to Alton Towers. I was excited about the trip, but I didn't want to give in to them.

After some pained discussion I agreed to go out with Mum for two hours only. Although I was still worried that

55

they would take me home, I knew I could always run away again. Mum and Kevin picked me up and I sat silently in the car as they tried to talk to me, as if this was a normal thing to be doing, like they had just picked me up from a long camping trip. We stopped at a Wimpy restaurant. I refused to talk or eat, but they still tried to make conversation. Kevin said I should show some respect to my Mum and answer her. I looked at him and said:

'You can't fucking tell me what to do.'

I was relieved I could talk to him like that and not get hit. He couldn't do anything about it except answer back, and he had to be careful what he said. I picked up a salt pot and tipped it upside down, spilling a big pile of salt, a defiance of white. Eventually Kevin grabbed the salt pot off me and said I was embarrassing myself.

'Fuck Off' I told him. That was enough for him; he told Mum it was time to take me back.

When I got back to Woodstock, children were on the roof rampaging around. The Alton trip had been cancelled due to a lack of staff anyway. I had let my guard down for the sake of a trip that never happened. I was as angry with myself as I was with them. The staff then tried another subtle approach. I hadn't been allowed to visit any of my grandparents; if I refused to see Mum, I couldn't see the rest of the family.

Pat took me into the office one day and asked me if I wanted to see my grandparents on my Dad's side. I was ecstatic at the idea: then came the catch. If I wanted to see them, Mum and Kevin had to take me there. I couldn't believe they were making me do this. I may have felt differently if it was just Mum, but to have Kevin involved was just one big slap in the face. It was as if I were shouting through a megaphone to a room of deaf people. It is the most frustrating experience to be called a liar when you are telling the truth and it is even more frustrating to have everyone around you believe the opposite of the truth. I had absolutely nobody in my corner. It was the loneliest moment of my life.

I wanted to see my grandparents. They already held Kevin in contempt for breaking up their son's marriage and never forgave Mum for breaking his heart. I could relax at their place, because they didn't write me off as a liar and troublemaker. I eventually agreed to the trip with Mum and Kevin, as long as I wouldn't have to see them for the rest of the weekend. I was good at silence. I said not a word during the entire journey.

The minute I got to my grandparents I went into the kitchen. Mum called out, telling me to give her a hug before she left, but I refused and she began to cry. This made me hate her even more; I felt it was just part of her act to get people to believe I was the devil child she made out.

That weekend I began to feel normal again. I didn't need to scream, shout and rampage. I was safe; I got lots of hugs from grandma. It was a reminder of how happy my childhood had been all those years ago.

My grandparents on Dad's side were middle class and very religious. They offered compassion, understanding, love and forgiveness. Though not millionaires, they were relatively wealthy. Grandma had been a District Nurse and Grandad a corporate accountant. They hadn't started with much, but had saved all their life, making shrewd investments. They had a bit of money, a nice house in a nice area and two children. I used to love the weekends we spent with them. I would always cook with Grandma, baking some kind of cake; she taught me how to make Banofee pie from scratch with evaporated milk.

The weekend ended and the horrors at Woodstock resumed. One of the experiences that would change my entire life happened on a camping holiday in Blackpool. I was excited to be going to the bright lights of Blackpool, 'the Queen of Seaside Resorts'. Dennis came from there and had spent weeks building it up. Blackpool, he would proclaim, had the best fun fair, the best Tower, the best beaches and the best fish and chips in the world. Only the boys were going on this trip as the girls went on a separate holiday. We set off overnight in our minibus and made the five hour drive to Blackpool.

When we put our tents up I realised that I was going to be in a tent alone with the boys. At the time it made me feel uncomfortable, but I didn't say anything. I didn't want to separate myself from them again as in the past that had just made them hate me, causing more beatings. I think I was nervous because of what had gone on in the shed, which was stupid really as that had been with the girls. At some point in the night Michael started to talk about 'joshing'. I didn't know what the word meant. They laughed and explained it meant 'wanking'. Still I didn't know what they meant. He said he'd show me and pulled his trousers down exposing his penis. It was a little bigger than mine, but shrivelled, and covered in hairs; I had never seen one pubic hair before.

But then he started pulling at it and as he did it got bigger. The other two boys were naked and started to do the same. I had a horrible feeling in the pit of my stomach and a lump in my throat. I knew this was wrong, but didn't know why. I couldn't scream out because I didn't want to get beaten up.

'Why don't you try it?'

'I don't want to.' I looked away.

'Go on. It's the best feeling.'

'No. I don't want to. I think I'm going to sleep outside.' I got up to leave. Michael grabbed my arm and pulled me back. The others to laughed.

'I've got a knife here and you know what I'll fucking do to you if you go out there'. I was shaking with fear.

'Pull your pants down and try it.'

I edged my pants down slowly. I was too scared to even cry. I knew he was going to make me do what he was doing. The other two had now stopped touching their penises and watched Michael, laughing, egging him on even further.

'Just watch me. It'll feel good.' I felt stupid sitting there half naked. He moved his hand towards my penis and I shivered with embarrassment as he touched it. The other two laughed as he tried to pull it backwards and forwards. Nothing happened to mine. It just stayed small.

'He can't even get it hard,' one of them laughed.

Michael didn't care; he carried on yanking it with one hand and used the other to pull on his. I didn't realise I was crying until I could feel the tears running down my cheeks. I turned away from him.

'Fucking look at me,' he said.

I looked back. After what seemed like an hour, but was only several minutes, some gooey stuff came shooting out from his penis; I had no idea what it was. It just looked like glue. He let go of me.

'That's joshing. Next time you should try it.'

I didn't say a word. I couldn't say a word. I felt strange; empty, humiliated, sitting there naked while they laughed. I pulled my pants up and turned away to sleep. Eventually they too went to sleep. I lay awake for hours. I wasn't thinking about much. I was pretty numb by that point.

The next day I spoke to Denis and the other staff member

about what had happened. He laughed. I couldn't believe it; surely he would think this was bad and do something about it.

'It's normal Matthew. Everyone does it.'

'I don't. I've never seen it done before.'

I couldn't see how it was normal, especially as he had touched me too.

'It is normal. When you get older you will understand.'

'But I didn't like it. I don't understand. I don't want to stay with them again,' I began to cry.

'Look, don't cause trouble. We are on holiday to have a good time. If you want I'll talk to them and ask them not to do it.'

They completely denied it had happened. Denis told me I was just trying to cause trouble and it was three against one so I must be lying and seeking attention, he said. The others didn't want to spend time with me that day because I'd sneaked on them. I went to explore Blackpool alone.

As I walked through the maze of arcades I thought about the last eight months. It had all started at a seaside, like this, on a pier. I didn't realise how naive I was when I first went into care. I thought I had the worst family ever and hated every minute of it; I couldn't wait to leave. But I had come to a hell I hadn't planned for: a hell that had brought me the worst beatings of my life, exposing me to drugs, sex and now molestation.

I don't blame the other children for what they did. Just like me, they'd been labelled, penned and ignored. God only knows what they had experienced before coming into care, but, judging by their behaviour, it must have been worse than what I'd been through. They had spent years going from place to place; Woodstock was reserved for the worst behaved.

At the time I mainly blamed the adults – my social worker for keeping me there and not doing anything to get me out, the staff for not protecting me, Social Services for listening to my Mum, while not believing a word I said. I blamed Mum, too, for staying with Kevin. While she was with him, I was never going home. It was because of her, I thought, that I'd ended up in this place.

Now I don't even blame the staff. They were paid a pittance and completely unsupported in carrying out their duties. At that time, you didn't need any training at that time to become a residential social worker and there were no police background checks. They didn't know what to do when things kicked off and they couldn't handle a troubled eleven-year-old; their answer was to call the police when things got rowdy. They felt as unsafe as I did.

When we got back from Blackpool I was determined to leave Woodstock. One night I tried to run away and Dennis caught hold of me. He restrained me, but I screamed and shouted. He warned me to calm down or he would get Michael to come and deal with me. He knew that would scare me. I dared him to go and do it. So he got someone to go and wake up Michael, who came downstairs. I sat there, held tightly in Denis's arms and started to calm down as Michael stood there watching me. I didn't think they would really let him near me, but I didn't want to chance it.

The next day there were only two staff on duty, both female and one of them pregnant. I set off for the train station first thing to run away. Before I could get on a train the police came and got me. They took me to the police station and restrained me until I calmed down; I kicked out and spat in one of the officer's faces. I said I didn't want to go back to Woodstock, but they took me back anyway. That day I ran away twice more and both times the police took me back. The third time I even told them I was being beaten up at the home, but, when they found out it was only the other children and the staff explained I was always winding them up, they just took me back.

When I was taken back the third time two staff tried to restrain me. As they were scared that I'd harm the pregnant woman they put an armchair over me and sat on it, squashing my small body. I found it hard to breathe and screamed for them to let me go. Michael was in the room and the pregnant woman was his key-worker. He'd kill me, he screamed, if anything happened to her and her baby. I lay there, trapped, terrified, fearing that I was going to die. Eventually the other children went to the Notting Hill Carnival on their own as the two staff had to stay with me. Once the children had gone I convinced them I would calm down if they let me go. They pulled the armchair off me. As soon as they did I ran out of the room, grabbed the golf club that had been used on me before, ran into the office and phoned the police. I told the police operator that I now had control of the building and they should get here quickly. I then climbed on to the roof and waited. I knew we'd go through the same routine. They would either talk me down or come up and get me. I would be restrained and then normal life at Woodstock would resume with another black mark on my file. Not this time. When the first police car arrived they started to try and talk me down. By now several residents from the surrounding area were out watching and the staff had come out to watch too.

'Matthew, we're here to help. This isn't helping anyone, you being up there, is it? Why don't you come down here and we can talk about all this?'

'You won't fucking listen. I have been trying to talk all

day. I said I didn't want to come back here but you just brought me back, again and again. I'm not coming down this time. I'm in control now.'

All the months of pain and anger, humiliation and abuse had been brewing away. Every incident, every beating, every foul word spoken to me flashed before my eyes in rapid succession, as if I was about to die.

'If you don't come down we are going to have to come and get you.'

A police van turned up with many more officers.

'I'll kill any bastard that comes up here'. With that I smashed a window. Destruction felt good. Power surged through me. I was definitely in control now. I smashed another window. It felt great.

'Calm down, Matthew.'

I could see them gearing up to get me. I lost it and just started smashing all the other windows one by one, screaming like a crazed lunatic as I did it. My screams of anger and the shattering of glass, one break after another, were so fast that it sounded like machinegun fire. I smashed all nineteen windows around me. I could see several of the police coming towards me asking me to drop the golf club. I was scared of what they might do. I dropped the club. They ran towards me, grabbing me and forcing me to the ground.

'That's it, calm down now. It's all over'. I no longer struggled. I just sobbed. I knew I had done enough to make them move me. As I sat in the back of the police van, handcuffed to the bar inside I could hear the officers talking with the staff. I could hear them saying I was crazy and should be locked up. The best place for me was secure accommodation. I had no idea where I was being taken to. To think I'd be locked up scared me, but it scared me less than spending another night at Woodstock.

4

Aged Twelve – Caldecott 1992

When I got to Caldecott it took a long time for me to speak at the weekly group therapy meetings. I wasn't convinced I was staying anywhere permanently and I didn't believe I could be helped.

Caldecott did give me some hope, though. The brochures made it sound like a holiday camp with horse riding, pottery classes and a fantastic on-site school. But the best part was the huge, castle-like mansion I was to live in with the other eighty or so residents. When I first arrived I was overwhelmed with a sense of adventure. As I walked up the steps, which seemed to have been built for giants, to the main door with majestic columns and statues either side, I didn't notice that the building was tatty and run-down. The main reception room was as grand as a palace, with a huge aged rug; the dining room was the size of a football field. The stairs wound up five floors to the top of the building.

The place felt mysterious, part magical, part spooky. The offices were in the east wing which was the spookiest of all. I hated climbing up the cramped stairs to the Director's office. The top room on the East Wing was said to be haunted; Jan, who ran the stables, once stayed over there and recalled being woken by a ghost. She didn't seem like a liar. We used to play 'Dungeons and Dragons' in the East Wing 'ghost' room which made the game even more fun.

The bottom part of the mansion had been the servants' quarters and was now a maze of tunnel-like corridors leading to kitchens, offices, laundries and a gym. It was easy to run away from the staff and hide. The grounds were perfect for escapades and escapes. There were several large fields, where we would play football and rugby and hold our annual fetes. Out back there was the biggest natural park I'd ever seen, a mass of trees and dens managed by the local game keeper. Magical, magnificent surroundings, but Caldecott was still much like an open prison, with strict rules and boundaries, and many lurking horrors.

In my first days, I heard all-too-familiar sights and sounds, the painful screams of a child being restrained, a child being pursued across the fields by staff. At Woodstock, the rules were erratic. But Caldecott was different.

The home manager, Diana, was a young woman who looked like a kind angel but had a tone of voice that suggested there was a whip under her wings and she wouldn't hesitate to use it. I liked her but she unnerved me. She told me exactly how it was going to be. I would be happy at Caldecott, but they wouldn't tolerate the kind of things I'd been doing. There were rules and I had to adhere to them; if I didn't, they'd work with me to change my behaviour. But under no circumstances would they let me leave. I was here to stay, for better or worse, and I couldn't do anything to change that. *That's what she thinks*, I thought.

Your first few months in Caldecott were called the 'honeymoon period'. Every child, Diana said, is well-behaved when they first arrive, but eventually, the real 'them' comes out. That wilful child would find Caldecott ready for them. It took longer than she expected with me because I enjoyed my new home. They didn't tolerate bullying or violence of any kind, so I didn't have to worry about being beaten up or molested. On my second day, they took me shopping to buy some things for my room; a lamp, a rug, a duvet and curtain set and a special teddy. I got to choose the colour I wanted my room painted. I had known nothing like it before.

It took some time to get used to the rules, though. Everything about Caldecott was routine; everyone had an agreed bedtime (the younger group 7.30, lights out 8.00 and the older group bed 8.30, lights out 9.00). We all woke up at the same time, had our rooms checked for tidiness and ate together before school. Even the breakfast was prescribed; no more than one bowl of cereal and two slices of toast. One of the staff didn't like white sugar and insisted on brown sugar and, then, only one teaspoon. This rule, although small and insignificant, always bugged me. I thought it stupid one person's preference could be considered right for everyone just because she was an adult.

Lunch was like a scene from *Oliver*, with long tables for each group and the same sloppy food; mince and potatoes, pies and stodgy deserts. Not that I ever complained, it was what I liked to eat: a diet high on starch and fat, low on vegetables and vitamins. The difference between Caldecott and *Oliver* was the noise; Mr Jinks, the Director, would stand up at the head table and bang on the table. He was a man with a heart as big as his stature; as he said grace, his voice boomed across the room like a foghorn and his chin wobbled from side to side. Once he finished and the go ahead to eat was given, the noise would start; chattering, laughing, the banging of tables. Sometimes someone would kick off, start screaming abuse or chuck their plate on the floor. Everyone would suddenly hush. The staff would remove them and the noise would resume. In that honeymoon period, I used to wonder where they took those children and imagined them being taken off to some depository, never to be seen again. I can't remember seeing children who kicked off in the dining room again, but that was probably more because they were too embarrassed to come back than any sinister child-snatching conspiracy!

There wasn't a place for me at the on-site school at first so I stayed at home and got something I had never had before – full-time attention. I made massive tent constructions in the lounge, organised major disasters with the play mobile and read endlessly. Funnily enough, I missed school. Before coming to this chaotic world of 'care', I liked to learn and I was bright. My grandparents would always set me sums when I came round and make sure I read books; they always gave me the confidence to believe I was bright. Now I had to wait for an educational assessment before I could start at the school.

In the meantime I got used to life at Caldecott, exploring the house being my favourite activity. There was a secret passage disguised as book shelves that led into the grand library filled with dusty books. Oil paintings of grand dukes and regal ladies from centuries gone by hung in gilt frames. A door reminded me of one of my favourite childhood books, *The Lion, the Witch and the Wardrobe*, and I would imagine entering a new world each time I went through it. We'd often play group games in the library, tag and table tennis. Next to the library was my favourite room, with a hand-painted ceiling that seemed out of place in what was otherwise a very traditional, but grand residence. It was the most peaceful room in the mansion and I would go there sometimes to just sit and think, while no-one knew where I was.

I was told Caldecott was a 'therapeutic community'. I

understood the community bit right away. Every Sunday we had chapel; it was supposed to be a non-faith based worship. However, we sang Christian songs and Mr Jinks would read from the Bible. My favourite, though, was when he would read us stories; fables with moral codes. His body shook with animation as he presented each character with a different voice. I have never heard a more engaging storyteller. We did lots of activities too. Each year there was a talent show in the library. Each group could enter themselves for different slots; West Wing dominated the show with the most slots. We would sing Beatles songs, act out sketches and read poems. One moment I was John Lennon singing 'Help!' and the next I was dressed as a snake. I think our group contributed more to this because we had a few dramatic types, myself included, who liked to show off.

The culture of West Wing was also different; the staff were more serious and the standards higher. Lots of noise and banging wasn't tolerated at our tables; rarely was one of our children dragged off kicking and screaming away. We always attended chapel in our smart clothes and participated fully in the talent shows and other events. Just like in a family, such high standards came with pressures. Whilst other groups had more relaxed rules about outings or bed times, we were very restricted in our free time. We were seen by most of the children as the 'boffin group', the ones that never got into trouble, when there was chaos around us. But it wasn't that we were calm; we were just contained.

Only one time did things really explode in West Wing, in a riot that took over our house and spread across the mansion. One of the older members of the group, Sean, got into trouble for something. He was the one we all looked up to, cheeky but smart. You could like and respect him, but also have fun with him; his humour was a little too much for the adults and used to get him into trouble. I liked his common sense back chat to some of the stupid rules. Sean kicked off with the staff, which ended up with him restrained on the ground. The average staff count for ten children was two or three at any one time and more in times of crisis. That would be enough to handle one difficult child like Sean, but not many more.

This day everything exploded in the house. It might have been because there were quite a few new children in the group, myself included, as well as new staff. Several staff and children had recently left. A lot of the other children had been at Caldecott for a long time, years, and some of the older children, like Sean, had seen children come and go. They saw others leave to new families but they were stuck in this restrictive place, fed on a diet of textbook therapy and rules; it was hard to see others get what they so desperately wanted. Caldecott had become a holding pen for them, a prison, and every child who left was a reminder that they were unwanted. I know now that people speak of triggers; a child leaving the home often triggered violent incidents.

This time though, everyone turned violent. All ten of us let rip, overpowered the staff and took over the house. As they called in reinforcements, most of us scooted out the windows and into the deer park. One by one the staff found each of us and took us, kicking and screaming, back to the house. The place was unrecognisable. Windows were smashed, tables were overturned, fire extinguishers had been let off. The screams reminded me of my recent past, the hell hole that was Woodstock. I wondered how it had got to this point so quickly. Now they had found out who

I 'really' was, I didn't want to be there any more. I was angry that I let myself appear to be the psychotic little boy described in my files.

I tried to run off through the dinning room, but was grabbed by the angel-like manager, Diana. She threw me to the floor and I hit back. I punched her in the face and tried to bite her arm. She pulled my hair, breathing hard and shouting.

'Your honeymoon period is over, Matthew. Where's that polite little boy gone?'

'Fuck off, you bitch! I'm not staying here any more. You wait until you let me go.'

We struggled around on the floor.

'You are staying here. You won't be going anywhere, Matthew. You're not big and you're not clever.'

She had me pinned to the floor with my arm up my back, her full weight heavy on my legs. She was panting, out of breath. I was calming down, exhausted and defeated. Diana was right. I was not big, I was not clever and my honeymoon period was definitely over.

That night I went up to my room and barricaded the door with my bed. The staff tried to break down the door, but couldn't get through it. I went crazy inside destroying everything in sight; I ripped apart my wardrobe and threw it out my window. I urinated all over the floor. I smashed my mirror and threatened to cut my wrists.

The problem about rioting is that it's bloody exhausting. By 3 a.m. I was so tired that I opened the door to one of the staff, a new woman called Jessica. She slowly calmed me with her soft Irish tones. It was too late to do anything about the room. That night I slept in the staff room with one staff member awake and another sleeping right outside the door to stop me leaving. When I woke up in the morning and remembered my madness from the night before I felt as ashamed as I had that morning after the couch fire. Again I had gone too far; so far I had scared even myself.

But it didn't make me feel I needed help or could get it here. It just made me more determined to flee. And flee I did.

Later that day I ran off up the busy dual carriageway. Jessica and another staff member chased me up the road. I was weaving in and out of the cars. They caught up with me and Jessica tried to pin me to the ground but she was too petite to handle the kicks and punches alone. A bespectacled man stopped his car and offered to help; the three of them bundled me into the car and held me down as the man drove us back to the home. I kicked out and hit him in the face breaking his glasses. The car swerved, horns blared and the cars wheels skidded, but we didn't crash.

We arrived safely back at the home. I was taken to my room and restrained by staff for what seemed like days. Every day for about a week I lashed out. One day I put my hand right through a window, cutting my arm. Later I barricaded myself in the lounge and bit off the head of a rubber Noddy toy, then urinated over the two house hamsters, Bubble and Squeak. I had no control. I was doing anything and everything to get them to chuck me out. But, the more I did, the more they stuck with me, convinced that there was a reason for my mess and 'madness'. Something had happened and they wanted to know what. I realised that there was nothing I could do to make them send me to a new place.

They wanted me to talk. But they didn't push me. In my first few group meetings I didn't have to say much at all. I could just say something about myself if I wanted. But I had to listen and I realised other kids had had it worse. I often felt a fraud living at Caldecott after hearing their stories; like I didn't have a right to be upset with my lot in life. I heard stories of torture, yes torture, not to mention endless stories of sexual molestation, rejection, hate and violence. What is done to children can be so awful. I can't remember every story and some are not mine to tell. Many of the children I listened to in those meetings, week after week for four years, are a blur to me now. That doesn't mean I'll ever forget their pain.

A small group of us arrived at more or less the same time. We were the new ones; or the 'younger ones' as we were called. The older ones, by age and length of time at Caldecott, were either preparing to leave because it was coming up to their sixteenth birthday or because they were finally making the giant leap into a family.

Hilary was one of the lucky ones. She was the brightest child in her house and charming to all those around her. Her head was a mess of curly blonde hair and she smiled constantly. She was clearly the adults' favourite and was held up as an example of what we could become and how we should behave. She went to a local grammar school for girls, brought home 'A' grades and, in group meetings, she was the first to offer the perfect text book psychology to the rest of us. Sometimes I liked her, and at other times it bothered me that she could do no wrong in the eyes of the staff. A few months before she left I could sense it bothered her as well. She started to answer back and to support some of the younger ones when they had problems with the staff. I think she felt under pressure to be such a perfect example when she was still only fifteen. Despite being near-perfect, she had to come to all the group meetings, be in bed by a certain time and abide by all the house rules. But she was the staff's favourite; two of them, Jo and Peter, fostered her so she could stay with them until she was eighteen. That was the first and, as far as I know, the only time any staff from Caldecott fostered any of the children.

We all had our annoying traits; Dicky was my age and would make up wild stories of his life before Caldecott and his future with his Dad. Any stranger could be forgiven for thinking his Dad was James Bond away on a long term secret mission. The truth was much more painful, and he only admitted it rarely, under duress and after long periods of silence in group meetings. As long as I was at Caldecott his superstar Dad never visited. We all annoyed each other, but we also tolerated each other. Because no matter what happened during the week, the tantrums, the broken windows, the abuse, when it came to the group meeting we would each relive the horrors from our past. Then it would become clear why each of us behaved the way we did. We could reach an understanding as we shared our pain. But that didn't mean we became friends, just the most intimate of acquaintances.

By Christmas, 1992, I had accepted that I was staying at Caldecott for some time. At least they listened to what I wanted. Shortly after I arrived, Mum and Kevin came to visit. When they left Kevin gave me a hug goodbye; I pulled away. Later I told the staff I never wanted to see him again and didn't want to see my Mum, either. That was the last time I ever saw Kevin.

A few weeks later, Mum turned up to see me unannounced and the staff got really angry with her. They had a strict policy about planning visits and this was definitely one that hadn't been agreed. It gave me a feeling of safety to know that she couldn't just come and get me. For the first time since I had come into care, I knew that I wouldn't be forced to go home.

Later Mum sent me a horror comic book with a few spooky toys. I thought it was a bit of fun; I didn't like them, but that was because it wasn't my thing, rather finding it sinister. One of the staff thought that there was something more to it and replaced them with something less spooky; they thought it inappropriate and strange for a parent to buy a young child something so scary. To be honest I still think, as I did at the time, that Mum didn't give it a second thought, or mean anything by it. But, at the time, I was comfortable with the staff's view as it placed Mum firmly in the wrong for a change.

My first Christmas at Caldecott was a mass of contradictions; as magical as it was depressing. I had always loved Christmas. As a young child, before Kevin, it was the special time of year that brought our family together. The night before Christmas we'd listen to Cliff Richard's *Mistletoe and Wine* and open one of our presents around the Christmas tree. We would leave out mince pies for Santa and carrots for his reindeer. In the morning we would have a special breakfast. Mum would be extra nice; her voice would be sweet all day and she would try her best not to lose her temper. Boxing Day was spent with my grandparents and the rest of the family. All twelve of their grandchildren in one small house enjoyed the pile of food grandma had spent hours, if not days, preparing.

The Christmas periods just before I went into care, though, were marred by the violence that erupted at Kevin's parents, but it still remained the best time, a time when I always felt loved and didn't need to worry about doing anything wrong.

But this was my first Christmas away from home and I knew it would be different, though I didn't know what to expect. Most of the children were staying at the home for Christmas. The thing I remember most was the Christmas tree which took centre stage on the centre of the spiral staircase, drizzled in glittery balls and twinkling with lights. On Christmas Eve the community gathered around the tree, up the stairs and along the corridors, and sang Christmas carols. We all held small candles stuck in tiny tangerines, I felt warm inside.

I was so excited for the next day that I asked one of the staff for a sleeping pill as I knew I wouldn't be able to sleep. After some persuasion he relented and gave me half a sleeping pill as a compromise. After playing *Mistletoe and Wine* as a reminder of one of the best bits about home, I went off to sleep. The next day he asked me how the sleeping pill had worked. Brilliantly, I told him. Then he confessed it had been a vitamin tablet, not a sleeping pill!

Christmas morning, there was a burst of excitement as we all sat around and opened our presents. As the last presents were opened and the paper bagged away, we realised few of us had presents from people we loved. It is the loneliest feeling in the world not to be wanted by your parents. You can't do anything to make them want you, and even if it's through no fault of your own, you can't help but blame yourself. Christmas is probably the biggest reminder of that to most children in care. You can't avoid the adverts promoting the special family day. And the only way that *your* family is special is that it's abusive, and you no longer live with them. To be faced with the painful reminder that you don't have a family on Christmas day re-opens the wound. As I looked around at the faces of my housemates I could see the pain and disappointment on their faces. Louis had his head down, silence saying more than if he shouted and got angry; Dicky couldn't ignore the fact that his 'James Bond' father had been too busy on secret missions to send him a present or card. The only way he knew to ignore the truth was to start an argument with one of the staff which ended with him hitting out and being restrained; I think he wanted to be restrained so that he could scream and cry out his anger at his father without reality; that he just didn't want him. I couldn't bear to look at Shirley. It always hurt me so much to see her upset; she didn't cry or get angry at first. She just stayed silent and refused to talk. When one of the staff challenged her to talk, she swore and spat in their faces. She started screaming and biting. By now I was crying, but this time not for me.

For the first time, I saw that the children around me were experiencing things I could not imagine. I had not been completely neglected. I always felt like I wasn't wanted by Mum, Dad and Mum's boyfriend. But she acted like she wanted me now. And I had wonderful grandparents. I missed my family that Christmas day.

Later in the afternoon we went for a walk through the grounds. One of the children, Darren, found a baby bird that had fallen from its nest and broken its leg. Darren wanted to help it. This seemed strange as he had always been so hard and aggressive, but he was cradling this baby bird delicately in his hands like a concerned parent. He was crying. The staff said he couldn't bring it back to the house, that the bird was going to die and we should leave nature to take its course. He began to get angry and upset, insisting that he wasn't going to just leave it dying. He ran back to the house. When we got back inside, the bird was in the kitchen sitting in a small box, barely alive. Darren, saviour of the bird, meanwhile, was being held down on the floor by two staff. Eventually, when they let him go, we were called to a group meeting.

Darren had been born prematurely, as had a baby cousin of his when he was just a few years old. He remembered his cousin's tiny hands and feet, from his one visit to the hospital. Shortly after that, his cousin died. For many reasons this had affected Darren; a reminder of his own mortality and his brush with death as a baby. When he saw that small bird in such a vulnerable state, with no one there to help it, he couldn't bear to leave it dying like his cousin. The staff had been slow to realise this, but they were quick to make amends. We all agreed that it would be the right thing to give the little bird a proper burial. All of us gathered around a tree and Darren prepared the ground as we stood around in silence holding hands. As he put the bird into the ground and covered him up, we began to break down and cry. I looked over at Louis and, for the first time since he came to Caldecott, I saw tears streaming down his face. For all of us the little bird had been a close reminder of our own loneliness and loss. We were as vulnerable and alone as that little bird had been. Like the bird's leg, our little hearts had been broken and might never be repaired.

I realised for the first time that Christmas would never be the same again. And it never has.

I have described the episode where Diana restrained me. At the time there was no training in safe restraint and most staff were very young as well as untrained. Staff now receive training in how to restrain children and young people.

78

5

Aged Fourteen – Recovery and Disclosure

Each child had two key workers at Caldecott who took the lead on all decisions to do with their case; school, family contact, even any specific rules or punishment. As well as Jessica, I was lucky to have a powerfully exciting influence in my life, Elroy. He was a big Scouser with stubble and loose flowing hair which he was proud to say he never washed and conditioned. He had been a police officer and then spent several years travelling across Europe in his old converted ambulance. In the back, he had an arrow and a crossbow for catching octopuses; for months I was intrigued by his tales of adventure in the waters of Portugal, catching giant squid and picking oranges in Spain; it sounded so romantic. I wanted to be like him. He would always play-fight with me, letting me hit him in the stomach which he'd clench tightly so that it hurt me more than it hurt him. He would tickle me relentlessly. He was such a free spirit when he first came to Caldecott, very different from some of the older staff who had been there a long time.

The new staff didn't speak in the same way as the old ones; they didn't say things like 'talk about your feelings Matthew' or 'you need to think about your actions'. They just talked normally. Elroy and I spent a lot of time together in those early days as each child had 'special time' with their key worker. My favourite time was 'special food' with Elroy. Twice a week you would have anything that you wanted at bedtime, with your key worker and they would read or chat with you. Elroy made me cockle sandwiches or beans on toast and would do a puppet show for me. I had this snake puppet that he would use and put on the scariest voice I ever heard; he would put the slithery horror over the door and say as slowly as possible 'Matttthhheewww'. I'd scream and laugh in mock fear, knowing what was coming. He would get closer and closer with the puppet until he came and tickled me like crazy with it. He would then read to me until it was time for lights out. Elroy always challenged me to try harder and think about things. When I went to Caldecott I never ate anything except for meat and potatoes; I wouldn't eat vegetables and was reluctant to try anything new. Slowly Elroy got me to be bolder. Eventually he even had me eating mussels. He was like a father to me in a lot of ways and I loved the attention he gave me, something I had never really had from a man before.

Elroy was a great influence on the others in the group including the staff. He had a guitar and a beautiful singing voice and taught us songs from his music books. We would all sit around and sing songs together as he strummed away at his guitar.

Caldecott was a mixed blessing for me. I had to get used to the affection that you got from adults. If you wanted a hug you just had to ask; if you wanted to hold an adult's hand you could. For months I couldn't do either. I hadn't had a hug since coming into care and it felt strange to have anyone hug me now. Eventually, though, I got used to the idea and gave Elroy a hug. Once I started hugging.

I couldn't stop and loved to cuddle up with Elroy or Jessica on the sofa.

The other side to Caldecott was that you were scrutinised with such intensity that it would make the most secure person turn paranoid. The new staff soon learned the language and the business of 'interpretation' and of investing meaning to things that didn't need any. Sometimes they were right in their analysis but more often than not they were wrong. Once I hadn't bothered to comb my hair so it was messy. Elroy made such a vast mystifying deal about it. He made me sit on my own in what we called 'the naughty chair', but the staff called the 'quiet corner', to think about my feelings. There was nothing to think about; I just didn't feel like combing my hair. It was not a sign of anything deeper.

Sitting in the quiet corner was the worst kind of punishment they could give me. It reminded me of Mr Taylor making me sit on my own in the corridor and write lines when I was late. I hated being alone with my thoughts. It was something they thought necessary, that it was wrong to want to be with people all the time. Sometimes I would have to spend ages there, one day over five hours, and I couldn't read or do anything else, just think. All I thought about was how stupid Caldecott was with its rules and rituals. I would often end up in the quiet corner for minor silly things. The alternative was worse though; if I refused to go there it would escalate and I would either be forced or taken upstairs to a room to be restrained.

After my first six months I got tired of being restrained and just wanted to get things right. The quiet corner, however mind-numbingly boring, was better than restraint.

My room was near the upstairs lounge where the staff would have their evening meeting to discuss all of our behaviour in detail. I'd sit by my door and try to listen, hoping to catch what they said about me. They played 'relaxation' music each night to help us sleep, which made it hard to hear – and ironically, made it hard to sleep. I hated having to listen to Enya and sometimes had to stop myself slinging the tape recorder out of the window. But I still heard most things they said. It would make me so angry when they got it wrong, when something I had said or done would be misinterpreted and made into a big deal. The worst thing about it was they would often not say anything about it to you at the time, instead just raising it at the staff meeting. When they did raise a 'pattern of behaviour' with me, I'd get angry and ask why they didn't just say it at the time so I could do something about it then. But I'd never correct them about those things I overheard from the staff meeting. I couldn't risk cutting my flow of information, which I now needed to ease my paranoia.

The new staff quickly fell in with the intense culture of amateur psychology and Elroy and Jessica became two of the most judgmental and sanctimonious of them all. Their way was the only way of doing things. If I disagreed with them, they trotted out their privileged defence of being right because they were the adult and I the child: *'Think about your feelings, Matthew'*, they would say. It made my blood boil over at times and I would get angry, not violent, just answering back and trying to defend my position. They sometimes slapped their thighs and said 'Ha! We were right, look! You are angry so there must be something wrong'.

Eventually I chose not to go into battle with them. I tried to keep my behaviour as constant as possible and use the information I got from eavesdropping on their staff meetings to help me adjust to their view of how I should be. When that didn't work and it started to become a disagreement I would accept my defeat, surrender and disclose some ill feeling about something or other. Once I had cried, talked about my feelings and got my hug, they would back off and everything would go back to normal again. But this wasn't therapy; it was just a game between two groups; adults, who had the power and children who did not. These things they chose to pick on simply avoided the bigger issues we had to face and prolonged our stay at Caldecott. Love and care were offered freely; but your feelings were not yours to make sense of. It was like an intense course of radiotherapy; it may cure you. But too much of it can have serious consequences to your health, and may even be fatal.

School eventually became my refuge. I finally got a place at the on-site school several months after I arrived. Everyone at Caldecott started at the on-site school as part of assessment before going to a mainstream school; the truth was that most of the children would remain at the school until they left. We had maths, science and art lessons. My teachers reminded me a little of French and Saunders. Val looked like Jennifer Saunders and shared her sarcastic style of humour; Bryony was beautiful and young and her only resemblance to Dawn French was her jet black hair. She acted as Val's comedy side kick. They entertained us with songs and dance and together we created our own 'in jokes'. They were both fans of *Absolutely Fabulous* and in our free sessions we used to watch it as a class. Everyone in the school was jealous of the fact we had Val and Bryony.

The school was more relaxed than a mainstream school; we called teachers by their first names, we didn't have to wear a uniform and there only ten of us to each class. The best bit about school was drama. Val and Bryony taught us English and Drama and they became my favourite subjects. They gave us confidence and were always so proud when we did well, so much so that we rarely misbehaved for fear of damaging their belief in us.

The work at the school was very basic and not very challenging. They knew this and always pushed for me to go to a mainstream school. As outsiders from the intense culture of West Wing they saw life through a different lens; a more rational one. You could be, or feel, a certain way with them without it being spun into something different or more than it needed it be. Several times they clashed with Elroy or Jessica about why I behaved the way I did. Sometimes a child being cheeky is just a child being cheeky, not a revelation of deep-seated trauma. They would listen sympathetically when I had a grumble about life at West Wing, without rationalising my complaint away. It made me feel a little more normal and believe that I wasn't going crazy.

My other favourite class was art. Peter Hodgeson, my art teacher and a deputy head at the school, became a powerful influence in my life. He had a great sense of humour and endless enthusiasm. He looked older than he was with a fuzzy beard, slightly balding head and large rimmed glasses. He spoke with a slight northern twinge. He was very encouraging and would always remind me of what I could do in life. He taught me desktop publishing so I could design things. Two evenings a week he led the pottery class where we would make clay 'masterpieces' most of which would never see the light of day. We would go home covered in clay with a disfigured cup or a wonky bowl to offer some unfortunate soul as a present. I would try and spend as much of the time with Peter as I could. I felt like I had a connection with him beyond that of the other children; of course he cared about all of us, you could see that, but I felt then, as I do now, that he had a special place for me in his heart. He spent hours telling me stories about his life, where he had worked before and his adventures at Caldecott in years gone by.

The first year I was there he organised a 'green circus' with live bands and lots of green activities. Peter was an eco-warrior before green causes became cool. His influence rubbed off on me in many ways. He was a vegetarian and we spent a long time talking about the reasons why. For months I thought about it and became convinced it was the right thing for me to do. It wasn't just that Peter was a vegetarian, I had been a member of Greenpeace and, despite 'hamstergate', I'd always loved animals. I decided to become a vegetarian. I lasted a whole four months, until they served my favourite Steak and Kidney pudding at lunch one day. I was so ashamed but Peter didn't care at all. That special bond between us was confirmed when he and his wife invited me for dinner at their house. Nobody else had ever been asked before and I was so proud that day, I even remember what we ate; some kind of special pate with Melba toast and vegetables. He always came to my birthday parties.

Love is at least part of the answer if you are in care. I never played up with Peter because I knew he liked me for who I was, and genuinely wanted me to succeed. We talked about the crap at West Wing a bit and I knew the style of therapy they used bothered him. We used to joke about the phrases 'talk about your feelings' and 'let's discuss why you feel angry.'

His wife, Jan, was in charge of horse-riding. I felt scared of horses and was adamant she would not get me on one. But over time she coaxed me onto one of the smallest ponies, Portly, a small white Shetland with a long mane.

Sometimes I spent hours stroking him and chatting away like he was my best friend. When he died we buried him next to the stable arena. Slowly I progressed to one of the bigger horses and ended up riding Tango, one of Jan's favourites. I grew to like Jan and appreciated that you often knew where you were with her; if she was unhappy with you for something you had done she would tell you outright, not hand it to you when it became 'a pattern of behaviour'. My confidence with the horses grew and over the four years at Caldecott I even learned how to feed and comb a horse. Sometimes we do a 'jamboree' where two of us would be mounted, one standing and holding onto the other as the horse trotted in a circle. Several times I went on trips with Jan and Peter to horse shows. I loved being with them both and sometimes fantasised about them fostering me, just as Jo and Peter had fostered Shirley.

As my confidence grew, I had a wild idea. Caldecott needed a newspaper. I said that to Elroy on one of our long walks

'It's not a bad idea, but I don't think you will do it.'

'Why not?' I asked, surprised.

'I don't know. It's just a big challenge. I'm not sure you can handle it.'

I thought he might be joking, but he looked dead serious.

'How do you know I can't handle it? I think I can.'

'You just don't finish things. You always start projects and never finish them.' He was right; I had lots of different schemes on the go. Recently I had started putting my puppets together again, but hadn't finished them. But I began to get angry, although I wasn't quite sure if I was angry with him for being right.

'I can do it. I will do it. You can't stop me. I'll prove it to you.'

'Okay, okay. I'm not going to stop you. If you say you can do it, try it. But I'm telling you now I don't think you can.'

We walked on. I was determined to prove him wrong. How dare he tell me I couldn't do something.

The next day I went to the head teacher of the school, Jonathan Stanley, and told him about the idea. He liked it and asked me what I needed to make it work. He gave me fifty pounds to start it up and a small office to assemble my news team. My partner on the project was Mary, a beautiful girl I had a huge crush on, from my class. Mary was the cool girl from school and immediately got a group of six of her friends together for our first news team meeting. *Community News* was born.

The first job was to get the newsroom sorted; Mary and I were co-editors and had our own desks. We had a meeting table where we could convene our news team. We only had one or two meetings with them though. It quickly became clear that Mary and I were the only ones committed to actually doing it. Our first issue was cobbled together on A3 sheets of paper. We used the word processor to type the articles and cut and pasted them. That's how we photocopied the first issue. It looked clumsy and amateurish, but it was ours! We sold them for 10p and within hours were sold out. I took it straight to Elroy.

'Ha! I finished it. You told me I couldn't do it and I did,' I said.

He looked at me and smiled.

'Yes. I knew you would.'

'Then why did you say I wouldn't?'

'A bit of encouragement. I wanted you to prove me wrong. Now you have to keep it going'.

We kept it going each month, with each issue getting

better. We used desktop publishing to make it look more professional and as I got better so did the editing. Each issue came with a sweet taped to the front and it became a surprise for everyone as to what sweet they would get that month. Later we wrote to Lord Brabourne, the owner of the mansion in which we lived. He sent us a congratulations letter and a donation of ten pounds. That was the first time I proved to myself that I could do what I put my mind to.

I quickly started working on another project. After I went on a visit with our class to see *Joseph and his Technicolour Dream Coat* in the West End, I wanted to put on my own production of it at Caldecott. The whole group of children got involved. Just as in my play at the church as a young child, I was the director and the lead part, the narrator.

Several months later, a packed audience of Caldecott residents and group members' family and friends saw our production. I remember looking back on the video afterwards and being so embarrassed that I spent the entire time in our dances looking behind me at the floor of the other children's feet to make sure they were doing the same moves! But I was pleased we pulled it together and it was another boost to my confidence. Shortly after this one of the staff at Caldecott came in with an advert for a local theatre company, KHAOS, looking for child actors. I jumped at the chance. The first musical they were auditioning for was *The King and I* and I was cast as one of the children. I only had two lines but we had to learn all the dances and songs. I practised my two lines and my dance routines over and over again. The show was packed with several hundred people each night.

I was so excited that I would get to the hall at least two hours before everyone else to get ready. I loved watching everyone prepare; the build-up was electric. I watched the band rehearse from the wings and felt excited. The best feeling was always at the end when we bowed to a rapturous reception from the audience. I'd always end up crying from sheer pride. For weeks after the production finished, I would feel sad, lost and lonely because I missed the fun of rehearsing and bonding with everyone else involved.

I took a bigger part in *Guys and Dolls*, the production I enjoyed most. I stayed with KHAOS until I left Caldecott. It too taught me a lot and gave me more confidence and it was also another refuge from the intensity of the home.

I had very little contact with Social Services once I got to Caldecott. I saw my social worker, Haniff, just once, when he came before Christmas. He brought his daughter along; it felt strange to talk to him about personal things with a girl my own age there. I didn't say much. As he left, he told me he was leaving the local authority and I would have a new social worker. He didn't know who yet, but there would be a duty social worker allocated to my case in the meantime. Although I wasn't going to miss him, I did feel a bit left behind. It was as if now I was here there was nothing more for them to do. I still had so many questions about where I was going in life and he was the only one from the people in charge who could answer them. His parting words were 'what did you want for Christmas?'

The thrilling news was that I could choose from two presents which the local authority were giving children in care. A toy car or a doll. I chose the car. But I never saw it. I'm sure it was nothing special; we all joked about it. It seemed such an odd thing to say to a child – choose your Christmas present, either a doll or a car. Social work obviously had a box of cars and dolls somewhere in their basement.

I didn't see any species of social worker for a long time after that. My review meetings were cancelled at the last minute. I was clearly not a major priority.

After almost 18 months of waiting, Jo got fed up and wrote to the Head of Service, Hugh Pelham, to complain. Within days she got a letter back apologising and a new social worker was appointed. He didn't make me feel too wonderful. His face was stubbly and his moustache badly trimmed, his hair liberated from any kind of order. He smoked like a chimney and never wore anything smart, even to review meetings. The strangest thing about him was his accent; it was a mixture from all over the country and you could never quite place it. I treated my new social worker, Tony, with some scepticism. Caldecott agreed and the staff were just as sceptical of him as I was. I liked that. It was not just me against them; it was me and Caldecott against them. But once Social Services started to get their act together, Caldecott were no longer on my side.

The review meetings started again. I was never allowed to attend until they were almost over and the decisions, already made with professional wisdom, were fed back to me. It used to drive me crazy having to wait, sometimes for several hours, while they discussed every detail of my behaviour without challenge. I could only imagine how Caldecott would interpret my behaviour and the spin that Mum would put on it.

Part of the therapy at Caldecott involved one-to-one play time with your key worker. Every two weeks you'd go into the play room and have an hour to do an activity; it might involve just messing around with the play mobile models – which was my favourite – or something more serious like life story work. I hadn't talked much about my past beyond what had happened at home with Mum and Kevin.

Some memories came back to me during those discussions. I began to remember how Mum would handle me when I started at school and was naughty. She'd be so angry with me. We'd get home and she'd shout for me to bend over the bed and pull my pants down. I'd apologise and beg her not to, but she ignored my cries and hit me as hard as she could on the bottom with a vacuum-cleaner hose. It would sting like mad but it wasn't the worst of the pain. When she was finished she'd make me stay in my room and go to bed early, sometimes without tea. John would be up watching TV with her and when I went into to the warm cosy lounge, she'd scream for me to get back into my bedroom. I had forgotten about this until, in one of those play sessions, I started to talk about it. They suggested I speak to Mum about it and I decided to call her and talk to her.

The road to Hell is paved with good therapeutic intentions.

No matter how much you hate your mother for the things she has done to you, she is the only mother you have. After about a year at Caldecott, Elroy told me that Mum and Kevin had split up. 'It's about time' was my response. It still hurt that it had taken her so long to split up with him. She'd been prepared to leave me in care – sixteen months of loneliness, pain, abuse and chaos – for the joy of being with Kevin. Oddly, part of me was also angry that it hadn't worked out. If she hadn't found the special 'forever' love, then what had this all been about? How could she make such a monumental decision, choosing a man over her son if it was all going to end in 18 short months? Of course, she couldn't have known that at the time, and maybe it *felt* 'forever' for her when she loved him; I can never know her reasoning. I can only explain how it made me feel. I should have been happy but I was just angry. I felt worthless, that I meant so little to her that she'd chosen a man who didn't last long anyway.

One of the early phone calls to Mum went badly. Trying not to sound angry, I told her what I remembered about the spankings. She asked me why I was lying again. I couldn't believe it. My memories on this were not a blur; it was just that so much had happened since that time that something had blocked it out. I told her I understood I had been a bad child when I was younger; she was only twenty and it can't have been easy with Dad always at work, having to take care of me and a two-year-old. But she couldn't even admit that and got angry; she didn't understand why I was doing this to her, she said. In the end she hung up.

I ran off that night and hid in the school playground until one of the staff found me and brought me back. I was angry that I was being portrayed as the liar again; I knew she'd be believed and I wouldn't. I couldn't prove what had happened as it was a 'he said – she said' and who believes children? I never brought it up again whilst I was at Caldecott. I knew it wouldn't be worth it.

I missed Mum. No matter what she had done and how angry I was with her, she was still my mother. I had thought about that during my first lonely Christmas at Caldecott. The thought of spending another Christmas away from my family scared me. I also thought about my youngest brother, Danny, a lot. I'd never got on that well with John, but Danny and I were very similar, both daydreamers who always seemed to be in a bit of trouble. I sensed that he was lost and lonely in the world too.

One night, during 'special food', I spoke with Elroy about seeing Mum again. Caldecott went about arranging it, but they felt I needed to apologise to her for the way I had treated her. I couldn't believe it; *she* should have apologised to *me*, not the other way around. But I was tired of fighting. I was just an eleven-year-old boy who wanted things to return to normal. I agreed to the apology meeting, albeit through gritted teeth.

Gordon Brown should have spent a day at Caldecott. They believed in saying sorry. Elroy and other workers went through the things I should probably apologise for; they did not tell me what to say but they coached me in the subject of 'what has upset your mother and made her feel livid'. Poor mistreated Mum. I had said vile things to her. I had put her through terrible pain. I prepared myself to accept everything as my fault. It was the only way I could see things ever repairing themselves in our family. It was also the only way I could see myself getting out of care.

As I sat in the room with Mum I tried to rid myself of all the thoughts of anger and betrayal I had towards her. Elroy started things off.

'Matthew, would you like to start?' he asked.

I didn't know how to start, however.

'Your Mother has come a long way to see you today,' she went on. 'I think you owe it to her to talk about this.'

'Well, er, I've been thinking a lot about what has happened in the past. I've not been nice to you. And I'm sorry about that.' I kept my head down. I sounded genuine and I was. I was sorry for the pain that I'd caused her. That, at least, wasn't all her fault.

Graciously accepting the apology was not going to happen, I realised. She was quick on the draw.

'Matthew, it's all very well sitting there and saying sorry now. But you have to realise it's not as easy as that. You've said some very hurtful things to me.' She began to cry. 'You don't realise how difficult this has been for all of us.'

'I do,' I said quietly.

'Well if you did then you wouldn't have done those things, would you?'

Of course, I started to forget how sorry I was. It was exactly like her to be so sanctimonious. She was magnificent at being the victim; it sounded good in front of Elroy. She'd felt judged by Social Services since I came into care, she said, ignoring the fact that they had believed her version of events. This was her chance to make the point that they were wrong and my saying sorry was proof of that. I half expected the apology to be returned. I might as well have expected pennies from Heaven.

'It's going to take a long time to trust you again, Matthew. But I want you home just like I always have. This time it has to be right though; it won't be overnight.'

I was beginning to think it wasn't such a good idea for me to go home after all. It felt like all those times she'd made me feel guilty as a child. She'd hold this against me forever, yet another of the Crimes of Matthew.

If I wanted to keep things smooth, I wouldn't argue with her. I had been determined to keep things smooth, but she wasn't making it easy by denying any responsibility.

Bad children have to learn to shut up in the system even when it pretends it wants you to talk. I had gone from this crazy wild child who hit out at everything and everyone to this submissive, calm mini-adult. With insight!

So I sat there and didn't argue with her; I just took it. But as I left the room I felt like it had been forced; my apology wasn't all that real because there was a huge missing chunk of reality. The bitter truth was that we didn't then, or later, discuss honestly what had happened at home all those years and talk it through. I couldn't help feeling this was one big shortcut and at my expense. But at the time I was just happy it was over. As long as I could somehow get back to normal, I was prepared to take it.

Remembering the past doesn't fix it. Another time I was in a play session with Elroy and Jessica. I can't remember how the conversation started, but we began talking about my time in care. I'd never spoken about my time at Woodstock and had never really been asked questions about it. For over a year, I kept it as far away from my mind as possible. But after I had really settled into life at Caldecott I realised that there was nothing normal about Woodstock or the way I had been treated there. I just started talking about everything that happened there; the riots, the drugs and the beatings all spilled out of me. I told them about the shed at the bottom of the field and the sex that used to go on in there. I told them about that night when Craig restrained me naked on the floor in view of everyone. I held back the bit about being touched by Michael; I told them I watched them masturbate, but I couldn't bring myself to tell them any more than that. It was like I was part of it if I told them that; as if I must have wanted them to touch me. They just sat there in silence and listened; they didn't interrupt me or ask questions. At the end of it we all sat in silence. Eventually Elroy spoke.

'Thank you for telling us that, Matthew. It can't have been easy.'

I broke down into tears. I didn't realise how much I wanted to tell someone until he said that. I'd never thought about telling anyone because I didn't think anyone would care; I had told my social worker what was happening and he just told me to stop whinging. Why did I choose to finally talk about it? I think because I knew what happened in Woodstock was wrong and I felt safe enough at Caldecott to reveal it all. I didn't expect anything else to happen. Just being listened to was enough for me.

'What happened to you was wrong,' Jessica said, and held my hands, her soothing voice calming me.

I knew it was wrong, but having someone tell me was like being liberated from a prison sentence in my head; a prison sentence that I didn't deserve. But that wouldn't be the end of it.

6

Aged Fifteen – Leaving Caldecott

The familiar camera hung from the ceiling, the red light flashing, indicating it was on. I sat on a soft couch in front of a giant mirror. I knew that people were the other side; Jessica and Elroy had taken me there so they would be watching me through that mirror. What I didn't know was that Mum was also behind the mirror.

This time, though, it wasn't a psychotherapist in front of me but two detectives, a woman from the police child protection team and a man. They had their own camera, too. Jessica had explained that the police wanted to interview me about what had happened at Woodstock. But I had no idea what they would ask and what would happen next. I felt nervous as if I had done something wrong. Yet again I felt under some kind of scrutiny, like this was all some kind of ploy to catch me out.

These detectives were not like any police I had seen before; they didn't have uniforms and they didn't talk to me as if I had done something wrong. They were friendly and kind.

'Matthew, thank you for talking with us today. I know this must be very difficult for you. The cameras are here just so we can listen to what you say and not have to write anything down. They are nothing to worry about and nobody else is going to see the videos except us.'

The man did all the talking and seemed to be in charge.

'We just want you to tell us what happened to you at Woodstock. You can take as long as you like.'

'But I told Elroy and Jessica everything.'

'I know you did. But to do something about it you have to tell us yourself.'

'I don't want to talk about it again'. I kept my head down.

'I understand that. It is a very hard thing to talk about it. But if you don't talk to us we can't do anything about it. You see, what happened to you was wrong and should not have happened. We want to make sure it doesn't happen to anyone else. You can help us do that.'

I felt cornered; if I didn't tell them then I'd be responsible for something happening to another child like me and I didn't want that. I slowly went through the memories again. It was more difficult this time. It didn't just all come out like it had in the play session.

Intermittently, I'd stop and tell them that I'd said all I wanted to. Then the man started coaxing me on with more questions. His questions made me angry; it felt like he was questioning my version of the truth, as if I might be lying to him. Several times I got into an argument with him about it and would end up crying. Then the woman would speak.

'Matthew, this isn't about whether you are telling the truth. We're just trying to listen to you and help you tell your story.' She held my hand and passed me tissues when I cried. I liked her; I didn't like him. I realise now that was exactly what she was there for. Eventually we got to the bit about Craig – the bit I didn't want to say much about. I told them what I remembered; about finding myself naked on the floor with him restraining me, sitting on top of me, my body face down; seeing the others laughing at me through the window.

'What else happened that evening with Craig?' It was the man speaking.

'Nothing else happened.'

'Did he have all his clothes on when he held you down?'

'Yes. That's what I told you.' I was getting angry. We were just going round in circles.

'Why would Craig be holding you down naked?'

'I don't know. I'm not making this up.'

I started to fidget and I wouldn't look up at him. He didn't say anything and just waited for me to say more.

'I don't like this. I don't want to say anything else,' I said.

I couldn't see why this was the part they were most interested in. I'd told them about all the violence, sex and drugs. They didn't seem interested in that at all. We spent the next half an hour going round in circles; I didn't know what else I could tell them about Craig. There was nothing else that I remembered. Anyway, for me, it wasn't the most horrifying of my experiences at Woodstock. That was something I chose not to speak about; what had happened that night in the tent at Blackpool. Eventually they stopped asking me questions and thanked me for what I had told them. I never heard what happened with the investigation after that.

For years after that incident in Blackpool I'd convinced myself that sex and masturbation were a bad thing. I was never going to do any of *that*. In play time, when I was about fourteen, Elroy decided to confront this by introducing me to the 'facts of life'. He sat me down to read some books about how babies were made. It disgusted me that Elroy thought sex and masturbation weren't just okay but the best thing a man could do. He compared it to a footballer scoring a goal in front of a stadium of thousands of cheering fans. Every man masturbated, Elroy said. But I'd never do it. I never told him why I thought it was such a bad thing. I know now that I was scared because of my experience at Blackpool. Someone else had touched me and it had made me feel sick. I couldn't imagine now doing that to myself without that image of Michael with white goo coming out of his penis and the feeling of being used. But Elroy insisted. Masturbation was not just perfectly normal but rather good.

Over the next year I thought about what he told me and although I couldn't reconcile that idea with the feeling I had had in the tent with Michael, I wanted to try and experience it. Night after night I'd try, but it never worked. I'd wait for hours for something to happen but it just hurt. Eventually I gave up. It was only when I was fifteen, while watching a film with a sex scene that I realised I didn't need to worry about masturbation, in fact. Over time I blocked out the memories of the experience with Michael. But Blackpool would come back to haunt me when I started my own sex life with women.

After the interview with the police and various visits from social service investigators, I was happy to try and move on from my Woodstock experience. Although the issue had not been concluded – in the words of Caldecott I had not had 'closure' – it was something I never wanted to talk about again.

And sex was less important than what happened at our annual fete, where Caldecott's grounds opened up to the local community and parents and friends of children came to visit.

That day I had lots of visitors; Mum came with my

brothers and her Dad, my Dad came with my other Grandad. I was in a good mood; I'd prepared a brilliant monster costume for the fancy dress competition and was sure I was going to win. But before the competition started, I was taken upstairs for a meeting with Mum and Dad. They both looked serious and uncomfortable. I could see her struggling to hold the tears back. I thought somebody had died, but quickly realised everyone I knew was in the room and my brothers were waiting downstairs. The atmosphere was thick and they all seemed to be waiting for someone to speak.

I wonder now how many minutes the silence lasted. Then the truth tumbled out.

'Your father is really a man called Brian Phillips. He left before you were born and has never been seen since. We feel you should know, but it will not change anything with your family,' Jessica said.

She talked coldly, like she was reading from a press statement. For a while no one said a word. I could hear crying and knew it was Mum.

'This doesn't change anything, Matthew.'

I couldn't look up, but I knew it must be 'my Dad' speaking. I felt sick with a sense of betrayal, every word slicing my heart up piece by piece.

'I'm still your Dad and I always will be,' he went on.

I couldn't quite believe it. I felt numb; except for the tears that tore down my face, like blood from an open wound. I wasn't angry or disappointed. It was as if I had known – like it all made sense. That was why he didn't want to take care of me. I wasn't his son. Someone could have told me.

'I promise to be your Dad always,' he said.

More silence weighed on the room. Finally Jessica asked

the utterly predictable question: 'How does this make you feel, Matthew?'

At that moment it didn't make me feel anything. I was sad, but wasn't quite sure why. I felt betrayed, but not angry, just flat, flat, flat.

'I don't want to talk about it.'

'I think it's important you talk about it. This is a big piece of news,' she said.

I knew it was a big piece of news. I was furious that I now had to behave as Caldecott expected. Explore my feelings, dance with my anger, do the therapy high jump. Jessica had no right. I felt she was as much part of this as they all were. They must have known about this. It started to feel like one big conspiracy.

'I'm not going to talk about it and I don't have to'. Silence again. I had the moral high ground here.

'Okay'. Jessica relented. She didn't want a Grade-A flare up in front of visitors.

'I just want to go back downstairs. The fancy dress competition is going to be soon.'

'Okay, you can go.'

I went downstairs into the library where everyone was gathering for the competition and sat next to my brothers. Danny turned towards me.

'We have a different Dad to you.' I was shocked that they knew.

'I know'. I spoke without emotion. The rest of the afternoon went without a second thought about what I had learnt that day. I won second prize in fancy dress. Mum and 'Dad' – not my Dad – as well as my grandparents – one set of whom were not my true grandparents – came and said goodbye. I felt nothing; no anger and no pain.

When I went to bed I lay awake thinking and realised

no one had raised something rather personal. There was another person out there who *was* my Dad. I didn't wonder what he was like or whether I wanted to meet him. To me I already had a Dad even if he hadn't been there at the start of me. I was consumed more by the fear that he would no longer want to know me. He had said that nothing had changed and he would always be my Dad. But things had changed. I remembered a visit six months before. We talked about where I might live in the future. I saw my future with Dad; I had a plan hatched in my head that I had talked to him about many times that I would leave Caldecott in a few years when I was more independent and wouldn't need as much help from him. Until that day he'd seemed fine with the idea. Now he explained that things had changed for him. He'd met a woman and had fallen in love. She had children and they were going to live together. He wasn't going to be able to take care of me and it wasn't fair to keep the idea in my head that I would one day live with him. I needed to make different plans.

I now realised why he didn't want me to live with him. I wasn't his problem; I wasn't his son. I thought back to all those nights when I'd stayed next to the phone ringing and ringing waiting for him to answer so he could come and collect me. He never answered and he never came. I could never understand why. Now I did. I wasn't his son. They all knew that and must have been at a loss as to what to say to this little boy begging for his Dad.

I wondered how long they would have kept this lie up, if I hadn't been in care. Would I have ever known the truth? I lay there with all these thoughts swimming around my head and still I didn't feel anger or pain, just hopelessness. Part of me had been taken away and fathers aren't easy to replace.

103

Over the next few weeks living at Caldecott was easier to crack, but still hard work. My secret late night listening to the staff meetings helped; it allowed me to be just what they wanted me to be. Faking it is a big part of surviving care. If I heard them say I'd been too aggressive, quiet, rude or whatever, the next day I'd apologise as if I had come to that stunning insight by myself. Most of the time, I disagreed with their analysis. Often they got me wrong; things that I hadn't even thought about twice or words which were said off the cuff were twisted and given complicated meanings. It frustrated me, but I'd long since learned you didn't win if you piped up. Elroy was the worst to argue with as he'd say he was right because he was the adult.

I remember one conversation with him, in which I argued that everybody's views were surely worth listening to. He replied the adults here were professionals and were most definitely right. It made me so angry. But arguing with him or any of the other staff often resulted in time in the quiet chair. Be dumb, be numb seemed to be the best way to survive. I became as reflective and analytical as the adults and became a junior therapist, offering advice in group meetings to other children. Initially it was a way of endearing myself to the adults, but I soon realised that often my advice made sense and it did come from the heart. In each group meeting, I'd grow in my understanding of other people's emotions. As I listened to their stories of abuse and neglect, I would feel their pain. Often I would feel it so much I would cry as they told their stories; afterwards I would be the first to offer my thanks and feedback. My empathy was real and the staff liked it. The more I mirrored their language and met their expectations of me, the more they put me on a pedestal as an example to the other children.

Being on a pedestal made my life easier. I could be trusted and had more freedom; I was allowed to stay in the house on my own when everyone else went shopping or on group trips. I could have a lie-in on Saturday mornings. I was even allowed out by myself on Saturdays to go to town. These freedoms gave me the sanity I needed to survive. But they also led to pressures. If you are held up as an example to others, you have to keep your image up all the time. As a fifteen-year-old, that's virtually impossible.

When I made mistakes it was a bigger deal than if anyone else had done the same thing. Staff would tell me how disappointed in me they were and remind me that the other children looked up to me. It chipped away at my confidence. The only way I found to deal with this pressure was simply to accept complete responsibility when I did something wrong. I'd ask for forgiveness, hang my head in shame and admit everything, whether it was a minor or a serious offence. Then it would be their turn to give me advice; and after all the times I had used my wits and mimicked the staff to my advantage in those meetings they threw back every piece of pious advice and opinion I had thrown their way. Living at Caldecott had become a game and it was a game I played well; most of the time I won.

Then I got the news I'd wanted for ages. I was going back to mainstream school. I had a proper educational assessment, which placed my IQ at 'above average'. The staff knew, just as I did, that I needed to go to a mainstream school where I could actually sit some exams. It was already year eight in secondary school and I had missed almost three years of school. If I didn't get out soon I wouldn't be able to sit my GCSEs.

Mum, Elroy, Jessica, Val and the school head, Jonathan Stanley, went out searching for a suitable school for me.

As usual I was excluded though I desperately wanted to see the schools. I couldn't understand why they wouldn't answer my questions about the schools they had seen. They said they wanted to pick the right one before they told me anything. There was a debate about whether I should go to a grammar school or a normal school; I knew the difference then as the former was the harder and more challenging. I desperately wanted to go to grammar school. Elroy agreed. But the others – and Mum – thought it would be too much for me and decided to send me to a normal comprehensive in Hythe on the Kent coast, Brockhill Country Park School. A two day trial visit was set up before I was to start full time in year nine.

I've never found anything more daunting than walking into that school on that first day. As I was dropped off I could see hundreds of children of all sizes milling at the gates all wearing the same thing, their school uniforms, and I was wearing a smart pair of jeans and an unfashionable striped jumper. I was taken into my class by the deputy head. I felt everyone looking at me; I dared not look around and kept my eyes facing forward towards the teacher.

I was quickly introduced to the class, yet I was acutely aware that all of them seemed to know exactly who I was. I worried about what else they knew about me. As I sat down at the only desk available, right in the middle of the class, I took my first look around. The only person I saw was the most beautiful girl I had ever seen. Just as in a Hollywood film, everything around me slowed down. She was talking to a girl sitting next to her and laughing; she had the brightest white teeth I had ever seen and, when she laughed, she threw her head back. Her hair was golden with wonderful natural curls. She reminded me of a princess like the one I had seen only weeks earlier in the Disney film *Aladdin*. I couldn't stop looking at her. She stood up, still in slow motion, in my mind's eye, and took her jumper off to reveal her slender figure. My trance was broken by the sound of a shrill bell. I was going to like this school.

I was attached to a boy for the day and by the look on his face I could see he felt he was being punished. He showed me around the school in relative silence, giving only yes or no answers to my questions. This place was massive and nothing like I had seen before! Every corridor we walked along had dozens of classrooms packed with children. The long fields that split the upper and lower school were filled with children playing football or rugby. I was filled with a strange sense of excitement equalled only by the knot in the pit of my stomach that was screaming 'what the hell am I doing here?' The tour over, Michael took me to the canteen for break and looked relieved to be reunited with his group of friends; although still miffed that he had the new boy in tow.

'This is Matt,' he mumbled to the others. They introduced themselves but I immediately forgot all of their names. I stood uncomfortably. Everyone seemed to be looking at me. I felt out of place. To be honest I was out of place.

'You live in a children's home?' One of them asked.

I didn't quite know whether that was a statement of fact or a question.

'Yes,' I didn't know what else to say. I felt embarrassed.

'Why do you live in a children's home? You did something wrong?'

'No. Just couldn't live at home.'

'You abused or something?'

'Richard.' A boy intervened. I was relieved I didn't have to answer that one.

'What?' Richard asked.

107

'It's none of our business. Sorry, Matt, Richard's just nosy'. He seemed nice. Another boy, Gareth, looked on suspiciously. I felt like an intruder, as if I had turned up to a party completely uninvited. And I suppose I had. But I was too scared to go anywhere else so I stuck to them like glue for the rest of my two trial days.

I spent the rest of the summer almost exploding with excitement and anxiety at starting school. I was bursting at the seams to learn. Of course I had learnt things at Caldecott School but always knew that it was somehow going nowhere. My two taster days at Brockhill introduced me to a world of learning I'd never experienced before.

Despite my excitement I was scared stiff. There were so many children. I had no idea how I would make friends. I had only ever been in a class with eight or ten children since leaving junior school and got quite a lot of support from adults in such classes. Here I was going to be relatively alone with thirty other children and several hundred across the year. Also my experiences of proper school had never been great; I had always been bullied and never seemed to get on well with people. I didn't want that to happen again. But I was going to be a normal kid in a normal school. I had a chance at some kind of future and no matter how scared I was it would be worth it.

I had never worn a school uniform. We went shopping for my school kit and I was so proud to be wearing my new uniform; we took pictures of me standing as straight as a soldier with a beaming smile. The night before school I polished my new shoes several times until they shone and I could see myself in them. I laid my school uniform out after trying it on again to make sure it looked good and washed myself extra clean. I was prepared for my first day at school. As I looked at myself in the mirror for one last time, I felt like I could conquer the world and this day was the start of that journey. I felt smart for the first time in my life. My uniform was perfectly put together and my tie as tight as a knot could be. My blazer had all three buttons done up but there was a flaw. My trousers didn't quite meet the bottom of my shoes and if I lifted one leg up you could see my white socks. As I got into the mini-bus, emblazoned with the Sunshine Variety Club logo, I was completely oblivious to my situation; I was a lamb going to the slaughter.

Several months later I sat at the front of the class with Mavis next to me. She was the classroom assistant who had been allocated to support me and another child in the class. Initially she had only been in the class to support me from a distance, not wanting to attract unnecessary attention to the fact she was there for me; but over time I'd come to rely on her more and more. Mavis had become a comfort blanket that kept me feeling a little safer as things had become darker for me at school. She reminded me a lot of my Grandma Jean. Like her, Mavis spoke softly and kept calm in every crisis, never panicking, never shouting and never judging. Around me, the other children in the class were as chaotic as ever.

The class had moved to the upper school at the start of year nine and had been given a new teacher. Penny – I don't remember her full name as we all just used to call her Penny, even to her face – was young and fresh out of training. She was as much of a lamb to the slaughter as I was. She had no idea how to control this class and everyone knew it. They'd all be so abusive to her and use every opportunity to wind her up; at times I could tell she was at the point of crying.

This class wasn't Penny's though; it was art and for some

reason the teacher was out of the room and I was surrounded by mayhem. Children were shouting and throwing things around; cliques were huddled together chatting about their own private business and no one seemed to be doing any work. I could see that Gareth, the boy who had been so quiet with me on that taster day, was being talked to by a few of the boys in the class. The boys kept looking over. Before I knew what was happening I felt someone grab the back of my neck and start squeezing tightly around it.

'What you saying about my Mum?' It was Gareth. I didn't even think about answering; I just completely lost it, got up and started wrestling him. Immediately we were surrounded by people shouting 'fight, fight, fight' and I knew now was the time to prove I could hold my own. After some more wrestling I got free from his grip, grabbed his head and smashed it several times hard on the table. In no time at all I felt a second, much firmer hand, grab the back of my jacket and pull me up. I saw a second hand grab Gareth's jacket. It was the art teacher who had returned and, without stopping, he dragged us straight to the Head Teacher's office. It all happened so quickly and I wasn't sure why. I just knew I had completely lost control. As we sat waiting to see the Head Teacher, I wondered how it had got to this. I hadn't said anything about his Mum and Gareth probably knew that. And it wasn't Gareth that I had wanted to smash on to that table, but the boys who had been talking to him. But I was too scared to challenge them.

Things had gone fairly smoothly in those first few weeks at school. I had again attached myself to the group I'd been foisted upon at those taster days and I could still sense I was intruding on a clique that had formed when they started at the school together several years earlier. But it

110

was the best I could find and as the whole class had formed its own cliques, I didn't seem to have much of a choice. I didn't fit into any of the 'cool' groups and I didn't want to be one of the loners. This group seemed to be somewhere in between and although I could tell they were individuals, in the way they didn't conform to the norms that the other groups did, they didn't seem to get hassle from anyone. Dean had taken well to my joining the group. I liked him. He had a fun sense of humour and a big girly laugh that gave him character. He was well-liked by everyone. Richard seemed to just do what Dean did and didn't really have a problem with me, although I could tell he felt a bit threatened by the way Dean and I got on; they lived near each other and were best friends at the time. It was Michael and Gareth who didn't appreciate me joining their group. They didn't say or do anything in particular, it was a just a feeling I had, perhaps a paranoid one, but I felt it, nonetheless.

I got used to the routine of school pretty quickly. My crush on Lisa, the girl with the golden curls, grew every day and was perhaps a little too obvious, so I was teased. But I didn't care. I was already in love, as I thought then, and I was enjoying the feeling as I had never really liked a girl before. Every time Lisa came into the classroom I looked on, dazzled by her beauty. I had butterflies in my stomach when she was near. I loved her mannerisms – the way she laughed so heartily, the flick of her golden hair, the smile that made my heart melt into a gooey mush. Initially I think she may have been interested in me. She didn't have a boyfriend and several times, when I had plucked up the courage to speak to her, we held brief conversations.

I had no idea how to flirt with her beyond saying 'hi'

111

and a few pleasantries. I was more like a shy ten-year-old at junior school than a fourteen-year-old adolescent. I didn't understand the social norms that existed in the 'real' world, having been sheltered from it for so long. So I didn't quite fit in. I'd learned from my first day that looking smart wasn't considered as good a thing as I thought. My buttoned blazer was quickly unbuttoned by someone in my class putting their hand down the middle, breaking the buttons. I never buttoned it again. It turned out that white socks were not cool, but a sign that you were a virgin. It didn't matter that the rest of the class were probably virgins as well, it still led to name-calling, so I never wore white socks again. My trousers continued to be an issue. Several children from my class would walk past me and shout 'I'll give you a fiver so you can get the other half of your trousers' and call me 'ankle swinger'. For months I had no idea what they were talking about until Dean explained that my trousers came up the bottom of legs when I sat down and that they should be longer. I tried to get different trousers, but each time I had the same problem, so 'ankle swinger' was a name I put up with.

I also made the mistake of wanting to be the most intelligent kid in class. I was aware that I would have to do a lot to catch up and thought I would be behind in a lot of areas, having missed the first two years of secondary school. I wanted to try extra hard to demonstrate I could keep up. Fortunately, or unfortunately, as it turned out, I picked the work up quickly and in a lot of subjects I was at the top end of the class. So 'boffin' was added to the list of names I was called. That was considered an insult in this strange new world. Some could say, and often did, that I set myself up by trying to be the best and 'showing off'. But nobody ever sat me down and explained how

112

things were supposed to work. I thought the more you did, the better you got on; but it just wound people up, causing yet more trouble that I didn't need.

Where I lived didn't go unnoticed, either. I soon came to be known as the 'kid from the children's home' not least because of the variety club mini-bus dropping me off each morning. I'd beg for the staff to drop me off in the car, but only the van was available. I hated going to the pick-up point, feeling like everyone was watching me, and getting into that damn minibus. As time went on, though, the name-calling got worse. The bullies in the class would say things like 'your Mum doesn't love you' or 'you're not wanted, that's why you are in care.'

I felt bad inside and looked bad outside. As I hit puberty, my perfect skin became a volcano of spots. Every time they called me 'crater face' or 'spotty', I winced as if someone had slapped me, hard. I'd sometimes cry in class in front of everyone, as ashamed of my face as I was embarrassed by my tears. Some of the class would laugh and some would look on in pity. The pity was worse. I knew that someone as beautiful as Lisa would never want someone as ugly as me. I would go home each day and look at myself in the mirror. I'd stare for ages, wishing the spots would go away. I kept checking in every mirror to see if they had retreated, but they kept on advancing, covering more of my face.

I tried everything to kill the spots. I had already cut out sugar, on my dentist's advice. Caldecott being Caldecott, though, this was taken as an order, and I was only to eat sweets one day a week. It never really seemed to make a difference though. I used Clearasil three or four times a day and drank as much water as I could as I'd read that this also helped. That didn't work either. I even tried steaming my face each night with a pot of boiling water, but that only made the spots flare up more.

My hairstyle was also an issue. Everyone seemed to have an opinion on my side-parting, saying it was old fashioned. At first I refused to change it, but by the end of the year, I decided to have my hair cut short and put forward. The genius who said 'sticks and stones may break my bones, but names will never hurt me' deserves to be lined up against a wall and shot. It is the worst piece of advice you can give anyone who is teased and ridiculed. Insults burn into you.

There were a few hardcore bullies and the school. I'd get chased at times and beaten up for some reason: I never really knew why. The first few times it happened the school spoke to the people involved and punished them with detention. Most of the class frowned upon it. But after a while it became easier to blame me. The school said I 'gave as good as I got', which I didn't understand. The only time I gave as good as I got was when I ended up losing my temper. One time a wild ginger haired boy in my class, who most people feared, threw a sandwich in my face as we walked across the field. A switch flicked as it hit my face; *how dare he do that to me?* I jumped on his back and tried to pull him to the floor. In my anger I'd forgotten that he was much bigger, stronger and fiercer than me. He got on top of me and punched me over and over again in the face until my nose started to bleed. I ended up in the Head Teacher's office and was suspended for two weeks. They didn't care about the reason; we were both fighting and therefore both suspended.

To be fair to Caldecott and Elroy, they were as angry as me and Elroy fought my corner with the school. I was still suspended, though, and had lost my confidence in the school to provide any kind of protection from the bullies.

I was constantly humiliated, too. Another boy in the class, Oli, was clever, popular and a bully. It was obvious he felt threatened by me coming into class; I was as intelligent as him, if not more, and he didn't like that. Once when he was sitting behind me, he sneezed all over the back of me on purpose. Everyone found it funny; it just made me feel sick. I decided to deal with it in my own way. I was good at desktop publishing so, egged on by Dean and Richard, I designed an invoice from a dry-cleaner's firm for cleaning the jacket. I told my teacher, Penny, about it and she agreed to give it to him. Oli looked worried when he opened it and saw the invoice. When I told him it was fake, the whole class, and Penny, laughed. I felt momentarily better. But it was a mistake. A few days later Oli stole my jacket and cut an arm off. He was suspended for a few days. I didn't have the social skills to combat the bullies. No matter what I did I couldn't seem to make my peers like me. Whatever I did seemed to annoy people.

As I waited with Gareth outside the Head Teacher's office, I thought about the last six months. There wasn't that much difference between Gareth and me. We both didn't fit with either of the extremes in school, the cool group or the loners. Gareth was probably as lost in this world as I was. I didn't get a sense that he had wanted to come over and start a fight with me; he can't seriously have thought I was talking about his Mum. I didn't know his Mum, so what could I say that would hurt him? But he was just doing what he needed to do to fit in. He was as much a victim of the bullies as I was. They had taunted him, made him respond; if someone badmouths your mother you defend her. He was just playing the game he had to, in order to survive in this strange world of unspoken rules and power cliques. The difference between Gareth and me, though, was that he'd learnt how to play the game. He knew how to interact with people in the school in a way that didn't make him stand out too much or slink back too far.

'I'm sorry I banged your head on the table, Gareth.'

'That's okay. I'm sorry I started on you.'

'I promise you I didn't say anything about your Mum.'

'I know.' He looked down at the floor. I think he was sad that he had let himself be played like that. He shouldn't have been; in this world I'm not sure he had too much of a choice.

Shortly after that I had my first ever invite to a friend's house. Gareth had arranged for us all to come round his house for dinner and sleep over. When I told Caldecott I wanted to go, there was a problem as his parents would have to be police checked to see if they had criminal records. I was not sure I wanted to say to Gareth that his parents needed to be checked before I could visit. But I didn't want to be left out either. In the end I decided the embarrassment was worth it and it transpired that Gareth's parents didn't really mind being checked; of course they had nothing to be worried about.

I remember the Friday night that Elroy drove me in the van to Gareth's house in Folkestone. I was so proud. I felt like a normal child going to see his friend. It turned out that Dean, Richard and Michael all couldn't come so I was on my own. I was a little nervous. It turned out I didn't need to worry. His Mum Nicole was working that night, but his Dad Kevin made me feel more than welcome. He scared me slightly by painting a picture of Gareth's Mum as a giant, moody woman – he said it would take ten minutes to walk around her. The next day, though, when she came home, she turned out to be the smallest, kindest lady I had ever met. We all fell about laughing and she had no idea why. Gareth had a brother and a sister, both younger. Lucienne was about

Danny's age and I instantly liked her; she had a cheeky way about her and reminded me of Danny. Sam was a few years younger than Gareth and went to the local Grammar School. Gareth's Dad was a self-employed mechanic and his Mum worked at the local Safeways. They were not rich but had their own house in the middle of a nice estate.

We stayed in Gareth's room in the loft conversion and watched movies all night. He had all kinds of gadgets that dazzled me, including a widescreen television with surround sound and flashing lights. He asked me a bit about my life and why I had come into care. For some reason I felt comfortable talking to him and explained the whole story. He listened without interruption and at one point I had thought he had fallen asleep; but he just sat quietly until he broke the silence.

'God, that's shit. You know if you ever need to talk, I'm here for you. We're friends.'

Shortly after my first visit to Gareth's, I was invited over for a family dinner. It was the first of many occasions that would become treasured memories. Something about his family put me at ease. I'd never really sat down to family meals like they did with Mum, Dad and children all around the table. They chatted about their day and laughed and joked. We laughed so much at those dinners. It was there that I discovered I had a good sense of humour and could make people laugh if I wanted to. We'd always joke around and wind each other up. In their home, I felt good about myself. I felt not only wanted but liked and, over time, loved. After dinner we would clear up and then go on a long bike ride with Nicole and Kevin walking their neighbour's dog, hand in hand. It was the model family for me and I wished I could be part of it full-time.

Gareth and I became closer over time and did everything

out of school together with me spending as much time around his house as Caldecott would allow. Once, I invited Gareth around to Caldecott for dinner. I was nervous about the idea at first, scared of what he might think of this strange place. But the evening went well in the end and he came back several other times, too.

Things only started to get better at school for me when I had made some solid friends in Gareth and Dean. We were similar in our sense of humour and used to take every opportunity to wind up my classroom assistant, Mavis. She always took it on the chin, even when we went too far, and I think we even made her laugh at times. All three of us hated physical education and would bunk off PE, hanging out in the computer room instead. If we did go to PE for cross country running we used to take a short cut, making the run no more than five or ten minutes. The PE teacher, a former army instructor and Olympic coach, was always watching and would catch us out. We had to do it again and, after we cheated for the second and third time, would eventually walk the entire route.

The bullying never really stopped; it just got easier to handle. It became something that I just lived with and, most of the time, chose not to fight. At times I would get beaten up, fall to the ground and curl into the ball like a snail curling into his shell for protection. Gareth and Dean would ask why I never fought back; I don't know, really, why I didn't. It wasn't just that I was scared, I also couldn't bring myself to hit someone. I became a bit of a joke across the school. I remember walking from upper to lower school and would have younger children, who I didn't even know, shouting out my nicknames. At times I tried to adopt the strategy I had at Woodstock of joining in with the class chaos.

In year nine, we were considered to be the worst class in the school. I felt sorry for Penny, our teacher, who was obviously out of her depth with us and once fled the class in tears. The deputy head came into the classroom in a rage and told us we were destroying another human being with our behaviour. For the first time we all felt guilty. I can't remember whose idea it was, but we decided to buy her some flowers and write her an apology card. She cried when she got it. However, it was too late. She had decided to leave the school and was considering leaving teaching. I didn't feel great that we had done that to someone. I could tell that the others in the class didn't either.

Going into year ten I found I had more friends than before. The classes were now mixed, according to our choice of GSCE options and a lot of the people that bullied me were no longer in my classes. I was doing drama as part of my GCSE options so I was in a class with Lisa. I still dreamed that one day, maybe, she would love me and we would be boyfriend and girlfriend. I was infatuated with her. But in the meantime I was happy to be her friend. I got to know her social circle, the nicest kids in our class.

My life also changed in year ten and year eleven because of Gareth's love life. He started dating and had a few girlfriends that were from the 'cool' group. As I spent all my time with Gareth outside of school I got to know them quite well. So I was no longer the weirdo to everyone.

Since my success on stage at a young age, I'd always wanted to be an actor. But over time I convinced myself that acting was a risky profession, so I switched my attention to writing and became sure I had a future as a journalist. For work experience I got two weeks at the *Folkestone Herald*. Joining me was the clever bully Oli. The first day we went to eat lunch and realised we had a good deal in common.

He lived around the corner from Caldecott and by the end of the week had invited me round to his place. We talked about the last year and his bullying of me, and, to my amazement, he apologised. I realised then that all this wasn't as simple as someone hating me. I was a new boy when the groups in the class were well-formed, and the pecking order already established. Oli had felt threatened by me. He needn't have been; we were both as intelligent and ambitious as each other. In the end we became good friends, although at school we always remained slightly distant, sticking to our own cliques.

With me at a real school, life at Caldecott became a lot easier. I was even more of a model child in the staff's eyes and would always be held up as an example of how a child could improve. I had changed a great deal and some of it, I see now, must have been due to them.

All that made it easier to contemplate mending the great rift. Mum had moved to Chatham, she said, to be closer to me, although when I found out she had a boyfriend that lived nearby I realised it was more to do with him than me. But the plan was still to move home and I started going there every fortnight for the weekend. Things with Mum were the calmest they had ever been. We rarely argued and she hardly ever told me off. To be honest, I didn't do much to deserve a telling off when I was with her. It was as if we were always walking on eggshells around each other, both on our best behaviour. It helped that the time we spent together was so limited, with her working long hours through the night, leaving me to look after Danny and John. We often found things to do and it was fun going out with them on long bike rides. We'd take a twelve mile round trip to Maidstone to go swimming, which ate up the entire day. John and I loved the challenge, but Danny

120

struggled to keep up and would throw his bike to the ground and refuse to go any further as if he expected a helicopter to come and pick us up. But it wasn't all brotherly love.

John often bullied Danny. When Mum was at work both of them played up, saying I wasn't their Dad. Sometimes, when it got too much for me, I'd phone Mum at work. She'd get angry and say if I couldn't handle it she would have to leave and come home and deal with it herself. Is that what I wanted? Often I felt I couldn't win. I couldn't cope with them on my own, but if she came home, she wouldn't see a problem and be angry with me. So I put up with it.

The only time I was really happy at home was when she was around and we did stuff together, all four of us. She always made it special. We'd go out to a restaurant or the cinema. She worked so hard she had money to spend on us – and, to be fair, she did spend it. I think she knew she wasn't the Mum we needed, but spending money and treating us made us all feel better. Part of the problem was that John seemed to be Mum's favourite. They had a special bond that neither Danny nor I shared. They would cuddle up on the sofa, hug and say they loved each other. It wasn't that she didn't say that to me or Danny; it was just that the affection between her and John was more constant and intense. It always made me jealous and although he never said so, I think it made Danny jealous, too. John had the same special bond with Dad.

Sometimes we were packed off to our Dad's to spend the weekend. We went by train, just the three of us. The journey was a nightmare. Danny hated travelling and would always swing on the bars on the underground or put his foot into doors. It would be down to me to stop him. He'd scream abuse, telling me I wasn't his Dad and couldn't tell him what to do. Other people would stare and some would tell me to get better control of him. At times I'd just cry, not knowing what to do. John wouldn't help. He'd wind Danny up and was a bit of a bully. When I tried to step in, he'd take it out on me. By the time we got to Dad's I was exhausted. I was too young to be dealing with this crap.

Danny didn't have it easy when we got to Dad's. Dad's girlfriend took every opportunity to blame or criticise Danny. He hated going to Dad's and said so many times. Mum insisted he still go, as it was Dad's right to see him. I became increasingly uncertain about whether I actually had a place there. It didn't seem like John wanted me home; my getting some of the attention scared him. For the most part I began to feel like a babysitter and didn't feel any closer to Mum. She wanted to keep most of her life separate from me and my brothers, as if there was a distinction for her between her duty as a mother and her life; I'm not sure she viewed us as a family any more. More as a responsibility she had to fulfil.

Mum kept her boyfriend, who she had now been with for several years, at a distance; he would come to the house late at night and leave in the morning. If he stayed the next day they would stay upstairs and Mum would come down and tell us to turn the TV down; 'James is sleeping' as if he was some kind of king. He had his own 'special' cutlery and plates that we were not allowed to touch. She even had that special voice for him that I had heard all those years ago with Kevin underneath the tree, except with this man she used it all the time. When I did see him he barely spoke two words to me. He was a big man and worked as a bouncer; I knew he was married with a kid and still lived with them. I didn't know anything else and Mum wouldn't entertain any discussion about it. It was a part of her life that she wanted to keep separate and given what had happened in the past, I understood why. But, exactly because of what had happened in the past, I needed to be as sure of the man in her life before I moved home. Keeping him under a cloak of secrecy merely served to heighten my anxieties about moving home.

Before long I knew that moving home wasn't the right thing for me. I was never going to fit back into this family. The decision came with a complete sense of freedom and ease about my future that I didn't have before. I no longer had to worry about what I would have to cope with in moving home to live with Mum. I could think about a future where I only had to worry about making things work for myself.

It wasn't long after that I began to think I had outstayed my time at Caldecott. Recently, they had announced in a group meeting that Elroy and Jessica were no longer going to be my key-workers; they would be allocated to some new children who needed their experience. I would be allocated two new members of staff. It may seem strange, but I felt it was the most painful rejection of my life, at the time more painful than Mum's. Despite the intensity and control, my relationships with Elroy and Jessica had enabled me to grow. To lose them now was a big reminder that I didn't have anyone for the long term. I argued that it wasn't fair, especially given that I probably wouldn't be at Caldecott for much longer. They argued that I was just being selfish and that I should allow some new children the same attention and time I had received over the last four years.

Something else changed. My friend, Hayley, had suddenly

gone completely off the rails and decided she had had enough of Caldecott and wanted to leave. She had tired of seeing child after child leave to go to a new family while she was left behind. She was in care because her stepdad had abused her, but now she said that she'd made it all up. Everyone knew she was lying, just so she could go back there and leave Caldecott, but she kept to her new story. Each night she would kick and scream and staff would restrain her. Eventually they kept her secluded in the family room day and night. After several weeks they relented. I was sad to see her go as we had spent so many years living through happy, sad, angry and playful times together. But it was even sadder to see her go back to live with the man she'd said had sexually abused her.

Louis was also preparing to leave and go back to the foster carers he had left years earlier to come and work through his issues at Caldecott. We both struggled with the intensity and control of Caldecott and used our time together to vent our frustrations with the place. The rest of time was spent talking about women, as teenagers do, a subject on which Louis seemed to be a bit of an expert, which always intrigued me.

With things changing so quickly I wondered whether or not I could handle Caldecott any more. The twice-weekly group meetings started to take their toll. After a hard day's work at school with several hours travel each way I was exhausted. Not only that, but in my GCSE year I had homework to do; I was getting behind. The five hour Wednesday meetings just added pressure I didn't need. It had been so long since I found the meetings of any use and I didn't want to listen to any more stories of abuse. I didn't want to cry any more. For several years I'd spoken about my own feelings as a matter of routine. But now my life was pretty normal. I went to school, had the same hassles as everyone else at school and came home. When it would get to my turn at the end of the meeting, I'd announce I had nothing to say this week. Having nothing to say was denial, of course.

'But you have to say something, Matthew.'

'I don't have anything to say. Everything is okay with me.'

'Everyone here has spoken and really opened up. I think you owe it to them to say something, don't you?'

'I would say something if I had something to say. But it's just ... everything is all right'. By this time the other children and staff would be joining in, claiming I was insulting them by not being prepared to 'share'. Eventually I got so wound up I'd give in and disclose some piece of minor information to get them off my back. Then everyone thanked me for being open and 'sharing'.

One Wednesday I had had enough. I came home in a bad mood from school and got into an argument with the house manager, Jo. I told her I wasn't going into the group meeting and she couldn't make me. I was too old to be there; I wanted to get on with my life and leave Caldecott. Instead of letting her get too much of a word in, I stormed off and went for a long walk. When I came back there were two staff waiting for me and one said:

'Where have you been?'

'Just for a walk.'

'You didn't have permission to go for a walk, Matthew.'

'I don't need permission for a walk; I'm old enough to do what I want.'

'Right, we want you to go to your room.'

'It's only seven, I'm not going to my room now.'

'Matthew, we have asked you to go to your room and if you don't, we will have to take you up there.'

'You're saying you're going to take me upstairs. I haven't been restrained in almost three years and you're going to take me upstairs, just because I disagree with you? You can't do that. I want to phone my social worker.'

'You can't phone anyone tonight. If you don't go to your room we are going to take you there.'

'Okay. I'll fucking go to my room then.'

'Watch your language, Matthew. You are getting very aggressive.'

'That's because you are making me aggressive.'

'You are making yourself aggressive, no one else is doing it to you.'

I walked towards the stairs and ran off towards the disabled toilet, where I knew there was a window I could escape through. The staff chased me, but they were too late. I locked the toilet door. But before I could try and open the window they opened the lock from the outside and dragged me out. I began to struggle, but they did their best to keep me pinned to the floor. They weren't that professional at it and, of course I was no longer a little boy. But eventually they had me on the floor in submission. As they sat holding me locked in a sitting position, one with their arms tightly around me as if in a hug and the other holding my legs down, I couldn't believe this was happening. This was a complete over-reaction; I didn't need to be restrained. It wasn't as if I had become a danger to myself or others. I had just had a strop and stormed off. Normal teenagers do that in normal circumstances. And this was no normal circumstance. If I could be treated like this when I wanted to take an unauthorised walk, I wondered what else lay in store for my future at Caldecott. I was supposed to stay here for another year. But, as they held me, I decided then and there that I couldn't stay any longer.

I wasn't prepared to play the game any more. I vowed that I'd never sit in another group meeting again.

The next day I phoned my social worker as soon as I woke up. I told him I wanted to leave and it needed to be now. Elroy spoke to him afterwards in private; I didn't know what he said at the time, but, when he came out and told me Tony wouldn't be coming today and I wouldn't see him for another few weeks, I knew Elroy had talked him out of it. I could hear him telling Tony that coming down today would just be 'colluding with Matthew's demands' and I shouldn't be allowed to 'split' Caldecott and Social Services. I was furious they still had absolute power over me.

I ran off to a phone box away from the building and phoned Tony back. I insisted he come and see me today. After some argument he agreed. Elroy still convinced Tony that I couldn't be allowed to dictate when I was going to leave Caldecott. There was a flat in Hastings that they sometimes used for seclusion purposes and they would take me there for several days with staff until I calmed down. I had seen Hayley fall apart when she had to leave. I didn't want to be in that position. I couldn't handle going backwards like that after I had made so much progress at Caldecott. I had to break free from the place that had helped me.

I ran off again; I phoned the police and told them the only thing I knew would get me removed from Caldecott; that I was being abused at the home and they needed to come and get me.

I could see Elroy running towards me; I ran across the field, but he quickly caught up and jumped on me. I kicked him as hard as I could. It hurt me as much as it hurt him. This was a man I'd grown to love like a father. But I think

127

kicking him at the time was my way of kicking him away so that I could move on. I wanted to hurt him so he didn't want me any more. By the time we arrived back at the house there was a police car waiting.

Elroy spoke with the officer before he spoke to me. I told him I was being abused and when he asked by whom I had to think quickly; I hadn't planned this. I thought of a staff member who had once walked in on me when I was naked, an innocent mistake, but it was all that came to mind. So I said it was him. He asked me for details and I could tell he suspected I was lying. Elroy told them this was not true and asked me if I was sure about this. Did I know what I was doing? Yes and no. I just wanted to leave, desperately. But things had gone too far and I couldn't take this back now. I told them I wouldn't tell them anything else until they took me away from the home.

The officer and Elroy talked and the policeman was obviously about to leave and forget the whole incident. I ran out the door and went straight over to the police car. I grabbed the windscreen wiper and snapped it in half screaming that he would have to arrest me now. He handcuffed me and read me my rights. Jessica travelled with me to the police station; she tried to talk about what I had done and how serious the accusations I was making were. She sounded deflated; disappointed. I couldn't cope with that. I loved her like a mother; she had given me more attention and care in four years than my mother had all my life. Now I had destroyed any kind of bond we once had. I told her to shut up. I didn't need to listen to her any more.

Once we got to the police station they told me I wouldn't be going back to Caldecott. It was then that I told them I had lied about been abused and nothing had ever happened.

To me it had been harmless. I made, and withdrew, the accusation in a few hours. But in reality a lot of harm had been done. As a matter of procedure, the staff member had been suspended and sent home. He had to tell his wife about the accusation as part of the investigation might have involved a referral to Social Services to look into his own family and interview his children. Most of all though, this man, who had done nothing wrong, had to deal with the anxiety of not knowing the effect this would have on his future. I can't imagine what it must have felt like to be falsely accused of something like child abuse. At the time I wasn't thinking about the consequences that might follow from my claim; I was just thinking about myself and getting out of Caldecott. It is now something that I look back on with regret, not just because of what I put him through, but also because making a false accusation made a mockery of all those children who had made true allegations – only not to be believed.

I spent the next few weeks in an emergency foster care placement in Romford. It seemed I had come full circle; now I was back in squalor and uncertainty. The house was tattered and undecorated, the carers loveless and cold. They were not abusive or horrible. They just didn't show any kind of understanding towards a child, despite having several of their own. They both lived on benefits and spent day and night watching TV. I didn't have any of my belongings and spent the entire time bored, my only distraction being thoughts of where I might end up next. I no longer cared where I'd end up. For so long, my whole future had been based around returning home to Mum. Now I lost any faith that I had in a worthwhile future. The only thing that I looked forward to was the knowledge that at fifteen it wouldn't be long until I had to go my own way.

I had rushed to leave Caldecott so quickly, pushing away those that had cared for me for so many years, that I hadn't taken time to think about all the things I'd loved about living there. I would miss the company of all the children I'd shared so many memories with, some good and some very painful ones. I would miss the trips and the adventures. But most of all, I would miss the little things that made Caldecott my home, even if only a temporary one; my room with its now extensive postcard collection; the hugs that I still received despite being too old for them; the long chats about life and the future with Elroy and Jessica. As I went to sleep that night, in a makeshift bed in Romford, I thought about the people I had hurt that day. I started to cry. It was then that I realised the person I had hurt most was me. I had pushed everyone who loved me away.

7

Aged Sixteen – Leaving Care

I was used to sitting outside the Head Teacher's office now and the secretaries were used to seeing me there. I hated the waiting; it was as if he would make you wait for ages on purpose, forcing you to think about what you had done. If that was his intention it worked. *Why had I been so stupid?*

This time, though, I didn't feel like I had done anything wrong. The buzzer of doom went; as I entered he sat behind his desk with a stern look on his face. There was no warm hand shake and no reassuring smile. Mrs Royal, my Head of Year, was with him and there was a secretary at the back with a note pad to record more Crimes of Matthew. But at least this was a new one.

'We have discovered that you have been using school property to run a business.'

'I have been using the computers. But Mrs Royal knew about that.' She didn't back me up. She just sat there in silence, avoiding any kind of eye contact.

'You were not authorised to use any school equipment for these purposes. We take this issue very seriously.'

'But I did have permission. The business studies teacher knew I was doing it and so did Mrs Royal. They have even helped me.'

Mrs Royal had talked to me about investing a few hundred pounds if it went well with the orders.

'I don't understand what I have done wrong'. My voice became high pitched. I was getting upset with the lack of support from Mrs Royal.

'That's enough' he shouted 'What you have done is serious. I have given you many chances in this school but this time you have gone too far. You have brought the school into disrepute...'

'But I was just...'

'BE QUIET.' Why was he so angry with me? 'I have been left with no choice but to expel you permanently from this school. You will be allowed to return for your exams but in the meantime you must not set foot on school property. Do you understand?'

'No. I don't understand. I haven't done anything wrong.'

'Get out of my sight.' I left his office feeling humiliated and helpless. I phoned my foster carer and told her the bad news. I could hear the disappointment in her voice. As I waited for her to pick me up I scanned the school grounds one last time. I knew that I wouldn't come back to sit my GCSE's. I was too embarrassed; too ashamed. I had messed up at a place where I'd felt I was really worth something, a place that could have given me a future.

Desperation in my home circumstances had led me to set up my own business when I was fifteen. I had been living with the Farrels for a few months. They worked for a not-for-profit agency, ISP, which seemed flush with money; all the staff drove around in multi coloured cars with the ISP logo plastered over it.

Sarah and Alan had five other children, two of whom had left home. The ones I got on with the best were Kelly and James, the two youngest. James was eight and Kelly twelve. It was like having a brother and sister and we enjoyed each other's company. Sarah and Alan liked me a

132

lot when I first came to live with them. They couldn't understand the picture that had been painted of me by my social worker and Caldecott. They didn't see a manipulative, angry boy, and understood that Caldecott had been a weird place to grow up. Sarah was a housewife and full-time carer. I enjoyed spending time with her; we would do the shopping for the house or go swimming with Kelly and James. Alan didn't get home until late. He worked as a jeweller. Their love for each other was clear to see; every evening they'd sit cuddling on the sofa and drink a bottle of wine together. Each night we would eat as a 'family' around the table once Alan got home. I felt like I was part of a family for the first time. They took an interest in my future. Alan constantly pushed me to work harder at school.

Just as Caldecott came with a honeymoon period so did the Farrels. At first I relished being part of a family. But I was soon reminded this whole set up was every bit as fake as my own perfect behaviour had been for the first few months of my stay with them. There were little things that annoyed me initially but nothing that made me want to leave. They had certain ideas about their status. Despite living in a modest house on a newly build estate, they were snootier than Princess Margaret. They often criticised me for yawning without covering my mouth or sitting with my elbows on the table. I didn't realise that I bent my head down to eat my food, perhaps because I didn't realise there was anything wrong with it. They didn't like that either. It wasn't that I ever had bad manners. I didn't talk with my mouth full, I always said please and thank you and I'd never leave the table without permission. My grandma had taught me that when I was young.

But you can never quite forget you are not really a family member. I remember going for dinner with them to a posh restaurant with the whole family; at the end of the meal, when Sarah wanted the bill, I called the waiter over, not thinking anything of it. She got very angry with me and shouted 'How dare you?' I felt like a child chastised.

I wasn't allowed a door key so when I got home from school I'd have to wait for Sarah to arrive, which could mean waiting more than two hours on the doorstep. I wasn't allowed to be left in the house alone. I might nick the silver – there wasn't any – or make phone calls to New York, I expect. So wherever they went I had to go with them, which often meant tagging along to swimming practice for the younger ones or some Brownie activity Sarah was involved in.

What hurt most was when they had family occasions and I was told I couldn't come. Sometimes they'd have special family dinners on a Sunday that I wasn't allowed to come to. I wasn't forced to live in a cupboard under the stairs like Harry Potter at least but the Farrels said it was important for them to have some family time.

Their daughter was getting married and the family was busy with the arrangements. Nearer the time I was told I couldn't come as this was a family day. A carer came and stayed for the weekend to look after me.

Things were not going so well at school either. I was getting more depressed and feeling very alone. I now regretted the way I had left Caldecott and started to think I'd made the wrong decision. I had been back once to have a leaving dinner with everyone, as Caldecott thought it was important to have closure. First, of course, we had to have a group meeting so everyone could tell me how bad the way in which I had left made them feel. I just sat there and took it. I did feel guilty about what I had done and I was pleased to have a chance to sit down with the staff member I'd falsely accused and apologise to him. He accepted my apology but I could tell from the look in his eyes that he had been very hurt by the whole business. I spoke to Louis on the phone – he was in hospital with alcohol poisoning. He also gave me a hard time about what I had done. I didn't really need anyone to give me a hard time as I had lost a lot by leaving the way I had.

The only time I ever felt I had closure on Caldecott was when I spoke to Jo on the phone several weeks after the dinner, as she couldn't be there. She apologised to me for the way it had all happened. She had thought about it and realised that it was all too much for me at the time and they should have given me more freedom. They shouldn't, she said, have taken Elroy and Jessica away as my key-workers at such an important time in my life. It was one of those occasions where I truly admired someone who cared for me and who could see that it wasn't black and white but grey and complicated. I was like a fox scared by the lights of independence and I had scarpered rather than face what was coming my way. Now I was paying the price.

I remember breaking down in school one day and going to see my head of year. I told her I never felt so alone and just wanted someone to love me. She just told me I needed to focus on school and get on with things. But I couldn't. I started to feel as anxious as I was when I first came into care. It was starting to boil over. One day it blew; a boy in my class started to bully me about my spots. The acne was still in full ghastly flower. I did look disgusting. I didn't need them to tell me that. The final straw came when he said to me out loud so everyone could hear 'let me get a vacuum cleaner so you can suck all the puss off your face'. I saw red, grabbed my chair and rammed him up against the wall. I'd have hurt him badly had I not been pulled off by several people in the class and held down on the floor. I was suspended again.

So many bridges had been burned. Going back home was now not an option. I saw to that in a review meeting with Sarah and Alan Farrell, when Mum turned up. I sat there as cold as I could and said I never wanted to see her again.

'I hate her', I said. She was sitting right in front of me. She broke down in tears and fled from the room. I could tell from the looks I got that every person in that room felt sorry for her and appalled by my behaviour. Looking back, it was heartless of me; but at the time I wanted to be heartless. I wanted to hurt her. I knew that saying it would end any hope of ever returning home. I also knew that my future wasn't with Sarah and Alan. I would be sixteen soon and would have to decide where to go. I never told anyone at the time but I was scared of leaving care. I did want to leave care and be away from all this control and judgement, but I desperately didn't want to be alone. I wasn't the only one thinking about my future; some friends and I started talking at school about what we would do after our GCSE's and how scary the idea of leaving school was. It had come around so quickly.

I didn't have much charm and even less money. What was I going to do? And that was why I had the mad dream of starting my own business and making enough money to go my own way in life. But it wasn't so mad. I left Caldecott having worked on *Community News* and with some knowledge of desktop publishing. I was handy with the computer and spent almost every PE lesson skiving off, practising my skills with desktop publishing software.

I was intrigued by *Free Ads*, a magazine of local businesses that was given away and thought there was a market for a similar publication which also provided discounts to people who took the ad into the shop. I printed off leaflets explaining what my magazine was about on the school computer with the charges for advertising. The lowest fee was about ten pounds for a small advert going up to a hundred pounds for a full page. If they booked for three issues they got a 20% discount. There was no financial rationale behind the plan; just figures plucked from the air. I printed off some order forms and some examples of the adverts and went out in my shirt and tie on Saturday to pitch to local businesses in Ashford. I didn't tell anybody, not even my friends; I wanted to prove I could do it first. The first day I went home having filled my first few pages with orders; I even had a few cheques and someone paid £30 in cash. Over the next few Saturdays I carried on taking orders until my Ashford issue was complete. I then went onto Folkestone where I had an even bigger response.

With all these cheques coming in I had to open a bank account. I went to the Midland Bank, as it was then, and met with the bank manager. I explained my enterprise and emphasised the educational part of it; he thought it sounded like a school business enterprise and was happy to help by opening a bank account. Within a week I had my own cheque book. It was then that I told my friends about it. They were impressed; had I told them sooner, before it had made any money, then they would have just thought it was one of my hare-brained schemes which could come to nothing. I even went to Mrs Royal, my Head of Year and Business Studies teacher. She suggested she might invest a little money in it if it continued to do well, although I thought this was more a way of encouraging me than a genuine offer.

I didn't know what to do with my immediate success

with the business; it seemed too good to be true. I did the calculations based on current progress and worked out what I could make if I did the same in five areas or more. I looked at an office in Folkestone that I could take on when I left school. With money in the bank, the £50 a week rent seemed more than achievable. Of course I knew nothing about business and didn't stop to think about printing costs, let alone things like business rates and tax! I was just excited about the possibilities; the possibilities of independence, not having to listen to anyone's orders; the possibility of proving to everyone I could be somebody and the chance that I may succeed beyond my own wildest fantasies.

Much to my friends' amusement I bought a pager; I didn't need one but thought that that was what real business-men had. I clipped it to my side and wore it all the time. Nobody our age had mobile phones back then and it made me feel special to have a pager. My friends would wind me up by going down to the phone box at the school and sending me rude messages to see if the operator would type it out. Those were the only calls that I ever got.

I was out of my depth, of course. I had eventually told my carers about what I had done and although impressed with my initiative they were concerned that I was letting my school work go by the wayside, which was true. Several weeks later, when the agreed print deadlines with advertisers had gone, the school started to get complaints. I'd also used the cheque book to pay for taxis and without funds in the account the bank, too, started to complain to the school. That was when I was called into the Head Teacher's office and expelled.

After that my carers started to treat me like the other boy in the house; like an unwanted misfit. I just responded by separating myself from the rest of the family completely.

I got a job at the local Tesco as a cleaner and started to work all the hours I could. I'd start at five in the morning and would work until late into the night. My boss, a fat man with a moustache, unnerved me. He was always slimy and always patted me on the bum. I ignored it at first, but the more I ignored it, the more he seemed to get angry with me for minor things. One day he just came in and was annoyed that I hadn't cleaned properly; he went around the store and shouted at me, pointing out all the things I had missed. Eventually I swore at him. He sacked me on the spot. I started crying and screaming back at him. Then the store manager came over and spoke to me in his office. I told him how I'd been treated and he assured me that he would be dealt with. It turned out that I was too young to be doing that kind of work and shouldn't have been working all those hours.

I quickly got a job selling Double Glazing by phone; that didn't last long either. It was not long after that that things broke down so badly with my carers that they no longer wanted me living there. I was too much for them to handle, they said. I was moved to a semi-independent unit for a few months until it was time for me to leave care. I was just sixteen and given a two hundred and fifty pound leaving care grant to help me survive in the real world.

8

Aged Sixteen to Eighteen – Early Independence

A fast food kitchen is a manic, stressful, even dangerous place. Boxes of fries are stacked up by the dozen, hundreds of buns sit by the fire-breathing dragon of a cooker. The frozen patties are fed through one side non stop and come out the other dripping with saturated fat, to be plonked onto toasted buns caked in mayonnaise, pickles and ketchup.

Each section of the kitchen and front of the store has a different manager, charged with coordinating the fries, maintaining the production line, keeping the burgers coming. Queues go right to the door, with around a hundred people waiting to be served. Most staff go for hours on a Saturday, sometimes their whole shift, without a break; it's loud, it's sweaty and it's punishing. I was the shift manager, which meant I got to wear a shirt and my own tie; it also meant I was at the 'chute', the hub of activity where the production line stops and the service begins; my command post for giving directions to forty plus staff, most of them not even eighteen years of age. But then again, I was only seventeen.

'Where are those twenty whoppers I asked for?' My voice carried across the floor. A fast food kitchen on a Saturday lunch time is no place to be shy. I could tell people around me were getting frustrated with my orders. 'FRIES,' I screamed, hoping someone, anyone, would take up the fries. I felt great; it was stressful, sure, but I was in control, General Matthew commanding the fast food army. Once battle is in progress, you can't stop and ask for a recess. The dining room is the battle field, the queue the adversary, and victory comes when there is calm across the restaurant and the tills ring out their last orders. I loved the pace of it, the sense of achievement that comes with taking thousands of pounds in an hour. You almost forget that very few of those pounds belong to you, and that someone else is the master of your destiny. Over time I was becoming more and more aware of that.

I hadn't got to be shift manager easily. When I left care a year earlier, a few weeks after my sixteenth birthday, I worked at a McDonalds in Folkestone. For the first few weeks I was on cleaning duty, which was exactly as much fun as it sounds. I took on as much work as I could, sometimes working twelve hour shifts; I had to, on a rate of just over £2 an hour, with rent and bills to pay. My flat was quite large, with one bedroom, a kitchen and a lounge, in a block near the Folkestone cliffs. Some of the friends my own age I made at work would come around every night and sleep in the lounge; they didn't seem to like their own homes. That summer was fun. I had left care and school behind me and was earning some money; I was free.

Eventually though they tired of coming and I was left alone. I'd go home and curl up on the chair overcome by a deep sense of loss; I suddenly felt so lonely, so deserted. It hit me that I was now on my own. I cried and cried and found myself calling out for my Mum.

A few days later I came home from work to find the street closed off and fire engines and police. I wondered whose flat was on fire and soon realised it was mine; the cooker had been faulty and a loose wire at the back had caused it to explode. Everything I owned was now gone except for the photos and postcard collection I had built up as a child, still unpacked, kept inside a wall cupboard. The manager of the restaurant, Mark, came down to the wreck. He felt a bit responsible as I'd rented the flat from a friend of his. He said I could stay with him until they sorted out a new place for me.

Two weeks later, as promised, his mate gave me a new flat, with the first month's rent free. But I had nothing to put in it and very few personal possessions; Mark and his girlfriend had bought me a few clothes and a pair of shoes for work, and they gave me an old TV and some bedding. The flat was massive but had no furniture, not even a bed or somewhere to sit. It was empty, dark and lonely. A few days later I stopped going to work; I watched TV all night until 5 or 6 a.m. and then slept all day. I didn't have a cooker, or money to buy takeaway food, so I just ate sweets and ice lollies.

I didn't have a phone so no one had any way of reaching me. Some days I heard banging on the door but I'd just ignore it. When I went out to the shop to restock on sweets I'd keep my head down, avoiding eye contact with anyone. I was depressed, shut away and alone. It had hit me, dramatically, on the night that my possessions went up in flames, that I was on my own and no one was coming to my rescue. I was sixteen, with no qualifications and nothing to look forward to.

One Sunday morning I had a strange dream that someone important had been killed in a car crash. I'd developed a habit of sleeping with the TV on so I wouldn't feel so alone with my thoughts in the night. I was aware that something bad had happened; as I looked up at the screen I couldn't quite believe what I was seeing. Princess Diana had died in a car crash. I felt strange; as if I had lost someone close to me. I didn't even know the woman, I hardly followed the news and I'd never cared much about her or the Royal Family. But I felt immensely sad, even bereaved. As I watched the tributes I couldn't help but think of my own Mum. She was from a different world than Diana, but it seemed to me they had certain things in common. Both were lost in the world, finding their own ways in life, against the odds. Diana had married into the 'firm'; my Mum had given birth to me and then got married. Diana could charm people when she wanted to. My Mum did the same; she could be charming, yet switch it in a flash to make you feel responsible or guilty if things didn't go her way. Was this naivety on her part, or just plain manipulation? Diana was accused of both.Without thinking I went to the phone box and phoned my Mum.

I woke her at 7 a.m.; she hadn't seen the news. At first, I don't think she believed me. After not speaking for a year it was the ultimate ice-breaker; we didn't need to explain anything to each other. She came to pick me up. Soon we were chatting over dinner in a restaurant and she told me how things were going at work and what my brothers had been up to. I felt nervous with her, like this was too much too soon. I was still angry about everything and it was going to be harder to forgive her than I'd thought that morning.

'I need to ask you something', I said. If I didn't do it now, I never would. She didn't say anything, just looked down at her plate, as if she knew a grenade was about to be lobbed her way and she would rather be anywhere else than here with me when it exploded.

144

'Why did you keep Kevin in the house so long after I went into care?' I asked.

I could see she was angry by the squint in her eyes, as if to say *why spoil it Matthew, why are you doing this?*

'It was complicated. It wasn't just about you. I needed to think about me and your brothers.'

'But I told you he was hitting me. I wasn't lying. I don't know why you chose him after you knew that.'

'Why are you bringing this up now? Why can't you just let it go, Matthew?' She crashed her fork down onto her plate.

'Because it stays in my mind. I need to talk about it if things are going to work with us.'

'But we have done all the talking. You got what you wanted; you had everyone running after you for years and ruined my life as a result. You didn't think of what it was doing to me did you?' She was starting to cry now. I hated it when she did this. It always stopped the argument.

'I don't know why it has to be like this when we talk about things. I had to say sorry to you for what happened, and I am sorry,' I said, 'It's just you have never explained to me why you did what you did.' I knew that she wasn't going to talk about this any more.

'Well I'm obviously such a bad mother, Matthew, as you have always reminded me. It's a good job I haven't made a dramatic decision like letting you come home, like I was thinking of this morning'. With that, in tears, she stood up, paid the bill and left.

I watched the news coverage of Diana every night, shutting myself off from the outside world as I sank deeper into depression. I barely ate, slept all day and didn't wash. The day after Diana's funeral, I was woken at midday by loud knocks. Gareth's Mum, Nicole, was shouting through the

145

letter box; I ignored her, hoping she would go away. Then there was silence for five or so minutes followed by a loud crash; four police officers burst into the room where I was still half-asleep. Nicole had called them and told them I was missing as she hadn't heard from me; she had checked at McDonalds, who said they hadn't heard from me either and that I had just stopped turning up. She thought I might be hurt or something and she didn't have my grandparents' number. She came over to me and gave me a hug.

'What's been going on? You've had us all worried'. She said as she held my hand. I was crying, relieved that someone had taken the action I couldn't.

'I just don't see the point any more. Everything's gone wrong. I just want to be left alone.'

'You should have called us, silly; we would have come and helped, you're not on your own. We've all been worried about you.' Her voice was so light and calming I believed her. They took me to the hospital to check me out; I was pale and thin. I hadn't been eating all week. After some blood tests they took me home and I stayed with them until I decided what to do next. The following Monday my grandparents picked me up; I'd live with them for a few weeks until I got myself sorted. After six years I was going back to Dagenham.

A year later I was proud of how far I had come in the jungle of saturated fats. I was smiling, the burgers were under control, the staff followed my orders, the customers were happy. A year after the fire had left me with nothing except my clothes, a smelly old quilt and a broken telly I was now the Shift Manager at Burger King. I noticed the way people, when they came in with their stupid complaints, talked down to me as if I were their servant. I suppose, to some extent, I was. But it wasn't just them, it was the staff too. Most of them were at school, and used this job for pocket money to subsidise their weekends. I was the youth leader who had to keep them in check; the un-cool adult, a mild annoyance.

Most of those kids looked at us full-timers as a joke. Some of the full-time staff were decades older than the teenagers, in their forties or fifties. There was one lady, a German, called Dot, who was seventy-five! But most of them did the weekday shifts, working nine to five. Us young full-timers, the ones who needed this job, not just as a job but our only chance of a career, had to work all the hours we could to earn anything like a living wage. Sometimes I'd do my shift, and then work an extra one for cash in hand to help one of the other managers out. We were proud of our work, too; we would try to be the best, increasing our takings, getting worked up over the inspections and mystery shoppers from HQ. Some of the part-timers thought of us as losers, no-hopers who couldn't do anything else in life, and would end up, at best, as restaurant managers. What kind of life would that be? 'Didn't we have any ambition?' they would say. It bothered me. Of course I had ambition; I felt proud to be a shift manager at seventeen, even if it was superficial prestige and other people looked down on me.

I had friends now, too, some really good friends. Matt was the assistant manager and had been working there since dropping out of his A-Levels. We got on well and soon after I started he would ask me to stay late on special jobs for cash in hand; cleaning the broiler which cooked the burgers and toasted the buns (one time we found lots of dead maggots in the bottom of it!), sorting out the back yard where all the rubbish would get compacted, or getting down on our hands and knees to scrub the toilets. He had high standards and took his job very seriously. When we worked together late into the night we chatted about life and I learnt a lot about his past, which had been a pretty normal childhood. Slowly I told him parts of mine.

I learnt so much from him about basic life; the kind of skills you never get taught in care. I didn't always know how to be with friends or girls. I was at my worst with girls. He talked to me about his relationships and would give me advice on how I should treat women. He was like an old gentleman in his ways; 'it's the small things that are important. Listen to something she likes, something small, then when she least expects it give it to her or do it for her. When Julie started college I bought her a nice pen. It wasn't a great big gesture but she appreciated it.'

I was never that cool in my taste for music, preferring the classics, such as *Queen* and *Dire Straits* to modern artists. He was the same and after we finished work, often past midnight, we would drive for ages, go to the Dixie Chicken shop in Ilford for a chicken burger and wings; he would always play songs that I had never heard before. He was a bit of a lad, talked and lived like an Essex boy. One day he took me for my first ever pint; I only managed to finish half! He was my best friend for eighteen months of working together and several years thereafter and helped to shape me into a better person.

'Come on, lets keep those queues moving,' I shouted at the tills.

'We're going as fast as we can. You don't need to shout' Tina, with her curly blonde long hair, was grabbing a coke. She was right, she was going as fast as she could and it was pretty fast, at that. It was partly the fact that she was so small that made her the fastest cashier we had; she would weave herself in and out of the way of her colleagues, and serve her food before anyone else. She wasn't one to bow to authority, especially not mine.

'Tina, can you come here please?' She looked at me as if to say, *who the hell do you think you are?*

'What?'

I scrunched up my face and gritted my teeth.

'Come here!' I shouted. She came over, making a point of stamping her feet.

'What?'

'Don't talk to me like that in front of everyone,' I said.

'You called me over just to say that?' She was smiling, her beautiful freckled cheeks looking up at me, her blue eyes all of a sudden alive. I couldn't tell whether she was mocking me or finding me endearing.

'You are so pathetic'. Yep, she was mocking me.

'Look, I just don't want you to talk to me like that. It looks bad.'

'Well, if you don't shout, then I won't talk to you like that. Anyway, Mr Huggins, what are you going to do, take me out back for disciplinary action?' I went red and smiled, hoping no-one else had heard.

I didn't fancy Tina when I first met her. She was always moaning about something; she liked to work the tills, and if I dared to suggest that she take her turn in the kitchen, she'd throw a near-hysterical fit and wouldn't speak to me for the rest of the shift.

It started when I fancied her friend; I had a major crush on her and was building myself up to do something about it. But when I went to Matt for advice he suggested Tina might like me. 'There's a way she is with you. I've seen her looking at you a few times too. You should think about it. She's got a nice bum'. Next time she was on shift I watched her a bit closer; she did have a nice bum. And she was pretty attractive too; but so short! Later that day I made a joke. No one laughed except Tina, who wouldn't stop laughing.

A few days later she came in to show me some new shoes she had bought; why she thought I would like to see some new shoes I don't know but it was a sign that maybe Matt was right. But I'd never been on a date. I didn't ask her out, I didn't have the guts. She took the initiative. She just said to me at the end of her shift that she would wait for me and we could go and see a film if I wanted to.

'But I'm not due to finish for another two hours.'

'That's okay. I don't mind waiting.'

With that she sat down at a table in the grotty dining room and read, although every time I looked up she just seemed to be smiling at me. For the first time since Lisa at school, I had butterflies in my stomach. The date didn't last long; we got to the cinema and I realised I didn't have any money on me. I was too embarrassed to say anything so as we looked at the films I made an excuse that there wasn't much on and maybe we should go another time.

We didn't see each other for another week when she came to a house party I organised. It took me two hours to kiss her but we got together in the end and I was ecstatic: my first ever girlfriend. Everything was my first with her; my first real kiss, my first real date and my first phone call from her after the night we got together, when I had convinced myself that she was never going to call.

The first time she took me home I was so nervous that when I met her Dad I forgot to ask his name and spent the whole evening worrying he would hold that against me. Tina's younger sister, who had been eyeing me

150

suspiciously all evening, leaned forward at the dinner table and said, in a matter of fact tone 'his name is Paul'. I could never work out with her whether she found me intriguing or annoying. Me and her sister argued a lot, a bit like if we were brother and sister, but I think she enjoyed the arguments.

The only thing I couldn't stand about Tina was when she would look down on me and my job. 'What are you going to do, work at Burger King all your life? What kind of job is that?' Her parents felt the same; they were very middle-class, with a big house in a rich area and a country home in Norfolk. But they always told her not to be so horrible, and Tina would make extra effort to assure me she was proud of me. Although I knew her sister was right to say that Tina 'could do better'. She went to one of the top grammar schools in the country and received A grades in most of her exams.

Despite that, Tina showered love upon me like I had never experienced before. Once she got the keys to my flat and decorated it in tinsel, like a big Christmas tree. For weeks every draw or cupboard I opened seemed to have another little surprise she had hidden. At first I didn't tell her about my growing up in care. I just avoided questions about family. I knew I had to tell her about Mum soon, or she would find out herself. I was so scared she wouldn't understand and would think she couldn't be with someone like me. Every time I talked about where I had grown up I didn't feel normal, didn't feel I was entitled to have a relationship like this. The years at Caldecott left me feeling guilty. I realise I sensed – and I didn't know the word then – the stigma. All these reasons made me lie about who I was and where I had come from.

I took Tina to the local park for a picnic and we sat

underneath a tree, the sun beating down on us, branches and leaves our only shelter. She was wearing a blue flowery dress and looked beautiful with her head in my lap.

'I need to tell you something, Tina.'

'What is it? You don't want to split up already do you?' Was she crazy? As if!

'No, of course not. I'm really happy we got together. It's about my family. I wasn't telling the truth about where I grew up. I lived in children's homes from when I was ten. Me and my Mum haven't spoken in a while either.' She sat up and took her glasses off. She looked me in the eyes, gave me the most reassuring smile I'd ever seen and threw her arms around my neck.

'It doesn't matter to me. You are who you are and I like you.'

She held onto me for what felt like all afternoon. I was happy. I was safe. I was loved.

I could easily have gone another way, and never known Tina at all. I almost took a completely different journey. A few weeks after moving back to Romford my grandparents convinced me that I needed to get myself a career. I liked cooking and thought that if I learned to cook I could get a job anywhere in the world. I enrolled on an NVQ in cooking at Barking College. We went to meet the Local Authority who expressed their disappointment at having to see me again; 'We will help Matthew get back on his feet this time, but we cannot keep bailing him out of trouble'. I told them about the fire in my flat but they treated me as if I was some kind of nuisance. They gave me a deposit for a new place to live which was a small room in a house in Dagenham with three other people; all middle aged divorced men, most of them drunks, and agreed to pay the equivalent of my benefits so that I could do the college course. I got a job as a waiter at Romford Dog Track to supplement the small allowance they gave me weekly.

One night I came home and tried to open the lock to my room. It wouldn't open. I tried again and could hear people the other side. This guy opened the door in his boxer shorts.

'This is my room. What are you doing here?' I said.

'We moved in tonight, mate. You have to speak to the landlord; I don't know about anyone that lived here before, he didn't say anything.' All my stuff had gone. The postcard collection I'd covered the walls with, my clothes, my photos. Nothing was there. I was shocked; I had only left for work at 5pm that day and it was now close to midnight. I walked to my grandparents' house and my Grandad answered the door. Tears were streaming down my face.

The next day we spoke to the landlord who said he had no choice, but to take all my stuff and let the room out; he had come to collect the rent two days earlier and I wasn't in when I should have been. He hadn't heard from me so he assumed I couldn't pay. He was going to keep everything I owned for one week's rent! All of my things, personal things like photos and memories, my only possessions that had survived the fire! He was going to keep them for the sake of £50 rent, overdue by only a few days! We couldn't reason with him and after a few weeks we gave up. I had to start from scratch again.

The Council moved me to hostel accommodation in Forest Gate, an old building owned and run by the Church. At meals there were prayers and all the staff were religious. I had a small bare room, with some sheets and a blanket; a no TV rule applied to the house and you had to be out from 10 a.m. until 5 p.m., like a bed and breakfast. It felt like a children's home for adults and I wasn't in the mood to be told what to do any more.

Barking College soon involved more than cooking. I saw a poster for student union elections and fancied my chances; I always liked politics and I wanted to prove myself to people. I stood for the election of Secretary and for some reason no one else wanted the job; so it was mine! I was ecstatic, thinking it gave me all sorts of powers to do things. We had a full-time student union President paid by the college and an office with resources. Steve was in his early forties and always had a cigarette hanging out of his mouth. He was muscular and had a foul mouth; every other word was 'fuck' or 'shit'. He liked my enthusiasm and tried to take me under his wing. One day he was going with a friend to a meeting in King's Cross. They invited me to come along.

We went to a dark pub with lots of scruffy white men, some women but not many, drinking pints in a fog of cigarette smoke. The chair of the meeting was talking about the next part of the 'campaign for free education'. We were about to hear a speech from an activist who was on the National Union of Students Executive Committee. She talked about the thousands of young people who wouldn't get to go and study at university as a result, and how those who did would leave saddled with up to £20,000 of debt. Everyone in this room had benefited from a free university education including members of the Labour Government such as the Education Secretary at the time, David Blunkett MP. Her words, spoken with passion, sometimes so much so it made my hairs stand on end, gave me a powerful surge of energy, a desire to get involved. When they asked for volunteers as co-ordinators I didn't hesitate; by the end of the day I was the South East Co-ordinator for the Campaign for Free Education. I was also a fully paid up member of Workers' Liberty, a communist, revolutionary organisation.

As the months went on, I spent more time at the Workers' Liberty office in Peckham in a dirty back street littered with rubbish, discarded washing machines and broken glass. The filth inside matched the filth outside. Piles of papers were covered in dust. There were big old tables with freshly printed black and white posters and pamphlets thundering against the government, capitalism or both. In another room graphic designers worked on books on socialist history or for ethical clients, income that would pay for all this. I liked the smell of the place; the paper, the machines, the wood. But more than that I liked the *taste* of the place; you could taste the excitement as much as you could taste the knowledge that resided there. I wanted to learn and there were opportunities all around me.

I used to sit down with one of the guys who worked there, discussing politics and history. He'd do most of the talking and I'd ask the questions; not that I disputed his views, I agreed completely with everything he had to say, whether or not I understood it. Profit was about slavery and oppression; capitalism was the polite face of that slavery; until we had a revolution, people would not be truly free. He gave me books to read to back up their theories; *The Making of the English Working Class*, *Stalingrad*, *The Bolsheviks* and the *Communist Manifesto*. It changed me. I started to look at things in a different way; it made me angry to see the homeless guys on the street, to see Labour Ministers on the TV, like Harriet Harman, trying to defend cuts to single parent benefits.

It wasn't just learning and talking. We took action and I was more than willing to take centre stage. I organised pickets against my local MPs, Margaret Hodge in Barking and Judith Church in Dagenham. At the Dagenham picket

I got into the building and refused to leave the room where Judith sat, trying to meet her constituents. I held onto the chair. A burly security guard with a sergeant major style moustache walked in, just picked the chair up with me on it, took it outside and plonked me onto the pavement. It wasn't going to be the last time I would see him.

The week that Tony Blair launched air strikes against Saddam Hussain in 1997, along with the US, we had a phone call from George Galloway's office. We had planned to take some action as part of the all-night vigil that evening outside Downing Street, but hadn't yet decided what. It was suggested that several of us handcuff ourselves to the gates of Downing Street.

I was selected along with Anita, the NUS Women's officer at the time, who was an active member of worker's liberty, and a young Iraqi girl. That afternoon we went to his office at Westminster and one of his staff briefed us on the arrangements; we'd be led across the street by a delegation of a few MPs under the pretence that we were giving a petition to the Prime Minister, calling for a peaceful solution to the crisis in Iraq. Hundreds of the world's media were waiting outside the gates, expecting some kind of stunt. It was show time again, but far more chaotic than my old theatre company, KHAOS, had ever been.

As we waited in the dark amongst the thousands of demonstrators lining Whitehall with their candles; songs were sung, there were only glum faces, no laughing or joking. We stood ready to make our way across to the gates; my heart in my throat. We had been issued with handcuffs and blood pellets, so I kept one handcuffed hand in my pocket while my other arm linked in with Anita.

'When I say go,' she said, 'you have to be quick, the pigs will jump on you the minute you show your handcuffs.'

We walked across and everything immediately started to speed up like in a Bruce Willis *Die Hard* film. I jumped to the gates and linked my cuff on a railing; within seconds three police officers pounced, dragging me to the ground; I screamed in pain as the cheap handcuff ripped from the railing and cut into my wrist. I didn't even have time to use a blood pellet or one of the patches in my pocket. The police pinned me to the ground, dragged Anita off to one side and the Iraqi girl to the other. My head, legs and arms were held down by force, my vision blurred by hundreds of flashing lights as if walking up a red carpet to a film premier. I seemed to be the only one on show.

There was absolute silence and I realised my job was now to speak; but I didn't know what to say. I started with the slogans; 'welfare not warfare', 'Tony Blair listen to your people' and 'war is not the answer'. It felt like I was there for ten minutes, but afterwards I realised it had been more like two or three.

I was picked up by the police and led through a mass of crowds to the waiting police van and put inside; I was too exhausted to resist or speak.

'You're quiet, all of a sudden' one of the officers said.

'I've done what I came here to do,' I replied. We were only held in the cells for about an hour, formally cautioned and then released. Outside the station, a few waiting cameras asked us how we felt. George Galloway MP, was there with his solicitor and thanked us for what we had done; we'd raised the issue in people's minds. I'm not sure about that but we did make the news that night; by the time I got home I had been on BBC news, ITN, Channel Four, Sky and Newsnight. I think out of everything I have done in my life that probably made my Grandad, an ardent socialist, the proudest.

My activities had not gone unnoticed by the college and its principal, Ted Parker. He invited me to talk in his office; I didn't know what about, but I assumed it was a telling off. I wasn't pleased that I might have upset him as I had a lot of respect for him. He was friendly when I entered, which was disarming as I had psyched myself for an argument; he just shook my hand warmly and asked me how I was.

'Sit down, Matt. I just wanted to catch up on things with you. You seem to be doing a good job with the Students' Union and I wanted to talk to you about that'. I got the sense that wasn't all he wanted to talk about.

'You know, you remind me a lot of myself when I was your age. In fact I was probably a lot worse than you. But I wouldn't want everyone to know that!' We both laughed.

'I can't believe that, Ted.'

'No, I was. And I admire what you are doing; you're campaigning on student fees. A lot of people here will have sympathy with the issue. I used to be exactly like that when I was your age. We had some battles to fight; I was part of the Socialist Workers' Party. We were fighting racists, though. Skinheads trying to cause trouble in the East End of London.'

'Really?' I was genuinely shocked. This grey-haired, respectable principal was a former member of the SWP? 'What happened?'

'We were marching against the racists in Brick Lane and when the riots started we all piled in. I couldn't work out at one point whether we were fighting the police or the skinheads; they seemed to be bashing all of us. I came up against a police officer and he whacked me around the head with his baton.'

'Wow. You don't seem the type to be involved in all that.'

'Well, in the end I realised there were other ways to

change things. I was teaching and life took over; when I think about it, if I had carried on with the movement I would not have the opportunity to change so many young people's lives here.'

I knew there was a message coming here.

'So I understand what you are doing and why you are doing it. I admire it even. But ultimately the only thing I really care about is running this college so the students can do what they want to in life. I can't have that threatened in any way by your activities, however honourable your intentions.'

He was clearly getting some pressure from other people and I later discovered that local politicians, who would have known about the demos, were on the college's governing board. I agreed to calm things down in the college, but I couldn't stop campaigning where I thought it right.

It wasn't long until I broke my promise to calm things down. As part of the campaign against tuition fees a national education shut-down day had been planned for colleges and universities across the country. At the crack of dawn on the day of the shutdown I arrived with my table and megaphone; a van load of police were already waiting outside the college. As I set up my leaflets, Ted came down towards me and picked one up. After reading it he put it down and smiled.

'You have a bright future Matthew,' he said, 'but not at this college.'

As he walked back towards the entrance I shouted at him through my megaphone, repeating the things he had told me about his past with the Socialist Workers' Party. Afterwards I felt guilty that I had betrayed his trust. But at the time he seemed to be the betrayer.

Most of the tutors supported the campaign I started that day and sent their students to join us. After a while they were getting restless and bored with shouting slogans and started to argue for a more direct form of action; something that would make the college listen to what we had to say. I decided to lead the students into the college like the pied piper and marched through the car park.

We arrived in the canteen next to the student union office and called for the hundreds of students to join us. Then I opened the door to the small union office to find Steve on the phone to security. He and the union had decided not to support the demonstration. As students we were livid that our representatives were betraying us.

Then Ted appeared with several security guards. He was no serene operator now. He screamed 'GET OUT OF MY COLLEGE!'

I was picked up by the security guards and carried out to the main street, behind me were the hundreds that had taken the journey into the college. The adrenaline was now running like a fountain and we decided to blockade the road. The minute we stepped into the road, I was arrested. The demonstration was over; our message lost through unnecessary disruption to the very people who might have supported our action; tutors, motorists, perhaps even Ted himself. My inexperience was the cause, I had let things become about us rather than the message we were trying to give the authorities; not the college, but the NUS and Government. Now they could just dismiss us as loony radicals.

A few weeks later I was expelled for bringing the college into disrepute. And that made me really think about how this was working for me. Workers' Liberty had quickly become like a family and I was totally loyal to its causes. I believed in them passionately, at first without question.

But Workers' Liberty provided – and acknowledged – only one worldview. Anyone who disagreed, or asked too many questions, was a counter-revolutionary, a bourgeois pawn. So desperate was I for a home to replace care that I didn't take the time to stop and think if I had found the *right* home with the right ideals. I'd even started my job at Burger King not only as a source of extra income but because people at the movement thought I could, over time, help to unionise the employees at the restaurant.

I began to listen to the few who had some doubts. One person asked, but what about Richard Branson, surely he's alright? Yes, I thought, he seems okay. Maybe that kind of capitalist is acceptable after a revolution! The books they'd given me to read had made me see that the Russian Revolution hadn't really led to the happiness of the masses. Then someone at Workers' Liberty said to me one day.

'You're getting in trouble quite a lot now. Don't get me wrong, you're doing a great job for the campaign, but you need to be careful; you have been arrested a few times and you will start to get noticed by Special Branch. You're only sixteen, you should think about whether this is really what you want.'

And this brings me round to being Lord of the Fries. By the time I was expelled from College I had already decided to end my involvement with Workers Liberty and knuckle down to working full-time at Burger King and building a life for myself, rather than pretending I could solve the world's problems.

Eventually, after 18 months of working at Burger King, I had a big falling out with the restaurant manager. I left soon after and a few weeks later ended up back where I'd started at McDonalds'. I'd lost a month's pay and didn't have enough to cover my rent, so I had to give up my flat. My grandparents on my Dad's side let me come and stay with them until I sorted myself out. I was depressed; I had lost my independence. I was not even a manager any more, I had zero stars on my badge and was the lowest burger on the team.

The only thing that was going for me now was Tina and our relationship was starting to go wrong. McDonalds was near her school and she and her friends would sometimes come in at lunch; there I was in my McDonalds uniform. We argued more. What was becoming obvious to both of us was how very close we were, maybe too close. It had become such an intense relationship. She was my first love and I was hers. We had changed so much together, too.

When I met her I had only left care seven months earlier; my life a year before had shown no prospect of ever being stable, let alone of my having a girlfriend, friends and a job. She had tamed me and introduced me bit by bit to life as a normal young person, someone without a 'care/social services' label, and the baggage it brings. But she was preparing to go to art college. I realised that we were from different worlds; I could never fit in with hers and I think, at some point, she decided that that was probably fine with her.

So we made a mutual decision to split up. Two weeks later we met up to go out and catch up and she told me that she had a new boyfriend. I was devastated. I couldn't believe that after we'd been together so long, held each other so close, she'd switch to someone else so quickly. The love that had helped repair the scars of my childhood was now gone with one sentence. Going home, I started to cry on a packed bus and couldn't stop.

Over the next week I tried desperately to win her back. I begged her, going to her house most days, and she tried to reason with me, explaining why we couldn't be together. I was devastated; not just because she didn't want to be with me any more – after all, it had been a mutual decision to break up – but because she'd chosen someone else over me. I was reliving the pain from all those years ago, when Mum had chosen Kevin over me, her eldest son.

Someone once told me that there is a thin line between romance and stalking and a hairline between love and madness. Things that Tina would have once thought romantic now scared her and I was too blinded by my own feelings of desperation and loss to realise it. I wrote her love letters like the ones she used to write to me; I even drew a picture for her of a frog, her favourite animal, like she'd made pictures for me when we were together. But the more I did the more she told me to stay away; after she got the letter with the picture she told me I was starting to scare her. I realised I needed to move on. But I couldn't; I felt sick, I couldn't eat or sleep and no matter what I did I thought of Tina, of her and her new boyfriend together doing the things she and I had done.

One night after drinking with some friends I went around to her house, very drunk. I banged on the door and called for her to come down; eventually her sister opened the door on the latch and told me to go away; Tina stood behind her, looking scared.

'I just want to talk to you,' I slurred my words through uncontrollable, undignified tears and snot. 'Is *he* here?'

'It's none of your business, Matt, but no he's not.' Her voice sounded cold, like I was a stranger, a nuisance.

'How can you be so cold to me?' I asked through my snot and tears. 'I just want to know why you don't love me any more? How can you just change from one moment to the next?'

'Just go away, Matt. I don't want to talk to you.'

'You used to love me. I have this letter to prove it.' I pulled out the letter she'd sent, explaining all the reasons why she loved me, and started to read it. She ran to the door and tried to snatch it from my hands, screaming for me to stop. Then this small blonde-haired guy ran down the stairs and came straight towards me; compared to me, with my spotty face, he was extremely good-looking, and I could see why Tina was with him. He tried to punch at me through the gap in the door but couldn't reach me.

In my anger and frustration I hit my head against the window pane. It shattered over my head. Tina and her sister started screaming and crying, retreating against the wall. Then her new boyfriend put his hand through the broken glass to hit me, slicing his finger. Tina screamed that her Mum was going to kill her. I couldn't believe that she didn't care about me; blood was dripping from my arm and the top of my head.

I'd never meant for the window to smash, but once I'd found out *he* was there, I lost control and there was no turning back. Hearing sirens in the distance, I just ran. I ended up at the railway bridge and sat on the edge. This had been my default position in life if things got bad; tempt fate, plan a suicide. As I sat there surrounded by police, I began to think about the last time I was in this position, on a bridge trying to plot my downfall. So much had happened since then, so many good things.

I didn't want to go through life labelled as a nuisance and a misfit. I'd had the chance to experience what love could be like and it felt good, but my mistake was to confuse it with unconditional love. It was too much to ask of a girl who was so young and maybe too much to ask of anyone in a relationship. That's what I had looked for in Workers' Liberty, but an organisation can't give unconditional love either. Constant, unconditional love, the love I'd never had and craved, only ever comes, in most people's lives, from two people: their parents. And my parents just hadn't been up to it.

The police had no trouble getting me down. I was taken to the hospital, assessed and then released. It scared me, just how close I'd come to losing it again. I told myself that whatever happened in future I couldn't break down. Suicide wasn't the answer and violence against someone who had stopped loving me wasn't either. I phoned Tina, apologised profusely and said I wouldn't be bothering her again – ever. She told me how scared she was and how crazy I had become; she never wanted to speak to me again. That sad little exchange by phone was our final conversation.

After we'd spoken I felt a glassy calm. More than that, though, I knew that I couldn't find my grounding in life through love, not the kind that I could get from any relationship. I had to get that grounding from purpose and I set about finding that purpose straight away.

9

Aged Eighteen – Breakthrough

The good thing about going back to McDonalds as a serf was that I was more motivated and had more time to think. I was desperate to get out of there. I had no qualifications, a tendency to get upset, and my only skills were in the fast food industry. But I'd still spend my days dreaming up ideas of businesses I could run, most of them total non-starters.

But one idea kept coming back. My idea was a talent competition. It would be Essex-wide and have a big prize for the winner to attract people to compete; the money would be made by charging an entrance fee for auditions, plus ticket sales for the final show. It was *Britain's Got Talent* rolled into the *X Factor* before its time, though on a much smaller scale. The more depressed I became the more I thought through the idea. Then, as if by good and bad luck at the same time, I slipped whilst carrying some boxes and dislocated my knee; I spent the next four weeks in plaster with nothing to do except think. I had decided that, whatever else, I could never flip a burger again.

I spent those four weeks drafting my business plan. The company would be called *Inspirations Production Company* and my vision of what we could do became our manifesto; the 'we' consisted of just me and Rob, who I'd made friends with at Burger King. We'd start with the talent festival, quickly find premises and then, within five years, have twenty talent fests all over England. Ambitious? Crazy? Of course, but I didn't see the point going in small. I had read Richard Branson's *Losing My Virginity* and thought if *he* could do it at 16, then *I* could do it now.

I phoned almost everyone I could think of for support including Richard Branson (he never did take my call!) I convinced a local nightclub to let us hold the final event there. We advertised a top prize of £1,000 with a £10 entrance fee, although we didn't have any money. The local paper and Essex FM agreed to promote the event in exchange for a mention on the posters and leaflets. But despite these initial successes, we had nowhere to work and this was becoming a problem. Meetings with Rob and his friends were conducted in pubs, where little business got done. I was staying with my grandparents from my Mum's side now, as my other grandparents were on holiday, and it was difficult to work from their house. I had to conduct my business from a phone box.

When I was seeking sponsorship, the Editor of the local paper suggested that I phone the youth service. The Arts Officer for the Council was intrigued and arranged for me to see the Principle Youth Officer, Steve Power. I headed straight over to the town hall. Steve was a tall, handsome man with dark hair and a warm smile. As I whirled through my ideas and plans for world domination, gesticulating all over the place he just sat back with his hand on his chin, listening intently. By the time I finished I thought I had blown it.

'So what do you need from us?' I wasn't expecting that.

'Erm, I'm not sure. We don't have any money and what we really need is somewhere to work; a phone and a computer.'

He thought for a minute.

'Yes, okay, I think we can do that.'

'Really? It's that simple? Are you sure?' I was shocked;
I couldn't believe it was that easy.

'Yes, it's that simple. The way I see it is that you are a
young person starting a business, we are a youth service
and we are helping you by giving you this space. It won't
cause me any trouble and besides, it's not forever, only to
help you get on your feet. Let's say six months and then
review it then?'

'That's great. Thank you so much, I didn't expect this.'
I was so excited and shocked I could feel myself welling
up. I had spent the last few weeks traipsing the streets,
getting turned down and fearing an eternity in Burger Hell.
Now, in the space of 20 minutes, I had everything I needed
to get things properly started.

'I'm just wondering. When would it be possible to start?
I don't want to push it; it's just really quite difficult to
work at the moment.'

'Well, how about you go and meet the youth worker
who runs the building where the office is tonight?'

I thanked him and he wished me luck, saying he'd do
all he could to help. With that he left for a meeting. As I
watched him go I wondered why he had done that, knowing
so little about me, yet letting me have an office after twenty
minutes together.

The next day I started in our new office. We had a whole
room with space for three. We had use of the telephones
and access to the computer room. It felt like a real company,
and I felt like a real businessman. People started to take
us seriously, too. Mum, with whom I was getting on better
now that I was independent, offered to invest £1,000 for
one fifth of the company.

One day I was walking past a derelict, boarded-up shop front on the corner of South Street in Romford. It had a 'to let' sign. I rang the landlord, a private agent, and arranged a meeting. I got the property rent free for four months, in exchange for promising to renovate it. Inside it was like a ghost house, frozen in time, stuck in the eighties. There was no front to the shop behind all that boarding, no fire system and no electrics.. It was a big building and would easily house a stage and a catering area. We would need new toilets and had to pull out the ceiling as well as carpet the floor. This was a mammoth task. It was late September and I set a date for opening on the 1st December.

Rob had to become full-time which meant finding the money to cover his salary. I was due a compensation payout from McDonalds, but this was nowhere near completion. Mum said that a friend of hers, owner of one of the biggest private security firms in London (the man I remembered with giant hands, her club bouncer when I was a child), might be interested in investing. He did so and I also got a small bank loan. In 6 short weeks we had gone from a vision document in the back of a pub to having a building and official help. Now we just had to make the Talent Show happen. We held our first round of auditions.

We had applied for finance for the catering equipment and the shop front windows and expected it to be approved soon. Then one day, all at once, things started to tumble down. First, the catering firm wouldn't give credit to a new company. The shop front window company followed. We would now need an extra £30k for the catering equipment and shop front. Without it we wouldn't be able to serve hot food, a key part of our business plan.

Rob came to the rescue on the shop front as his Mum's boyfriend was a builder. He'd build it as well as completing the internal works for a fraction of the price of the shop front company.

We scaled back our plans to provide hot food and hoped to God that we would meet our revenue plans for entrance fees and arcade machines. Still the budget would be extremely tight and there was no margin for error. But with no experience of managing a business or a budget there were some huge errors. Any sane person would have stopped there, saying, 'great idea, guys, but it ain't gonna happen. And you certainly can't keep to your schedule.' But I insisted we could. Some workers from the local youth service had complained to Steve that we would be taking their 'business' away. They didn't see the need for what they saw as another, rival youth club. Luckily it infuriated Steve as much as it did me and their complaints fell on deaf ears.

But I didn't always deal too well with those kinds of problems. The admin staff at the youth centre also resented us, and I responded with childish pettiness. At times I went out of my way to wind them up, which made *us* laugh, but just made things worse. So I had a lot to prove in opening the entertainment centre and doing so on time.

Oddly, this venture had brought me closer to my Mum. We didn't need to talk about the past now: with the business, we had a future to discuss. For the first time she told me she was proud of me; and I believed her. So when Rob and Matt came to talk to me about pushing the opening date back by a few months I wasn't prepared to consider it: my pride just wouldn't allow it, and I felt they'd let me down. But now I know the main reason I felt angry with Rob wasn't that I felt betrayed: deep down, I knew he was right. I just thought that if we stopped now, we wouldn't do it at all.

In the midst of all this mayhem we still had some fun.

Rob had been a real friend to me. During the break-up with Tina he'd helped me a lot, listening to my depressive ramblings. I remember when I left the hospital that day after they'd assessed me. I went to see him that afternoon and spent an hour trying to convince him I was sane! He'd heard that I had threatened to jump off a bridge the night before. Most people would have written me off as a nut, but he just listened and accepted where I was at. He saw me at my worst times and yet he never once ended or threatened to end our friendship. It was the first time I had a friend like that, someone I could have differences with and the world didn't cave in – even if it did in my head sometimes!

To save money we dumped our suits and put on our scruffy clothes to make the final preparations to the building. The final week before the launch I split myself between answering calls for opening night tickets and overseeing the works at the building. With no experience of electrics in my life I was wiring plugs and laying coverings. When the official electrician came to fit the main fuse box, he went absolutely crazy at us. An electricity cable from the main inlet to the building was completely exposed; had anyone touched it they would have been killed.

A day before opening the carpet was laid. The arcade machines and pool tables wouldn't be delivered until late on the day of the opening and we wouldn't have time to set them up; but it looked like the rest of the building would be ready; just, if we painted till the very last minute. I hadn't slept for four days by the time we opened.

I was a bundle of nerves on opening night. I was so anxious the lump in my throat wouldn't go; I had no idea if anyone was going to turn up. The theme for the night was a house and garage club night, costing only £2 to get in. Other than the entrance fee the only money we would make would be on the arcade machines, the drinks and snacks. By the time we opened at 8 p.m. a long queue of young people was waiting to come in. By 10 p.m. we had two hundred people in the place. I started to think we were home and dry – but it was never going to be that easy.

A scuffle broke out near the arcade machine. We didn't know at the time, but the kids involved belonged to a local gang. A fight kicked off inside, and while it didn't seem to matter at the time, it stopped a fair few people from coming back; parents want to know their children are safe when out and not at risk of getting involved in fights. By the following week we struggled to draw more than fifty people. We had a live band one night which attracted a couple of dozen people, mainly friends of the musicians. But without hot food and a low entrance fee, it wasn't nearly enough money to cover costs and debts.

Over the following weeks creditors started to demand their money and wouldn't wait much longer. The only people that came to the centre during the week seemed to be members of the Romford Gang and they caused as much trouble as they could, even trashing the place one night.

The staff were demanding their money, too, and I realised I had to take some action to get things under control. I just couldn't bring myself to do the decent thing and let several of the staff go; these were people who had helped make the business possible. I had sold them a dream and they had trusted me. What made it worse was that it was now only a few weeks before Christmas. How could I tell them they had no job and no chance of getting their pay at this time of the year? As I thought about what to say to people I felt physically sick.

The next day I met the staff in a local coffee bar. Before I started to speak one of them said they knew what I was going to say and it was okay. She was crying and seemed relieved it was over. They were all as exhausted as I was. I could get people to believe in dreams and ideas but I couldn't make them happen. It was only a few weeks later, when they realised that they wouldn't be paid for their last few weeks of work that they became angry with me. They couldn't even afford to buy presents that Christmas.

The final bit of the business we had that was making money was the talent festival which took place a few weeks after the centre opened. With my exhaustion and only a few us left, I was left de-motivated by the knowledge that the business would have to close its doors soon.

Ironically, the talent festival was a fantastic success with a variety of good acts; solo singers, groups, dancers and even a solo drummer. The audience enjoyed every minute, cheering and shouting. The only thing I regretted then was not doing a deal on the drinks as the bar was probably the only winner of this enterprise. At the end the producer called me and the other event organisers on stage and presented us, to applause. Again, we couldn't present the cheque then because we didn't have any money so it was said that it would be presented later, after the event. Standing up there on stage reminded me of my days in KHAOS as a child at the end of a production. Over the music system the song 'When the Going Gets Tough' came on and the presenter got us and all the artists singing along to it. I suddenly felt energised and proud. We had done it despite all our setbacks. For a moment, I forgot that tomorrow I'd have to face the creditors and close the company. But, for now I could just stand there and be proud of what we had tried to do.

The next day I faced reality – and called Steve. I asked him to come to the centre.

'Steve. I'm going to have to shut the business. It's not going to work'. I started to cry.

'I think you are doing the right thing. But this isn't a complete failure,' he said.

I laughed through my tears. 'Of course it's a bloody failure, Steve. I've let everyone down.'

'Who have you let down?'

'My friends, the people that worked with me.'

'I told you that that wasn't just you. They chose to be involved; anybody that gets involved in something like this as a new business and doesn't think there is a risk, they are stupid or fooling themselves.'

'And I've let my Mum down.'

'How have you let your Mum down? She should be proud of you.'

I'd never told Steve about my background in care. He only knew my relationship with Mum as the working partnership he'd seen.

'This is the first time she has ever been proud of me. But she won't be proud now. I have lost her money, and her friend's. For years I have wanted us to be close, for her to love me and now she isn't even going to want to know me.'

'Why would she do that to you?' It was then that I explained the past to Steve. Again he listened in silence.

'Matthew, this isn't the end of your life,' he said, 'you've tried to do something, something that was big and ambitious, and it hasn't worked out. But you've done a remarkable thing regardless; people didn't think you would get this far. You shouldn't give up.'

He then opened up about his own past and particularly

his relationship with his father. That story is his to tell, but I've never forgotten him saying that he'd spent years trying to make his father proud of him and at some point realised no matter what he did, it wasn't up to him to win his Dad's pride – it was up to his father to give it. I felt there was a bond between us, that we'd been through similar trials in our childhoods. He hadn't always been the senior youth officer he was today, he reminded me. I was no longer crying. I looked at this well-groomed man who had overcome his past and I saw a glimmer of hope for my own future.

'Can I ask you something?' I said.

'You can ask me anything.'

'When I came into your office that day, the first time you didn't know anything about me. Why did you help me?'

'You looked like you needed a break.'

'Thank you for doing that,' I said.

With that, he gave me hug like a father consoling his child. He dropped me off at my grandparents' that night, just a few days before Christmas and said, 'Remember, Matthew, you have a long life ahead of you. This is just a setback. I still believe in you.'

For now I had to sleep. I slept right through Christmas.

10

Aged Nineteen to Twenty-One, First Real Job

Things were difficult in those first few weeks and months after the business collapsed. Rob was still getting hassle at home because his Mum's boyfriend was one of our creditors. The first time Mum and I spoke after the shut-down was on the steps of her house, as she left for a Boxing Day party.

'I don't why you are upset,' she said, 'you haven't lost anything. This was your dream, Matthew, not mine. And because I let you have your dream, I can't now have mine.'

I hadn't forced her to get involved. She had been as convinced as I that this was worth giving a try. Now it was like she was saying she had nothing to do with it. But, as usual, I thought better of arguing back, at least face to face.

Our next conversation wasn't any easier. Mum cried on the phone.

'What makes me angry, Matthew, is you haven't once asked how this makes me feel. What do you think this means for my friendship with Ez? I trusted you with that money, trusted you to make it work and it didn't. And I'll get through it, but the thing that hurts me the most is that you haven't once talked about how we will get through it.'

'I have thought about it. It doesn't need to involve you. I'm sorry about your friend, but he knew he was investing in a business and might not get it back.'

'But he wasn't. He was investing because I wanted him to and because he is my friend.'

'Well, it doesn't work like that,' I said.

'How can you be so selfish about this?'

'I'm not. But, you're making it sound like you're the only one suffering. I've lost friends through this. I don't have a job to speak of. I have to deal with all the creditors making threatening noises about their money. Not you.'

'Fine, then, I'll leave you to deal with it by yourself,' she said, and hung up. I went through to my Grandma's bedroom. She looked at me and asked:

'Everything all right?'

'No. She thinks it's all my fault.'

'Well that's silly. She knew what she was getting into when she got involved. How can it be all your fault?'

'I don't know, but I don't think she is going to talk to me again.'

She was silent for a minute.

'I'm sorry about that. We're still here for you,' she said.

The Romford Youth Work Manager, Andrew, helped me to sort out the mess with the business. As I was calling creditors, he told me to not sound so downbeat about everything. But I was downbeat. I felt I had no future. One day I phoned Steve and pleaded with him.

'Steve, I can't do this. I don't think I'm doing anything worthwhile and I can't go from what I was doing to this. I need a challenge.'

'I understand.'

'Can I please come and work for you? You don't even have to pay me. Let me get some experience and I'll be able to find something.'

I knew if I didn't do this I'd end up back at Burger King.

'Okay. Come and see me this evening.'

I met with him and Andrew at the youth centre. As I went in the admin staff looked at me as if there was a bad smell in the room. I could tell they didn't want me there. And looking back, after the way I had treated them, I couldn't really blame them.

Steve started the meeting.

'Matthew, you have a lot of skills to offer,' Steve said, 'and, after speaking with Andrew, we can offer you something here. We can't pay you though and you'll need to sign on for benefits.'

'That's fine. Anything will help.'

I started work the next day, with an apology to the administration staff. After I'd eaten a bit of humble pie, they accepted my apology. But things were always tense with them; they saw me as interfering in their centre and they were probably right. I saw great potential for the youth centre; a place that could be used all hours and make money for the youth service. But I was never one to take my time with my ideas and bring people along with them. They always had to be my ideas and, therefore, my success. I was still trying to prove that I could make something of myself.

Andrew was skinny and had a bad comb-over that couldn't hide his baldness. He spoke theoretically, like a member of staff at Caldecott. He'd once been a residential care worker in a therapeutic home, a job, he said, that he'd hated. Andrew was something of a rebel himself – and he wanted to change the centre's whole approach to youth work.

Numbers attending youth clubs had dropped significantly over the years. Andrew was interested in the youth beyond the clubs, pondering how to tackle the likes of the Romford Gang and the disaffected teens getting expelled from school? They were not going to turn up on Wednesday night for a few hours to play pool and talk to us. We had to find new ways of going to them.

Andrew gave me three main projects to work on. The first was Expedition South Africa 2000, a plan to take ten disaffected young people to the Cape Flats to set up a computer centre. The second was a project called Spread the Net; a 24-hour event where young people from the borough would attempt to use the internet to communicate with one young person from every country on Earth. Third, the Council was opening a centre called Youth Zone to provide information and advice to young people. Andrew put me in charge of organising an art exhibition and the launch.

This was my first real job where I felt what I was doing would make a difference. I had a job title – Project Support Officer – and an office, but no pay. I reasoned I could live for six months or so on the £40 a week I got in benefits.

Inevitably there was some aftermath from Inspirations. There had been a press article slamming me and Steve was still getting some complaints. A lot of people didn't want to know me any more. Rob still wanted to be friends, but thought it best to keep his distance for a while – his family hadn't been paid for the building work. One of Mum's friends started threatening me about the few thousand pounds he had lost in investing in the business. I phoned her to talk about it – at first she wouldn't come to the phone, but eventually, she grabbed the receiver and snapped.

'What is all this about, Matthew?'

'You know what it's all about! I've just been threatened by Ez and I want to know what's going on.'

'I don't know anything about that. I didn't know he was going to speak to you.'

'I don't believe you.'

'Matthew, because of you, Ez won't even speak to me. I don't think you realise you have ruined my friendship.'

'Me? Why is it all about you all the time? You got involved in this knowing what the risks were. It wasn't just me involved in this. Then, when things get tough, you just go and blame everything on me. Don't you think it's difficult for me, too? I've lost friends out of this, people who won't even speak to me.'

'All I have ever tried to do for you, Matthew, is help you and you have always thrown it back in my face.'

'Help me! How was choosing Kevin over me and letting me go into care helping me? What kind of mother does that?'

She was crying now. But I didn't care any more. All those years I had wanted to say these things, but held back.

'Well, come on tell me. Why was it him you chose and not me after what I told you about him?'

'It was complicated.' She whimpered through her tears. 'The psychiatrist said we should not let you dictate things.'

'Dictate things! HE WAS BEATING ME UP! Why didn't you just believe me?'

'Because there were so many things going on at the time I didn't know what to believe. Anyway, things worked out okay for you. You went to where you wanted and had a good place to live with everyone running around after you. I lived through hell while all that was going on.'

'Are you stupid? Do you actually know what happened in those children's homes?'

'No, because you have never told me.'

'I wouldn't even tell you now, because you wouldn't believe me.'

'Okay, Matthew, I know I'm such a bad mother, you've made that very clear.'

She blubbered insincerely through her tears. She was trying to make me feel guilty.

'Yes, you were a bad mother. And not just to me, but to Danny too. He isn't happy at home. Why do you think he keeps running away?'

'Don't bring Danny into this.'

'I don't know why I don't just phone Social Services and get them to take Danny away from you.'

I was just trying to hurt her now. She completely lost it.

'If you do anything like that I will come and find you myself.'

'Now the real Mum is coming out.'

'You really hate me, don't you?' she was crying so hard that it was difficult to understand her.

'Yes I do hate you. You destroyed my life and I will never forgive you for that.'

'I put my house up as a guarantee to the loan for the bank. Doesn't that show how much I love you?'

'No, it just shows how guilty you felt. And you're not going to get a penny of that money back from me. You're a bitch and I hate you. You didn't have to pay for anything when I was in care, yet I had to pay with the things that happened to me.'

'So this is payback time is it, Matthew?'

'Yes it is. I didn't plan it this way, but as it's turned out it is payback.'

With that she hung up the phone. I sat back in my chair. I didn't feel upset. I felt a deep sense of relief. Like a dark, threatening cloud over my head had been lifted. Something told me I wouldn't hear from her for a long while. But, at that moment, I didn't want to ever hear from her again. Until she admitted she was wrong, until she said sorry for the things she had done, I didn't want to have anything to do with her.

A few weeks later my Grandad took me to Mum's house to get some of my things. She was out and two of her friends were looking after John and Danny. We found Danny down at the supermarket hanging around with a gang of kids who looked like trouble. Danny came back to the house with us. He asked why I was taking my things and if I would come inside.

'I can't come inside, Danny, sorry. I'm not allowed'. He started to cry.

He didn't understand. I couldn't explain to him what had happened; that Mum and I would probably never speak again. I didn't know what that meant for me and Danny but I knew she wouldn't want me to see him any more.

'Matthew, please don't go. I love you'. I was crying now. I hugged him; I remember how tightly he held me.

'I love you too. I just can't stay. I'm sorry'. Mum's friends came out to take Danny inside. As we drove away, Danny just stood there crying. It was the third time he had seen his brother leave. After that day he phoned me several times a week until suddenly he stopped. I can only imagine Mum had found out he was in touch and either told him not to call or talked him out of it. We never spoke again. Out of everyone; my father, mother, all the people from my past; Danny is the one I still miss the most.

During the long hours I put in at the youth service I couldn't help but think about my experiences in care. They haunted me and manifested in my anger towards almost everyone around me, my paranoia and my bouts of deep depression. I was convinced that I needed to find some closure on everything I'd been through in the homes of my childhood.

I had tried to complain to Social Services many times and asked for access to my files. Every child in care has files, sometimes thousands of pages long, with minutes of review meetings, reports and memos, as well as psychiatric and medical reports. They provide a useful, but often painful, insight into what happened to you as a child from the adults' perspective. For years my files were extremely difficult to get hold of, but recent legislation made the process much quicker and easier.

After sending many letters over the years asking for access to my files and hearing nothing, I decided to take direct action, as in my days with Workers' Liberty. One day, I went to the Social Services reception and demanded to speak to somebody about my files; I wanted to make a complaint about my care and I wanted to do it today. The receptionist made a few calls and then said it wouldn't be possible to see someone today. I got angry, fed up with being fobbed off by Social Services and refused to leave.

About 10 minutes later the Sergeant Major lookalike, with a huge moustache walked in. I remembered him from the time he'd removed me from the MP surgery. I told him not to lay a finger on me and fuck off. He simply picked me up, while I kicked and screamed, and threw me out. I tried to bash my way back in, but he just stood there pushing me away. In my mind, I was back on that roof at Woodstock screaming for somebody to listen. I went around the corner to the big glass windows and I banged on each one, screaming as loud as I could:

'Someone fucking listen to me. I was abused in the care of Barking and Dagenham Council.' After a few minutes, a man came out who calmly asked me what all this was about. I remembered him as one of the social workers at Woodstock who I used to see from time to time, Hugh Pelham. Through my tears, I told him I just wanted someone to listen to my complaint. He took me inside.

'Matthew, we have met before, but a very long time ago. My name is Hugh Pelham and I am the Team Manager here. Can I firstly apologise for the way you have been dealt with today? You shouldn't have been taken off the premises like that and I will be speaking to the person concerned and their manager.'

'Thank you.'

'So what is all this about? You are obviously very angry.'

'I am angry. Over the years I have tried to make complaints about what happened to me in care. I was in Woodstock for some time and some things happened there that I want to complain about.'

'What things, Matthew?'

'I was abused in care there.'

'By the children or the adults?'

'I don't want to talk about it today.'

There was some silence.

'Okay, I can see you are still quite distressed. Why don't we arrange a time to meet and go through things properly? I want to listen to your complaint, I can't speak for what has happened before but I am sorry about today.'

We agreed to meet that Thursday. And I decided to be careful.

I borrowed a dictaphone and hid it in my jacket. But the minute I got in the room, Hugh asked me what the bulge in my coat was. When I showed him, he refused to say anything with a tape recorder present. I put the dictaphone away.

'Well, I was abused in Woodstock.'

'Okay. I need to be clear what we are talking about here. Were you abused by adults or children?'

I started to talk him through the story. I didn't tell him about the sexual abuse by the children, but I did tell him about Craig holding me down naked. And I told him about the violence, the sex and the drugs.

'So there was no abuse from the adults?'

'No, not directly, but I was abused.' It seemed like he didn't care about the other abuse at all, only whether there was something that happened with the adults. I got more and more agitated until, finally, I said there was no point in going on if he wasn't going to take this seriously.

'I am taking this seriously, but because this isn't abuse from adults we need to deal with this through the complaints procedure. You need to put your complaint in writing.'

I left feeling no better off than when I'd started. At the time I blamed him, but later accepted he was just doing his job. His first priority was to see if there were abusive adults employed there, whether residents were in danger. But at the time, I just saw it as him not being interested in the rest of my story. Shortly after the meeting the demonstration at college took place. After that, I decided to try and move on from my past and forget it.

But after losing Tina and my business, I now had more time than I wanted to think about all those years. When you have tried to push memories back for so long, suppressed so much anger, when you finally decide to do something about it you want to do it all right away. You don't want to have to wait through a process to get answers; you want to speak to people that minute and feel listened to. You want retribution.

Immediately, I fired off a fax to the Director of Social

Services at Barking and Dagenham asking for my files and an inquiry into events that took place in Woodstock. The Director was called Julia Ross.

I still had no trust in Barking and Dagenham and expected them to simply ignore my complaint or find some way of blaming me. I'd spent years trying to get a copy of my files and my requests had always been denied, with the excuse that they were held up in the lawyer's office.

At a Social Services conference I approached the Minister for Children, John Hutton, MP. He didn't stop walking but turned to me.

'Yes, you will have to keep talking as we walk I'm afraid, I'm late for a meeting,' he said.

'I'm Matthew Huggins and I grew up in care in Barking and Dagenham. I had a very bad time in their children's homes and suffered abuse.' He stopped and turned to me. He shook my hand.

'I'm sorry to hear that, Matthew,' He didn't seem surprised though.

'Well, I've been trying to complain and get taken seriously for years and haven't yet been listened to. I'm still trying to get access to my files and can't. I was wondering if you could help?'

'Well, that is not just good enough, Matthew,' he spoke without hesitation. 'I'm going to introduce you to this lady here, Jo, who works for me at the Social Services Inspectorate. She will make sure your case is dealt with the way it should. You should hear from her in the next few days.' He turned to the blonde, middle-aged lady by his side. 'I want you to report back to me on this.'

'Yes, Minister.' She gave me her contact details and said to call her the next day. For the first time, I felt confident that something was going to happen now.

The next day I had a call from Julia Ross saying she had heard from Jo Cleary, but already planned to get in touch about my letter. She asked if I could come in and meet with her the next day.

'Matthew, it's Jo Cleary here.' She sounded sweet and motherly; warm.

'Jo, thank you for sorting this out. I got a call from Julia today to set up a meeting for tomorrow.'

'I bet you did.'

'What did you do?'

'I didn't do anything. It was the Minister who insisted they take this case seriously and what the Minister wants, he gets. He has asked me to personally report back to him on the progress of your complaint. If you ever have any questions about anything then give me a call or if you think they are not listening to you get back to me and I'll help.'

When I went into the social service department it was the first time I had ever been through those doors beyond the meeting room. It felt strange and somehow empowering. I was bypassing all those offices with people in them who had known me as a child and written so many derogatory reports about me. I was half hoping to bump into one of them so I could tell them I was on the way to meet the Director. When I got to the Director's office, I was greeted by two women, an attractive, middle-aged woman who introduced herself as the Director, Julia, and asked if it was alright to call me Matt. The other lady I recognised as Maggie, the woman who had taken me to Balgores all those years ago with my Mum in the car.

'Do you remember me?' I asked her.

'Yes I do. Is that okay, Matthew?' She spoke with the warmth and kindness I remembered.

'Yes, of course. I always liked you'. We settled down with tea and had some small talk before Julia started the official stuff.

'Matthew, we have received your letter. We also received a call from the Minister's office and I know he is as concerned as we are to hear your complaint and deal with it as best we can. I know you feel you haven't been listened to before and I want to start by apologising. I also want to make clear that I will take what you have to say very seriously. The reason I have brought Maggie here is so that she can take a lead on dealing with your complaint, if you are happy with that. I have full confidence in her ability to treat this confidentially and deal with it as rigorously as possible.'

With that she turned the tape recorder on and said that I would get a copy. I went through the whole story. As I relived some of the moments I cried. The only moment I couldn't relive was the sexual abuse from the children. I wasn't ready to talk about that.

'Thank you for been so honest with us.' Julia said, it seemed, genuinely. 'I know your experiences have been bad and I just want to reassure you that I take that very seriously.'

I wiped away my tears.

'Thank you,' I said.

'I just wanted to talk to you about your personal circumstances at the moment' Maggie said. 'As you know, we didn't have a Leaving Care Service when you left, but now we have, I think you have a right to access the service. It is still in its early days, but there is someone I would like you to meet who may be able to help while we deal with the complaint.'

I explained I was working for Havering Youth Service,

virtually for nothing, and so I couldn't pay my grandparents any rent or even give them much for food and bills. At first they were kind about it, but it was now beginning to put a strain on our relationship. They were pensioners and only had a small amount of money coming in. They thought I should get a 'real' job. I could see their point, but I knew that if I got a job now, it wouldn't be a decent one. I was taking a chance with Havering, but it was a chance worth taking if it provided some opportunity.

My Grandad understood my desire for achievement as he had once been ambitious himself, but had a family at an early age. He could never have worked for Havering for free. Nor could my Grandma. Her childhood had been tougher than his. Her mother never paid her much attention and at the age of twelve she ran off with a man from the army leaving her parents, her younger sister and brother behind. Her father died when she was just fifteen and she went to the only job she could find, working as a live-in nanny in Newcastle. Her employers didn't treat her well and she wasn't happy there. Even the electricity had it in for her; every time she touched the light switch it gave her an electric shock!

Eventually she came to see the only person she knew would love her and take care of her; my Grandad who had returned from his two year service in the army. They got married, bought a modest house and worked hard to bring up the three children they had. Grandad worked full-time as a clerk at the 'May and Baker' company and my grandma worked various jobs, as many as she could get. She cleaned for people and was also a part-time dinner lady at Barking College.

One day my grandma did something that demonstrated such compassion as could make the hardest of hearts melt. A friend of hers came round to the house and told her about a young girl that had just returned to work from maternity leave, after giving up her child to foster care. With my Grandad at work and, without a second thought, she went with her friend to the mother and offered to take care of the baby.

The mother wrote a letter handing over care of the baby to my grandma. They went to the foster carer, who could hardly speak a word of English, and eventually explained it to her. By the time my Grandad got home they had a new addition to the family; my mother. She phoned Social Services the next day and said she had the baby, with permission from the mother.

'Oh, you can't do that, Mrs Huggins.'

'Well, I did.'

'Okay. Well, you sound like a good family. I will need to come out and sort out the paperwork with you, but won't be free for another few weeks.'

And that was how they adopted my mother. For whatever reason, my Mum was not the easiest of teenagers. When she got pregnant with me at sixteen, they took care of her and we both lived with them for the first year until she met my 'dad'. Their support for us never wavered, and I owed them a lot. But now things were tense and I could feel the tensions rising; I didn't want to lose them, too. They were the last of my family left in my life. So I explained to Maggie I needed a flat.

'Well that's something I think the Leaving Care Team can help with.'

'What's going to happen next, Matthew, is that we are going to start some initial investigation into your complaint and decide how we are going to deal with this. We will also attempt to find your files so you can look through them. Once that has happened, at some point, you are going to have to put your full complaint in writing, but I appreciate this will be easier when you have your files.' Julia reassured me more than anyone else had ever done. I still wasn't completely at the point where I trusted Social Services but this was a good start. Maggie gave me her number and told me to call her any time.

I should have been happy. But I wasn't. I had no friends any more and Rob and I were still not talking much. My only company now were my grandparents and Andrew at the youth service. Having no money didn't help either. It was difficult living on forty pounds a week, with paying for lunch (a 'chip butty') and travel to and from the youth centre. At times before I picked up my benefit I'd only have a few pounds left. One Sunday, I had no food and only sixty pence. I went to the local shop to see what I could find and bought an out of date quiche and a cheap packet of biscuits.

At least work took my mind off things. The major project we worked on was the opening of Youth Zone. Andrew, at the time, had a huge portfolio of responsibilities, so a lot of the time I was left to organise things myself. I was told I was in charge of the arrangements for the launch.

The launch went without a hitch. It was well covered in the local media. Again I should have been happy, but I just felt even more depressed. I didn't know what was wrong with me. I felt like I did when I was child before a big build up when I would do something silly. Steve gave me a lift and I tried to explain to him how I felt. He told me about a youth officer that worked for the Council who had suffered from depression and might be willing to talk to me. A few days later I met him, but he just seemed angry with me. Not for any particular reason; he just said that I had rubbed people up the wrong way in the youth service. It wasn't his problem to sort out if I was depressed. I said I realised that, but I was only talking to him because Steve told me. He went on about his own story of how he had been so depressed before his nervous breakdown that he had to go to a mental hospital and refused to leave until they admitted him. That was the only option he seemed to be presenting to me and I didn't see the point in that; I didn't feel that bad, did I? But, the idea took root that I was headed that way. That left me even more depressed than before.

As Maggie promised, the Leaving Care Team moved me into a bed and breakfast immediately. Whilst I wasn't keen on leaving my grandparents to go to a bedsit, it was time I stood on my two feet, whatever that meant I had to deal with. It was a horrible room with a bed, a wardrobe and a sink in a typical Department of Social Security hostel full of strange people. I avoided them, scared to talk to them. The strange thing is that a lot of them were probably just in the same position as me. But, rightly or wrongly, I saw myself as different.

To make it worse, I now had all my social work files to read. As I read through them I grew increasingly angry, most of all at the black lines put through certain passages by the lawyers. I couldn't believe what I was reading. The files seemed to describe another ten-year-old child; a violent, manipulative, disturbed boy no one could help. My mother was painted as a loving mother who had done everything she could to help, but had it all thrown back in her face by this evil child. Kevin came across as a loving step-father. The reports blamed me for the attacks I received in Woodstock and at school. They predicted a future of hopelessness and despair. As I waded through the paperwork I couldn't help but start to believe the things they were saying about me. Every word they had written felt like a punch to the head and a kick in the stomach. But still I carried on reading and slowly I realised that the majority were twisted tales of other people's versions of events; the one version missing was mine.

I wanted to go to the Civic Centre right then and throw a brick through the window. But, as I cried myself to sleep, I saw that would just prove them all right, show I was a crazy child with a temper. And if that was the case, they wouldn't have to listen to me.

The next day Andrew asked me what was wrong. I explained I had spent the weekend reading my files.

'I'm not sure you should read those alone, Matthew.'

'What do you know about it?' I snapped.

'I used to be a residential worker in a semi-secure therapeutic home. Children would ask for their files and whilst we'd advise against it, the advice would be ignored. And I'd be the one to clean up the blood after they'd read the files and cut themselves.'

I was silent. That was exactly how I'd felt, reading them. I wanted to hurt myself.

'If you need help you don't have to do this alone, Matthew. I'm always here to talk.'

One thing I couldn't understand was how people could write exactly what they thought, without any facts to back it up. My files were full of opinions about me and my character from Social Workers, Team Managers and Psychologists. Not once did I read anything positive, and they all focused on my behaviour, rather than its causes. They'd ignored everything I said about what happened to me at home or at Woodstock, and when they did, briefly, mention my version of events, they quickly dismissed me as a manipulative liar. No wonder Janette wanted to pump me full of medication.

I wrote to Julia to express these feelings and she called me shortly after. She said she wasn't accepting these opinions about me as fact and neither was Maggie. I met with Maggie, who explained what was happening next. The police would investigate the allegations and so would the Social Services Inspectorate. On top of that, the Council was commissioning the National Society for the Prevention of Cruelty to Children to investigate Woodstock and Balgores.

'I have asked where my files from Woodstock are. That would help me put together some of the incidents that took place there and put names to them.' I said to her.

'I have personally looked everywhere for your files at Woodstock in every possible place they could be. We simply can't find them, which is unacceptable.'

'Can't find them? Any of them?'

'No.' She replied. I was shocked. I remembered that shortly after I left the home there was an inspection. There were accusations at the time that the night logs had gone missing and the blame had been laid at the door of the children. We were all asked about it.

'So what happened to them?' I asked.

'We don't know.' I could tell that Maggie knew more than she was telling me.

'What do you think happened to them?' I asked.

She paused for a moment.

'I think they were destroyed. We can't know that for sure until someone is back from sick leave, and that may be a while.'

It gave me even more confidence and respect for her that she didn't lie to me about this. Many years later I found out that one of the senior managers had destroyed the files. I do not know the details but I know that he was disciplined for it – though he didn't lose his job.

195

As I continued with my complaint I prepared the trip to South Africa for Expedition South Africa 2000. I was the project manager. The idea was to take 10 fourteen-year-olds who were doing badly at school – the youth service jargon termed them 'disaffected' – to the Cape Flats. We were working in partnership with a community based organisation called Resource Action Group (RAG). I was ecstatic to be involved. I was the pusher and Andrew the puller; he would have to pull me back at times and it took him a while to realise just how much I needed to be pulled. It sometimes caused tension in our relationship. I'd never been managed before, except at McDonald's. So, when Andrew told me no, I would fight tooth and nail to get what I wanted. Sometimes, in frustration, I swore at him – he would usually stay calm and respond constructively. I wanted him to fight back. But when we sat down to work on ideas together, it went well.

Our group were 'hard knock kids'; not the type that join gangs and brandish knives and guns that you see in the media. Believe it or not, those are the minority. No, these are the kids that you don't read about in the press. Not causing society any problems but not contributing to it either. Most were from poor working-class families. I was surprised how many of them had never ventured into Central London.

As part of the preparations Andrew and I had to go to South Africa for a week to work with the Resource Action Group on preparing for the kids to arrive. That week was one of the most amazing experiences of my life and a turning point. The people that we met, the things we saw and the people we worked with who became good friends were to have a profound influence on my life, building my confidence and self-belief. Soraya Mentor, my South African equivalent on the project, was an amazing woman. She cared deeply about the people at the rough end of life; those living in dire poverty in the shanty towns and the street kids used as drug runners and as pets for the criminals. She came from a similar background and could have easily gone that way were it not for her own determination. She grew up in a small shanty style house with her parents, who were strict Muslims. She didn't see eye-to-eye with them on many things, but remained absolutely loyal. She was educated, having gone to university and studied journalism and was regularly in the press, writing articles, or on the radio and television talking about poverty and youth development. Her parents would refuse to watch her unless she wore the traditional veil, as required by her religion – though she was an uncompromising atheist.

We talked for hours about the problems facing the world, particularly young people, and came up with endless ideas of how we might work together. The memory both Andrew and I still hold closest to our hearts from that trip was when we went to a local restaurant for lunch in a shanty town in the Cape Flats. The 'restaurant' was the back room of a man's small house; with ten of us eating it took no less than five hours for him to cook up a feast of curried goat on his small cooker. As we waited we all talked and laughed. Then someone put some music on and we all just got up and started dancing, without a care in the world – just danced with each other, hand in hand, black, white, male, female, old and young.

When I left South Africa, Soraya handed me a personal poem expressing our close relationship and the aspirations we shared for our lives and what we hoped to accomplish.

After the trip I finally moved into my permanent council flat. I felt I had the energy and the time to see through my complaint to Social Services. Maggie had been kind and patient in waiting for it, but I'd been slow, mainly because the dusty box of files under my bed was like a monster that only comes out at night to haunt you. After the first time, I decided not to keep reading the files – the pain was too much to bear. But to write the complaint I had to relive those memories. I highlighted the bits I thought pertinent and then sat down to my computer and spent several hours just writing. The emotion I felt tore across the pages and expressed exactly how I felt.

At the end of my statements, which included excerpts from files, I would list question such 'Why did this happen?' and 'Was this really necessary?' I asked questions such as 'Could you not have thought through the long-term effects of this and predicted my reaction?'

The complaint I wrote wasn't like a complaint should be; it was a disjointed list of things. In the words of Cathryn Williams, the Deputy Director at the time, in a memo to the Council Solicitors, it wasn't so much a complaint, more of a 'social services ruined my life' statement. That was how I felt at the time. I know that many others, who have gone through far worse experiences than me in care, will wonder what I was so upset about. Compared to their horror stories, my experiences of the care system were pleasant. At the time, though, I didn't know that it could have been worse. To be fair my constant emotional turmoil wasn't simply down to my time in care. It was the result of things that had started long before Social Services had even heard of me. But they had played a part in it; and at any rate they were the only ones I could level any blame to at that time. I could hardly complain to Kevin about how he treated me or Mum for the decisions she made.

Maggie assured me my complaint would be dealt with

quickly. She always listened to me and gave me her honest opinion about things. But, even with my trust in her and despite Julia, the Director, demonstrating an eagerness to treat the issues I raised seriously, I still had a conflict. My conflict was with the Social Services Department I had known all my life; one that was set against me in a battle between what I wanted and what they insisted was right for me. The listening Social Services Department I was now dealing with didn't reflect that. I would have days when I felt my complaint was taking too long or I would convince myself they were not going to listen to me in the end.

One such day I decided to do something I had thought about doing many times; I called a journalist at the *Daily Mirror*, Rosa Prince (now deputy political editor). I spoke to her about my time in care and specifically Woodstock. I explained I had been abused at Woodstock but was cagey about the details. She was keen to print the story and sent a photographer down that day to take some pictures of the old Woodstock building with me standing outside.

It was now an old people's home and they had built on the field where the shed used to be. It was uncomfortable being back there – I felt dirty from the memories. Later that day I got a call from Rosa saying they couldn't print the story. When they had gone to Social Services for a quote they had been told my complaint was under investigation by the police. Rosa said her editor was unhappy about printing it whilst that investigation was continuing. I spoke to Maggie later that day: she was polite, but I could tell was disappointed I had gone to the press.

'You have to trust me, Matthew. We are doing everything we can to deal with this,' she said.

The police and the NSPCC interviewed me again. I was now confident in explaining what had happened during my time at Woodstock – though I struggled to talk about the details of the sexual abuse I experienced. Talking about it left me feeling exposed, as though I were naked, and I clammed up. I don't remember whether I ever told them the full details of what happened with Michael and the others and there is no record of the interview available. I know that they'd interviewed all the other children from the home they could find as part of the investigation, presumably including Michael. I have always wondered what he said and whether he ever admitted what he did to me. I no longer blamed him. He was as let down by the care system as I was. Several years later, I saw him on my way to a town hall meeting; He was fat, wearing shabby clothes, and had his own small child and wife with him. I recognised him immediately and my heart pumped fast. I knew I had to say something.

'Do you remember me?' I said with a smile on my face, hiding my anger inside.

'No, I don't think so.'

'I'm Matthew. We spent some time together at Woodstock. Do you remember me now?' He stood there quietly for a moment.

'Oh yeah,' he said hesitantly, like he had struggled to remember, yet I could tell from his uncomfortable body language that he knew exactly who I was. 'How are you?' he asked.

'I'm very good thanks. Does your wife know what happened at Woodstock?' He shifted uncomfortably and his wife looked up at me. Just then my stop came up.

'Anyway, I have to go. Look after that child of yours.' With that, I got off the bus. I felt no anger towards him. I saw, by the way he reacted to me, that he knew what he had done and regretted it; or maybe that's just how I want to remember it.

After the investigation the Head of Service, Bob Kedward, who Julia had delegated to respond to my complaint, wrote to me. When we met he accepted 'I can quite see that your childhood and adolescent had been painful and difficult and that you would have hoped that the individual members of staff from Social Services who were involved with your care might have been able to 'tune in' to what was happening to you'. But, he couldn't provide an answer to a lot of the questions and he was unable to make any solid statement that they had got it wrong. It was all hedged with 'I can understand that in your opinion this was...' and 'I accept that from your point of view'. I didn't want him to accept that things had gone wrong from my point of view: I wanted him to accept that they had got it wrong. He made several references to the fact that, as my behaviour was so challenging, it had been difficult for the professionals to make the right decisions.

Bob said he couldn't give me what I wanted; yes/no, right/wrong answers to my questions. It was a complex matter and the only evidence we had were the files and memory; and I was the one with the memory. I was naive to think he could say anything different. It was clear, from the files, that my care had been a complete mess; but the details of who was responsible were too murky to state. He didn't get it; I just wanted an apology. The letter, which had come out of the blue after several months of waiting for a response, was factual, cold and wasn't even signed by him. Julia later told me she was furious at Bob's letter and overruled the Council's solicitors and insisted that he apologise. I went in to meet Bob to discuss things further.

'Firstly, Matthew, I would like to apologise for the way in which you received my letter. In retrospect I could have dealt with it in a more considered and personal way and

I am sorry that it left you feeling angry and disappointed. I wanted to make clear to you that I acknowledge absolutely that there is every reason to believe that your account of the care you received at Woodstock and the fact that the placement did not fully meet your needs is accurate and truthful and that there is every reason to believe that for a variety of reasons your interests were not well served while you were placed there. I apologise if you feel my letter did not go over this. I believed that it had been previously acknowledged.'

I started to cry. I felt he was accepting some responsibility for what happened; I was being believed. After spending my childhood trying to convince adults that I was telling the truth about what happened to me it was such a heavy weight to be lifted off my shoulders to have someone say, 'we believe you.'

'I understand from Julia and Maggie that the most important aspect of this whole matter is for you to receive an acknowledgement that your period of being looked after in particular, in the early part of that period and while you were placed at Woodstock, was a distressing and unhelpful period in your life and you've quite naturally retained distressed and angry feelings about that period and about the care you received from a number of staff, managers and social work practitioners in the department. I am willing, formally, on behalf of the department, to offer a full and unreserved apology.'

I sat there, still crying. He asked me whether I wanted to take my complaint further and said I would be perfectly entitled to take it down a legal route if I wanted. Surprising though it may seem I no longer felt I wanted to take things any further. That would have been a disservice to the people that had treated my complaint so seriously; Maggie, Julia, even Bob. I also felt some closure about what had happened.

I knew from the files that I was a deeply troubled boy years before I left home and went into care. I hadn't remembered until I read the files, but when I was seven, I had taken an overdose of my Mum's medication; I don't know whether it was a serious attempt at suicide or a cry for attention, but it wasn't the normal action of a seven-year-old boy. I spent a week in hospital, and I remember not wanting to go home. Taking the complaint against Social Services further wouldn't have given me any more understanding about my troubled childhood. With Bob's apology I now had closure on one part of it. It would take years to understand the rest.

11

Jamaica

There was still a great jumble of emotions in my head. There were two sides to me; the side that could see opportunities, take risks and achieve, and the side that saw a bleak future, hated myself and felt depressed. It was like being on a rollercoaster. At my peak I could achieve anything and through the trough I felt in despair. Whether I was at a peak or a trough there were traits that remained in place; I was often paranoid about what people thought and said about me. I sought reassurance from everyone to feel good about myself, and often felt people didn't like me. I always put this and the peaks and troughs down to my past. Many years later I found out that I had bipolar disorder, what they used to call 'manic depression'.

Most people with bipolar disorder have a peak – hypomania – in which they think they can conquer the world; delusions of grandeur don't seem delusional in such a state. Optimism and adrenaline pump through you. At those times I'd set about grand schemes to change the world and myself. Many bipolar sufferers fail constantly because their dreams are too wild, but something about being bipolar seems to have been a positive influence in my life. If I hadn't had those peaks, I wonder whether I would have made it through the worst times, or if I would have achieved the things I have in life. There is a consoling book, *Great Manic Depressives*, about bipolar sufferers including Winston Churchill and, on a rather less-earth shattering scale, Alistair Campbell and Stephen Fry.

When I started working for Ed Berman I was at one of my peaks. I met him as a sponsor of the South Africa Expedition. At the height of his success with an organisation called Interaction ten years earlier, he'd had over 200 staff. I was excited to be working for a man like that and didn't realise that the charity was, by that point, a shadow of its former self. A few years before I joined, it had gone into voluntary receivership and Ed had lost most of his staff.

The charity was based on the docked HMS *President* boat in the Thames and Ed worked in the dark, historic captain's office surrounded by memories of the glorious past. The only activity that kept the charity from going into bankruptcy was the ship itself. It was now a venue for corporate functions. The ship was often eerie. When you explored the dozens of rooms below the decks you found materials from the past thirty years of charity work. Pictures on the walls showed Royal Visits, and young people flocking around the latest Interaction scheme. There were old sound studios which had once been state of the art, but were now archaic. Ed did rent out space cheaply to start-up companies, but getting a deal out of him was not easy. He'd question every aspect of their plan and spend hours telling them about his glorious past.

One of the projects Ed gave me was to change my life. It stemmed from an unexpected visit from a Jamaican Theatre Group, Jambiz, to the HMS *President* at the end of 2000. The people in Jambiz were smooth, likeable and easy. I spent time with Lenny and the main funder of the project, Sydney Bartley, Director of Education for the Jamaican Government. Lenny and I talked a lot about the problems facing young people and children in Jamaica, particularly Kingston. Young people were not only often deprived of a good education; many had also lost their fathers to gang wars, AIDS and drugs. Lenny had a vision of a project that could train young people to become leaders in their own community and develop their computer skills. I was just as keen and believed I could get a grant from the British Council for the work. Ed was happy to agree as I sold it to him as his vision for establishing an Interaction International Youth Centre in each country. Luckily, the funding opportunity only allowed someone between the age of 18 and 30 to go out and deliver the project so Ed had to stay on the Thames.

The weekend I arrived in Kingston there were political riots in which 26 people were shot dead. Oddly enough, though, it wasn't long before Kingston felt like home; the people I worked with and the friends I made gave this whole city a special place in my heart. At first it was a bit of a culture shock, being the only white guy. The young people I worked with were in their late teens but many of them were forced to grow up fast and take on caring for their siblings or their own children. I heard some terrifying stories of children seeing their fathers shot dead in front of them. State care and protection of orphaned or abused children was fairly non-existent. There were few social workers and little legislation against abuse so many children suffered appallingly and ended up on the street, running drugs and acting as servants to crime barons.

One day, I was taken to one of the poorest shanty towns in Kingston for a street fish party. Despite their poverty out came the giant tin cans to cook fish and speakers from local community projects to play reggae. The streets bubbled with dancing, laughter and an amazing community spirit.

We worked and we had lots of fun; they taught me 'patois' which is Jamaican dialect and laughed hard whenever I tried it out loud. They taught me the meanings behind Bob Marley's music – the lyric 'emancipate yourself from mental slavery' meant a great deal to these young people; I had listened to 'Redemption Song' a hundred times or so but had let the truly powerful meaning behind that word pass me by. These young people believed that in order to make something of themselves they had to learn and question.

Despite their horror stories what was most striking about a group of younger children I got to know was how like any other children they were; they played, they asked and they laughed. They even started to call me Uncle Matthew. I took an assembly one day with the sixty plus young children, meaning to give them a talk on life for children in Britain. Quickly I realised I had lost my audience. I stopped what I was talking about and decided I was going to teach them The Matt Dance. It was a short, easy routine of cheesy eighties dance moves. The Director of the Institute came in to find out what the noise was about to discover all of the children following my dance moves. I'd found the right level on which to engage them; fun! Jamaica gave me confidence.

12

Entering Politics

I still had a burning desire to prove myself. Back in London I started to put my new found confidence into practice. I got involved in children's rights more and stood for election as Trustee and Secretary of the Children's Rights Alliance for England. I won. Susanna Cheal, who had been so helpful in promoting the International Youth Voices project to children in care, introduced me to a Labour MP and former social worker, Hilton Dawson. He was a tireless campaigner for reform of the care system.

At one meeting I heard a presentation from several members of the Care Leavers' Association (CLA) who were campaigning for a Prime Minister's apology and compensation package for adults who had been abused as children in care. One woman on the platform brought me to tears with her harrowing account of abuse in a North Wales institution where she had been continually raped and drugged. A high profile inquiry supported her story, but nobody had ever apologised to her. And apology matters. People suggest victims want financial compensation. But what most victims want first and foremost is to just be believed. Making allegations is not a way of trying to make a fast buck. Many of those who come forward do so with great hesitation as it brings back traumatic memories. There is a complex psychological literature on how victims develop false or fractured selves.

Victims also often then have to 'confess' (though what do they/we have to confess really) to police, wives, husbands and children who knew nothing. They get little support to cope with the emotional and practical fall-out; as a result some see their families torn apart.

Afterwards I approached the Chair of the CLA, Phil Frampton, to see if there was anything I could contribute to their work. Several months later I became their National Secretary and got funding for a full-time post to develop the organisation. I was given that job.

It was a tremendously difficult organisation as each member had personal experiences of care. Some were against fostering because their own experiences of it were appalling. Others were against residential care for similar reasons. This made it near impossible to come up with effective policy decisions. Age was also a factor. Many members were in their 40s, some in their 60s. I will always remember the 62-year-old who found out he had been given the wrong birth date by his carers and only discovered when he was in his 50s that he was actually two years younger than he had believed all his life. He also discovered that he had had two brothers who'd died years earlier; someone had decided he shouldn't have the right to know when he was born and that he had brothers.

Hilton Dawson MP inspired me and made me feel I could make a difference to others. I got involved in a few election campaigns and through that met Cameron Geddes, Deputy Leader of Barking and Dagenham Council. I was ready to step onto a new journey for my life. For someone who'd been through what I'd been through and whose C.V had large dollops of McDonalds and Burger King it might seem arrogant. But youth sometimes is about arrogance. I was going to stand for public office – and I was going to make waves in the Council that had placed me in care ten years earlier.

On my return from Jamaica I had passed the Barking and Dagenham Labour Party's Local Government Committee's candidate selection interview. I could now look for a local ward to accept me as a candidate for the next elections. Shortly after, I was introduced to Goresbrook ward by Liam Smith. He had been a Councillor for the ward, which he won on a Liberal Democrat ticket, but he later switched to Labour. The ward seemed to trust him and, as he vouched for me as a good candidate, I felt confident. Bob Tappin, the Ward Chair had been on the selection panel and also spoke warmly on my behalf. I was lucky to be selected for what was, at the time, one of the safest seats in the borough.

The first thing I wanted to do was talk to people and find out their problems. So, I spent the next months attending meetings. I went to the local residents' association meetings and community forums to find out what people were concerned about. What immediately struck me was how unrepresentative and undemocratic these groups were. The same people attended the same meetings and the discussions would focus on their issues, local parking and traffic being the major topic for discussion. Parking matters, yes, but it didn't seem the most important issue in the 24th most deprived borough in the country which had some of the most underperforming services, like Social Services. Social Services had been in Special Measures. The members of these groups were largely elderly white men who got more time and attention from Councillors and Council Officials (also elderly white men on the whole) than other people, perhaps with more pressing problems.

You could argue, and many did, that these forums are

open to anybody. But, that doesn't address how politicians engage with local people about local issues. It is easier to assume that you are doing enough simply by attending the institutions that exist as a forum for consultation and the fact that, because you live locally, you know the local issues. After several months learning from this I was determined to actually consult local residents in depth.

I was struck by how passionate people were about their area and how much they really cared about changing things. These were hard-working family people, who had lived and worked in the borough all their lives.

I've had those moments where I feel like there is no future, no hope whatsoever. At those times of complete darkness I have felt so hopeless and lonely that I have thought about the various ways I could end it all. Then there are those other moments when I believe that I can do anything. I can change the world. That is what being bi-polar is all about. In the up state, I can be the man that I have dreamed I can be. Election night in May 2002 was one of those moments.

I was the youngest candidate for Council election in the whole country.

An election count is an amazing experience for anybody. But for the candidate it can be electrifying, particularly if you know you have a chance of winning; and I knew I had that chance. I had bought a new suit, making myself as smart as I could. Around me stood my colleagues from the local ward, whom I had got close to over the months of electioneering. Bob Tappin, my ward chair, was a family man and a true grass roots activist. He had tried to teach me to drive over the previous months and had persevered despite my terrible, and sometimes terrifying, driving skills. Bryan Speake was taking pictures that night, a Labour man all his life and passionate about his community. I could tell he was proud of me by the way he just kept beaming. Gordon Brown could take lessons from him in how to smile and look like you mean it. Bryan did mean it.

The best bit was having my Granddad with me, pristine in his suit and tie, smiling all night; I can see the pride in his eyes in the photo he has of me and him standing side by my side, me with my red tie and red election lapel, on his wall. The one thing that saddened me about that night was that I hadn't let him bring his camera. He naturally wanted to capture the moment. But, I was so aware of how I might come across to people that I didn't want to look like I was enjoying this too much, like I thought I was 'it'. So, I begged him not to take his camera, but I could tell he was disappointed when he saw Brian taking pictures. And I did think I was 'it'. It was difficult not to feel puffed up. I'd got some good press in the run up to the election, with *The Barking and Dagenham Post* running a piece on me grandly headlined 'From Edge of Ruin to Role Model'; a rags-to-riches account of my life.

I could feel all the Council officials, drawn in from their day jobs to count the votes, looking at me and I knew they were thinking one of two things. Either 'jumped up so and so, what is he going to do on the Council?' I was told that one senior manager in Social Services, who had known me as a child, had said that 'if that guy is elected I am going to write to the Leader of the Council insisting he is not on any Social Service committee. He would just be prejudiced.' I was so incensed at hearing this, as was the person who told me, that I phoned Julia. She had heard something similar and told me not to worry about it. Council officers didn't decide who sat on committees.

The other view about me was extremely positive; that I

would bring much needed fresh blood and energy. I didn't care. As long as I was elected, it didn't matter what they thought; I had a mandate to get on with the job.

As I waited for the returning officer to announce the results I started to panic about what would happen if I didn't win. There was already some talk from the observers that the Lib Dems had more votes than expected and that it could be closer than we thought. I stood by my two colleagues, also up for election – Alan Thomas was in his seventies, but looked younger. He was a man of pure principle and, although he appeared to be part of the old establishment of the Council, having served for for sixteen years, I could tell that he was independently minded. Jeff Porter was different; I liked him, but I found it hard to trust him completely. He was a tube driver and had only been a Councillor for one term; later he became a hero when he led his passengers to safety in the carnage of 7/7.

Now, standing on stage with Alan and Jeff, I hoped to God that I would be elected so I could do all the things we planned to do. I closed my eyes as the returning officer announced the results for Goresbrook ward.

'Matthew Huggins is duly elected Councillor for Goresbrook Ward.' The hall exploded into cheers all around me. As I went off stage people shook my hand congratulating and hugging me. Then someone clasped my hand.

'Cllr Huggins, congratulations. I'm from the Barking and Dagenham Post. How does it feel to be elected the youngest Councillor in the country?' I was stumped by the question; chuffed, proud, like I had shown everyone what I could do. I had the good sense not to say that though.

'Well, now is where the real work starts and I'm looking forward to getting on with it'. I couldn't have prepared a better answer. But, it was true; as I was led down to have my official Council picture taken, in the early hours of the morning, I was bursting to get on with the job.

After the count I only got a few hours sleep. As soon as the Council opened for business, and two days before I officially took office, I went to meet the Chief Executive, Graham Farrant. Graham was young for a Chief Executive and didn't quite fit with the politics of the Council. He was a moderniser and had risen through the ranks of Local Government very quickly; from health and safety officer to a Housing Director in the space of ten years. He replaced a very 'set in his ways' Chief Executive of the Council, Bill Smith.

Unlike a lot of the other officers, Graham was completely new to the borough when he arrived; most of the officers had been with the authority most of their working life. He also didn't quite fit because he was well spoken and you would describe him as upper middle class. He played tennis rather than football; preferred not to drink, but if he did would choose wine over beer; and he would be as uncomfortable in the Dagenham Working Men's Club as they would be with him. Despite all this, he had somehow managed to transform a largely failing authority into a performing one. And he did it in such a clever way that he brought people along with him and met little resistance from the politicians.

I liked Graham and learnt a lot from him. He agreed to have fortnightly meetings with me, something he didn't do for all Councillors, but he felt I would benefit from the chats; it would have been inappropriate to call it mentoring because as a Councillor you are responsible for holding the Council's management to account and not the other way around, but mentoring is exactly what it was. I would use these meetings to discuss my dealings with officers and

215

give him my opinion on various aspects of the Council. Sometimes he'd be honest about what he thought, often agreeing with my observations of weaknesses in the Council, and at other times, particularly on political matters, he'd keep his cards close to his chest.

Graham was the most politically savvy Council executive I have ever met. Not in the way other officers were; sidling up to Councillors and offering snippets of information to serve their own benefit. He was savvy by the way he would listen to each and every Councillor, treating each with the same level of respect. He would never take what one said and report it to the other. He would cover himself by keeping copious notes of every meeting and phone call he had with people. He said it was something he learnt early on in his career; the need to be able to refer to the facts at a moment's notice. As I sat with Graham for the first time, though, he didn't take notes. He gave me a rundown of how the Council worked and what my functions were as a Councillor. Then he said something I know was out of character in that it gave slightly too much away in terms of his views. He thought I was going to bring much-needed energy to the Council and help to shake things up a bit.

A family of people support the Councillors in their duties; most had served for over twenty years and were totally loyal. The drivers delivered the twice weekly mail package to each of the fifty-one Councillors' home addresses; it would contain the confidential papers for the next week's meetings. Then there was Members' Services, a, team of four secretaries that supported the Councillors in their administration, with one committed completely to the Mayor. Lastly, there were the security team and porters, who staffed the reception areas of Barking Town Hall, Dagenham Civic Centre and other civic buildings. One of my first encounters as a Councillor was with the burly mustached security manager, who had dumped me on the steps of Social Services when I was sixteen and removed me from the Judith Church surgery protest. Getting my security pass from him was a pleasant experience. I could tell, by the way he dealt with me, that he remembered who I was. But he had a personal and professional code, a respect for the office of Councillor even if he didn't like the individual. I was surprised when he greeted me with 'Good Morning, Councillor' when I came through the doors of the civic centre.

My first experience of Council life was the annual ceremonial Council. This packed event in the Town Hall chamber was both a constitutional requirement, to inaugurate the new Mayor, and on this occasion a celebration for those of us of who had just won or held their seats in the recent elections. The borough had a Cabinet system with the Leader of the Council, Charlie Fairbrass, at the top and an Executive Committee of seven other cabinet members elected by the ruling party, Labour, each with their own portfolio. The rest of the Councillors were referred to as 'back bench' members and their job was to scrutinise the executive's work. The Cabinet met weekly and any Councillor could attend to ask questions; the entire fifty-one Councillors met at the monthly assembly meetings.

The Mayor was purely ceremonial and elected by the assembly for one year. In 2002, Pat Twomey, initially an Independent Councillor, who had switched to Labour some years earlier, was Mayor; she was different to many the other Councillors and I immediately liked her because of it; she was independent-minded, a powerful leader amongst the women members of the Council and the first female Mayor for years. Unlike previous Mayors, she had a lot of fun at the Mayoral functions. That night, she let her hair down and dance the night away.

I also let my hair down, perhaps stupidly given the number of older, traditional Councillors there, and I danced my craziest of dances. Later I cringed at the pictures of me dancing provocatively with Pat and some of the other older female members. But on reflection I think it was then that some of the other Councillors saw just how young I was and saw me as vulnerable. One thing that didn't help me was the amount of free drink at these events; all night we would have a free bar at the taxpayers' expense and it wasn't until after I left the Council that I questioned how much money was spent on entertaining members in this way. After every assembly meeting members were invited back to the Mayor's parlour for drinks, for example. (The mayor is given an allowance each year. Some open their parlour readily, others less so. Any money not spent from the allowance stays with the Mayor. At first, I couldn't understand why some mayors were described as 'generous', as I thought it was just from taxpayers' pockets. Of course it *was* from tax-payers' pockets, but it still depended on the individual mayor whether or not they spent their allowance on being generous with drinks, or backing a charity or, in the best tradition of our noble MPs, using the money to fund some pet project).

It wasn't just the pictures of my dancing that made me aware of my youth; it was also the way some officers responded to me. Some were put out at being challenged by a 21-year-old. But I didn't let it hold me back if I felt there was an issue, but I was more assertive than I would have chosen to be had I been older. I was determined to be taken seriously and I didn't want to show any sign of weakness. Several officers that I met, ghosts from the past, were not happy to see me elected. Or so I suspected.

At first, I was keen to attend all Council meetings and went to most of the Cabinet meetings. I sat behind the manager who had written such derogatory things about me as a child. He was now a manager in older people's services and, whilst I was disappointed to see him still working for the authority, I was determined to not let my past determine how I would deal with him. The best bit was that he now had to listen to me, so I didn't feel the need to seek retribution. The other ghost from the past was someone I didn't expect to ever see again. I was going into a meeting in the Town Hall when someone with only one arm came over to talk to me.

'Cllr Huggins, I just wanted to congratulate you on your election'. I suddenly had a weird, anxious feeling and I felt vulnerable; I knew this man from somewhere. He looked at me through squinted confused eyes.

'You don't remember me do you?' I thought hard. I did know him but I couldn't place him. Then I looked at his arm and had a flash back to the manager of Woodstock, who had a hook on his left arm. Now, he was Equalities Manager for the Council.

'Ah yes. I do remember you.' I said pointedly.

'Well, I hope your memories of me are not that bad.' He half stammered as if he already knew the answer.

'I am not here to talk about that. That's in the past. I'm elected now and I have a job to do.' And, with that, I left him and went through to the meeting. It was an experience that marked a turning point in putting Woodstock and my time in care behind me; knowing that I had proved all that they said about me in my files wrong was a good feeling, more cathartic than any therapy could offer.

I got off to a positive start in my duties as a Councillor. I decided to hold a day surgery, as well as an evening surgery, in order to be accessible to my constituents. I held my day surgery at a supported accommodation centre for the elderly, Catherine Godfrey House. The residents and the warden of the house, Anita, got on well with me, but it took them some time to trust that I could actually help them. There were a couple of simple issues that they wanted to resolve, that seemed to take an eternity to fix. When it came to young people we always talked about the need for the Council to do more and to provide services that meet their needs. Yet the elderly, in supported accommodation often missed out because they belonged to the 'mustn't grumble' generation.

One surgery, Anita's daughter, Sarah, came to see me. She had recently had a baby and had been surprised at how little support there was for mothers, particularly young, single mothers. It was something that immediately touched me, because of my own mother's history. But, it also seemed absurd when I spoke to Julia Ross, Director Social Services, that we invested so little in such services, yet expenditure on dealing with the problems of poor parenting was so high. I wasn't able to give Sarah the answer she wanted; that the Council would invest in support services like this. But, I was able to say that if she wanted to set up something like a support group to new mothers, we would do everything to help. I saw something in her – a desire to achieve, regardless of her problems as a young, single mother – that made me want to do all I could to encourage her. She was up to the challenge and set up the support group. Within a few months we had secured some small start up money and convinced the local community hall to give its space free of charge for two meetings a week. I was so proud of her the day she officially opened the centre. With Julia Ross by my side we made opening speeches and congratulated her on her work. Surrounding us were a dozen or so mothers with their new babies playing together and I was struck by how much could be achieved with a little support.

So much talk in Councils, particularly poor working class boroughs like Barking and Dagenham, is about helping communities by 'doing to' rather than by engaging local people, inspiring and supporting them to make their own changes. For me, Sarah and the mother and baby group was a significant change in my own thinking about the role of the Council and a philosophy I hold today that I passionately believe is the difference between 'helping' communities and 'transforming' communities.

Another issue that still remained close to my heart was transforming social services, particularly services to children in care. Bryan Osborn, Lead Member for Social Services, was one of the most intelligent Councillors and, like me, a moderniser. He enlisted my support by creating an unofficial role of private secretary, similar to the unpaid role for backbench MP's in the House of Commons to support Ministers. It involved helping to organise Bryan's work, setting up meetings and advising on the political issues. I sat in on many of his weekly briefings with the Director and senior officers and helped to draft letters to the local press and prepare him for public meetings. I was keen to support fostering and I took him to several fostering support groups to hear foster carers' concerns. Many of the foster carers, some of whom had cared for the borough's children for over twenty years, had never met a Councillor before. I liked working with Bryan; he was always willing to discuss ideas and be challenged. He was also aware that many Councillors, who had spent years running the Council's services a certain way, didn't accept the fact that these were failing services under their rule. When the Minister for

Children and Young People, Paul Boateng MP, gave a speech to the Council about the need for improvement, he was interrupted by George Brooker, who had led the Council for years with an iron fist.

'Listen here, boy,' he addressed the most senior black politician in the country, 'we don't need you to come here telling us how to run our authority'. Boateng stood there for a minute and then responded firmly but calmly.

'I am the Minister of State and not only will I tell you how to run your authority, if you don't listen I will send people in to do it for you.'

So changing the culture wasn't an easy task for Bryan or the officers. Just as I was getting to grips with my new responsibilities, I faced a much more challenging situation; one that would consume the rest of my time in political office and make it politically impossible for me to support Bryan or do much else on the Council.

At the time I was being investigated by Bob Little (who worked for Jon Cruddas MP as his constituency caseworker as well as being the Council Leader's P.A). I knew nothing about what was happening. For some months I was completely in the dark, my suspicions raised only when things started to go wrong with the Care Leavers' Association (CLA) and I began to hear rumours about myself that were untrue. One problem was that I sent out a free post return questionnaire to all my constituents which received almost a 50% response rate. Charlie Fairbrass tried to stop my mailing for no other reason that it hadn't been done before. But I argued with the Chief Executive that if I was going to communicate with my constituents and deal with their problems, I needed to try new ways of finding out what those problems were. Graham was able to explain to Charlie that I was entitled to do this and it resulted in a phenomenal amount of casework. It turned out that rate-payers did have many problems they wanted sorted and just hadn't been contacted this way before. Unfortunately, not being a full-time Councillor and with only three of us covering the ward, it was impossible to deal with every response.

It wasn't just the Leader, Charlie Fairbrass, I was upsetting with my new ways of generating case work. One member of the Council's Top Management Team commented in a meeting that he was having to spend seventy percent of his time dealing with case work from me. Graham reminded him that I was just doing my job and if the case work was there then, there were clearly problems to address. This was the first time I started to hear rumours that Council officers were getting unhappy with my creating an additional workload for them. I hadn't realised that a lot of officers had been with the Council a long time, as had the Councillors, and, as such, had close working relationships with Councillors that sometimes crossed boundaries; some Councillors would go drinking with senior officers regularly. It was then that I began to think that I would have to start watching my back.

I also upset people by not following the unwritten rules of the Council politics: 'Buggins turn' rules. I was a new member and the youngest. Children should be seen and not heard. I was expected to sit and learn from my elders. I was advised at the Mayor's dinner by John Davis, Chair of the Assembly, to keep my nose down, learn from the wise old men and keep quiet in meetings. For the first few years at least. He kept referring to me as 'son' and said that if I stuck with him, I'd learn a lot. 'In twenty years time you could be deputy leader of this Council,' he said, grandly. As an ambitious 21-year-old who wanted to change the world, I had bigger plans.

I made a point of speaking at the first Council meeting and then I did something which I realise in retrospect was not going to endear me. At the first group meeting I stood for Group Secretary. It wasn't insane ambition or the result of being in an up mood. I'd been encouraged to stand by several people, whom I later realised wanted to prevent others from getting the job. The Group Secretary was powerful, involved in all the group decisions the ruling party made, controlling the agenda and supporting the Chair at the Council meetings by calling on new speakers. Less significant, other than as a sign of status, was that the Group Secretary sat near the Chair at the front of the assembly.

There were four other candidates and the vote was split. I won because the other candidates didn't have enough support. As my second victory in a few months was announced I looked around and there were some nods of approval from people. My ward colleagues and supporters and those members considered the modernisers, even cheered. But, across the chamber sat John Davis staring and, I could swear, gritting his teeth through a smirk that said 'you have really started something you didn't want to'. At 21, and with no political experience, I didn't realise how outrageous my success was in a very traditional Council.

The second naive position I took was on the Euro debate in July of that year at a Dagenham Labour Party meeting. There was a lot of talk in the press about whether or not Britain should join the Euro. I felt passionate about Britain joining. I spoke to some colleagues, including the Leader and other senior members, who agreed with my position. I spoke to the local press and announced I was setting up a support group for Euro fans. I was asked if there were colleagues who supported my campaign. Stupidly, I gave the names of those who had said they were for such a campaign, but at that point they were unaware that their support would soon become public knowledge. I also didn't know at the time that the recently-elected Dagenham MP, Jon Cruddas, who was later to stand for national Deputy Leader of the Labour Party and is now, of course, a 'major player' was strongly against joining the Euro. The article got a lot of anger from those I'd named. Jon Cruddas had to organise a local debate on the issue. I went and got my chance to speak; getting into a to and fro with Jon, me saying he was wrong, perhaps undiplomatically, given my audience. Eventually John Davis stepped in to say I could no longer speak.

After that debate, however, Bryan Osborne went with his wife to a local British Legion club with other party members, including Bob Little, the Dagenham Labour Party Secretary and assistant to Charlie Fairbrass, who was also on Jon Cruddas's staff and was later to become a local Councillor. During the evening Bob received a call, Bryan doesn't know from whom, but he over-heard the words '... he doesn't realise we have friends up-town ... make no bones about it, he's going to get a good kicking'. The kicking I would get was, of course, political not physical.

Bryan remembers another discussion prior to a meeting. It was alleged that I had used the members' secretary to distribute political meeting minutes to group members. Someone said 'it's no good, he's got to go.' It was then, in September, four months after I had been elected, that Bryan was so worried that he approached Charlie and Jon Cruddas. He expressed concern that Bob Little, who was also his friend at the time, had started to attack me very personally. Despite his intervention no action appeared to have been taken by either the Leader or the Dagenham MP.

Over the following months a number of strange things happened which led me to believe there was some kind of investigation going on into my actions. First, one of the Members' Secretaries took me to one side and said she had something difficult to tell me.

'I just thought you should know that someone has being going around and saying that you have lied about growing up in care. He says he met your parents coming out of your flat.'

'My parents?' for a minute I was confused. It seemed unbelievable somebody could make this up.

'Who is it?' I asked.

'Councillor Sid Kallar'. I was even more confused now. I thought I got on well with Sid. I always took him as a nice, charming man, full of integrity. . He had always been supportive and friendly to me. How could he make up something like this?

'Where did he say he saw my parents?'

'He was leafleting your block of flats a few weeks ago and bumped into them coming out of your flat' Now it all made sense. My Grandparents had gone to my flat to drop off some washing and it must have been them he saw. But they would never have been mistaken as my parents, in their seventies, and certainly wouldn't have introduced themselves as such. This was not an innocent mistake. He had chosen to interpret it this way and for several weeks didn't raise the issue with me. I saw him later in the corridor of Dagenham Civic Centre and asked him, as calmly as I could, why he had said that. He said he had got confused, but, if he had got it wrong, he was sorry. I had to accept that. I wasn't prepared to argue with him in the middle of the civic centre.

My relationship with the Care Leavers' Association started

to go awry. The new National Secretary, who had only got involved six months earlier, was not returning my calls, which was frustrating as I was now working full-time as the National Coordinator. When I did finally get through to him, he said I had some questions to answer. They wanted the cheque book back from me and the account details for the CLA. I went to see one of the executive committee in Leeds. There was an ongoing issue about £500 worth of outstanding receipts for purchases from the account that included sending postal orders to Phil Frampton, the Chair for his expenses, as well as travel tickets for Phil and me for various meetings. I no longer had these receipts. My only defense is that I had never been great at keeping receipts and seem to lose paperwork too often. There was certainly no dishonesty on my part and, until that time, nobody had raised any questions about it. There was £25,000 sitting in the CLA bank account which I could have removed at any time. I didn't touch one penny.

At one point, I got so frustrated with the lack of communication and what seemed to be going on behind my back that I called Mary, the national secretary of the CLA. I demanded to know who she was talking to that was souring my relationship with her and the CLA. She said she had spoken to Ed Berman and Bob Little. It was then that I knew there was an investigation going on behind my back.

I realised that my work with the CLA was over and I needed to resign and focus on sorting out this problem. What then happened in Leeds did not help. I had gone to meet a CLA Executive to hand over some paperwork, but at Leeds Station. I found my laptop had been stolen. I immediately reported it to the police and phoned the Council's emergency phone line to record it as stolen. It was later claimed that I sold the laptop to Cash Converters to avoid getting caught out on 'financial inaccuracies' in the CLA accounts. I resigned from the CLA, but was told later that they considered dismissing me because of what they had heard about my problems in London. At no time, though, did they come to me and ask if any of the accusations had any merit in them.

Two other issues came up that didn't help my relationship with Dagenham Labour Party. The first was an unpaid invoice for a celebration and fundraising event I had organised for Young Labour in London on the HMS President. Ed Berman had agreed to give me a discounted rate so the venue wouldn't cost me more than five hundred pounds. Unfortunately, not enough paying people came which left me with a bill at the end. InterAction sent the bill not to me but Dagenham Labour Party and added another £700. The letter read like I had booked the event in the name of Dagenham Labour Party. As soon as I heard about this, I sent Bob Little an e-mail explaining this was a personal issue and nothing to do with the party. I apologised for what had happened though I was not responsible for Ed sending the bill to the Dagenham Labour Party. Although I later paid off the amount personally, at the previously agreed rate of £500, it remained an issue and Bob Little pursued it.

I became aware of the second issue when Charlie Fairbrass, the Leader, rang me early one morning. He explained that he, and other leading members, as well as the press, had received an anonymous letter detailing my rent arrears, which I did have at the time. Charlie had already spoken to me a week earlier about this as it turned out he received the rent and Council tax accounts of all Councillors. I was angry that my private business had been leaked. I wasn't happy about these arrears but I was in a bit of financial trouble at the time and didn't have anybody to go to for help; a problem many care-leavers face. After ascertaining that the press were running with the story I decided to be upfront and honest and I sent a letter, approved by Charlie, to everyone explaining my situation and what I intended to do about it. Surprisingly, I had quite a lot of support from colleagues with members of all political parties contacting me to tell me how disgusted they were that my private information had been leaked to the press. And leaks have their sources. Ask any MP whose expenses have been all over the papers.

I still formally knew nothing about and had no details about what I was being investigated for. I got on with life as best I could while constantly hearing the 'drip drip' of rumours and accusations, never knowing exactly where they were coming from. My private life began to improve at least. I got a consultancy job working for Hugh Pelham, who was now Chief Executive of East London Foster Carers. My first task was to look at the educational attainment of their children and how it could be raised.Hugh and I raised over £250,000 through grants for a leaving care worker, education worker and other projects.

I also moved in with a friend, Alex Hilton, a Redbridge Councillor at the time. We had become great friends, spending a lot of time in the House of Commons, where he worked for an MP. Alex is now editor of the official website www.labourhome. I liked Alex's pure confidence; the way he could approach anyone and be their friend within minutes. He was intelligent and we could discuss the ins and outs of politics from a perspective I couldn't get from most colleagues in Barking and Dagenham. At times, though I felt a lesser man than Alex and it did get me down; I couldn't understand why I couldn't be as confident as him. It could cause tension in our relationship, when I would let my own jealousies about what he had, get on top of me and show. But, I was glad to be out of the flats, out of Dagenham and living with Alex in Gants Hill.

A few weeks after moving in, I had an anonymous letter arrive for me at Lesley Hilton's house. Lesley is Alex's mother and at the time was also a Labour Councillor in Redbridge. She just passed it on to Alex to give it to me. He watched me open it. My heart beat fast when I read who it was addressed to; Matthew James. I hadn't used that name since I was sixteen and the type of people who knew me as 'James' were people I wouldn't want to hear from. Inside there was a piece of paper with typing.

'Hello Matt, we haven't seen you for some time. Just to keep track of you. I bet Lesley doesn't know your past. Don't forget 'you must not live a lie'. See you soon. Old Friends.'

I was freaked and scared. I had no idea who this could have come from. We checked the postmark. It was sent from Romford on 7th November. Letters from Dagenham have a Romford post-mark. There were no other significant markings. No handwriting and a normal stamp. Alex immediately wrote a statement that he had witnessed the opening of the letter, and we took it to the police. Of course, they couldn't do anything, but they said they would keep a note of it in case anything happened in future. I wasn't sure it had a direct link to what was happening to me behind the scenes at the Council, but had a strange feeling it did.

The rumours circulating about me didn't stop. I spoke to the Chief Whip, Len Collins, who I got on well with and respected. He said he knew what I was talking about and wasn't happy about it either and would look in to it straight away. Cameron and Bryan also put their concerns in writing to Len. Cameron went as far to say that if there were charges that warranted investigation then they should be put forward so they can be answered, or, all rumours should stop. That night I went to Bob Little. There were some of my ward members around.

'Bob, what is going on? I'm hearing all kinds of things and I have no idea what is happening. Who have you been talking to about me?'

'I can't tell you that Matt. All will become clear soon.' Now I was angry. He was admitting that something was happening, but wouldn't tell me what it was. This was against the rules of fair play and justice let alone the rules of the party. I raised my voice.

'Bob, you have to tell me. I am hearing all kinds of things and I deserve to know. I even had an anonymous letter to my home, actually not even my home, but the home of my friend's mother.'

'I know nothing about that.'

'Well, tell me who you have spoken to?' Now there were a few members watching.

'Okay, I'll tell you who I have spoken to. Ed Berman, Phil, Caldecott and Steve Power'. Caldecott? That didn't make sense. Why would Caldecott talk to him?

'What is this all about?' I was now on the verge of tears and feeling vulnerable in front of everyone; Bob kept calm, like this was nothing.

'I'm not talking about this any more,' he said, 'we have a meeting to go to. All I can say is all will become clear soon.'

A few days later I received a letter from him and John Davis asking me to attend a meeting to discuss some matters of concern they had. I did not have any details of the meeting and didn't know whether I should attend. I had conflicting advice. Cameron said I should attend simply to clear the air as they had no powers to take disciplinary action against me. On the day of the hearing though Cameron had been told that a letter of resignation from the Council had been drafted and that I wouldn't be allowed to leave the meeting until I'd signed it. He phoned and told me not to sign anything, no matter how difficult the meeting became, as it would immediately be handed to the Chief Executive and I wouldn't be able to do anything about it afterwards. After discussing it with my ward colleagues I decided I shouldn't attend the meeting at all.

A few days later I received a call from Jeff Porter who had been at a meeting of the Party's Local Government' Committees Executive. I had not been aware of the meeting and people attending were not aware of the agenda in advance. Bob Little presented a full dossier of evidence against me, which he had spent the last three months compiling. Jeff couldn't tell me much, just that it had been a long meeting with many damning accusations. The main claim was that I was mentally ill and had manipulated everyone into believing in me. The truth was that I was dangerous to the party, and to myself, and Bob Little recommended that the LGC members vote for my resignation and for me to seek medical help or give permission for the Chief Whip to suspend me. Everyone voted in favour of this, despite not hearing from me, except my two ward colleagues present at the meeting, who abstained. They didn't know what to believe. In the face of Bob's many serious accusations, I admire the fact that they didn't follow everyone else. I was amazed that such accusations could be presented in such a way; no advance warning to the accused and no opportunity to defend against them. No papers had left the meeting, so I still had nothing to go from except for the snippets of information Jeff was able to remember.

I spent that weekend talking with Alex, Cameron and Hilton Dawson about how I should approach the meeting I had been summoned to with the Chief Whip, Len Collins, the following Monday. Len said it would be a quiet meeting and I had nothing to worry about if I hadn't done anything wrong. When I asked if I should bring a witness, he said he wouldn't stop me, but that was not really how he liked to do things.

Despite pleas from my friends and ward colleagues, I decided that playing along with Len's wishes might mean he would deal with me fairly. That weekend was a long and miserable one; full of worry. The only thing was that I still didn't know exactly what I had to worry about.

That Monday morning I went into Len and we agreed to tape record the meeting. He presented a dossier compiled for him by Bob Little. Len gave me a chance to read through the dossier and as I did, I became more and more angry. The transcript of the tape is on the website as well as the dossier compiled against me.

There were quotes from people in the dossier that had come from people that I considered friends; there were some from Caldecott and a lot of lies.

'I can't believe some of the people have said this'. I said.

'You're being given the chance now. What you're doing is answering something that according to you...'

I interrupted him. His voice sounded so accusatory and I started to wish I had brought a witness.

'I will answer it all in writing and I will confirm with these people. I can't believe some of them would have said these things. I need a photocopy before I go.'

'You won't get a photocopy of all that before you go. You will stick to proceedings.' I was getting more agitated and trying to keep my cool, but doing a bad job of it. I was already upset by what I had read and Len's tone with me was making it worse.

'I am entitled to it. I am entitled to it.'

'After this Matt...'

'I am entitled to it and there are various accusations I have to answer in writing.'

'After this I will then report as regards our meeting to the Labour Group; you will then be given the opportunity to state your case properly'

'I have no copies of any paperwork. This is wrong. I am asking you officially as to whether I can have copies of this.' There was silence now. I started to read the addendums to the dossier which included emails from Ed Berman, who said he was a personal friend of Nelson Mandela and Tony Blair.

'Do you realise this man is a liar and has never ever met or discussed anything with Nelson Mandela or Tony Blair. I can prove this.'

'That would be your right to do so.' The way he was looking at me was like he thought I was guilty and had me caught red-handed. I read another addendum which had lots of crosses and 'no' written against various achievements I had listed. One was that I had written the application to the Tudor Trust for the Care Leavers' Association. Bob had just written 'no' next to it. Another one was about the work I had done in Jamaica and South Africa which had 'not true' scribbled across it. I was amazed he could just randomly put lines through things, which had seemed to me, he knew nothing about?

'These references to my CV are all true. I wrote the Tudor

Trust Application, which Hilton Dawson as an MP can confirm.'

'Who is this MP you keep referring to Matt?'

'It's all right he's going to attend any future meetings with me.'

'You see, there you go, you talk about trying to…'

'Len, you have obviously made your judgement. You have obviously made your judgement about me'

'I am not but you are helping me to.' If he was basing his judgement on me from my attitude in this meeting it wasn't going well. I wasn't prepared for any material of the sort I had read.

'I am reading all these lies and you expect me to respond in a rational and logical way?'

'No, no, you're the one that picking that up. You're the one that's turning round halfway through reading then making comments. When I go to give a civil answer you want to "no, no I'll make no comment"' I realised I wasn't going to convince him of anything and I needed to calm down.

'All I am saying, Len' I paused for a moment. I thought this wasn't worth arguing about, I was losing. I sat back in my chair defeated and started crying. 'I'm sorry.'

'If you sit here and talk properly I will try and discuss it properly, but don't keep on reading little bits and then, when I go to say something, you carry on.'

'I am saying' I tried to get my words out without shouting them, 'I am saying that Hilton Dawson has known me for three years. He was part of setting up the CLA and that I was the one that wrote the Tudor Trust Application, which Bob Little says is a lie.'

There was also list of car journeys I had taken as a Councillor, as was my right for Council business. What I was looking at didn't make sense.

'What are these to suggest?'

'Well, just have a look, it's there. It's quite open and honest if they've written it down as to the journeys that you have taken in Council vehicles. They're the dates, but at the side of it you will see the question mark as to whether or not it was a Council duty.' I still didn't get what they were accusing me of.

'I have not misused any Council vehicles.' He then referred to a number of journeys from my house to the civic centre – a journey of 250 yards. He had a smile on his face now like he had caught me out again. I couldn't believe that was right.

'I've not.' I looked at it again. 'Hang on a minute, there's no way I would have got a car from the Civic Centre to my house. Where does it say that?' He pointed at the paper.

'Home to civic centre. There.'

I started to laugh. 'It hasn't. It's got Barking Town Hall to home. There's nothing here about the civic centre to home.' He didn't say anything as I read on. (For readers not familiar with the geography of the borough the trips I took were a 20 minute drive).

'With all due respect Len I need a copy of this.'

'With all due respect,' he began. I started shaking my head at his words. 'No, no, don't start sitting there shaking your head,' he added.

'I should have had a witness. I knew I should have had a witness. I didn't because I trusted you.'

'You don't need it. It doesn't matter, it's on there, the tape. What I am saying to you, Matt, is this, as far as I am concerned all the evidence that I have got is there. What will happen is that, yes, quite rightly, you will have the right to respond. You will be given the opportunity at a proper meeting to discuss it and say 'yea or nay' that is

236

right or it isn't, but you will have to prove it and put proof there in the same token as our people will and that is the only way, because it can go on and on and on. I mean you are denying everything that's in there!'

'I am not denying everything, There are things in there that could be half-truths, or whatever.'

'There are a lot of grey areas in there.' He conceded.

'Look, I know how it looks'. I was trying to reason with him to see that this looks bad at face value, but that he had only heard one side of the story so far.

'And so that's all I have got to go on. Now it is up to you to prove otherwise'. I didn't realise it at the moment, but what he was saying in effect was that I needed to prove myself innocent, having already been proved to be guilty.

'Which is exactly why I need a copy of what's here.' I argued again.

'You will get a copy when I have finished talking to you because I believe that is only right and proper. What I said to you earlier on when I said no is because halfway through a meeting when we were supposed to be talking and discussing something very, very serious.'

'I'm sorry Len, I am trying not to let my emotions guide my actions, but reading this, you can understand I am very angry.'

'And so would I be if it was me, because I would hope that I would not be put in that position as an individual. But you have obviously let yourself be put in a certain position. Now that's the problem and it builds up, one thing after another. Now me, as a person sitting here trying to do a job and I am presented with all that, what else can you expect, Matt? What would you turn round and say? And so what I am saying to you, with the tape on, I have said to you time and time again I think you are a very intelligent person. I think you have got a damn good future but you have got to tidy yourself up. I think you are dwelling too much on this care leavers stuff, I really do. There are other people that have been in the same position as you.'

'I am not. I am trying to promote the positive image of a care leaver and what's turned around in this is the fact that I am a horrible, evil, disturbed person.'

'Everything there is pointing to it. Everything there'. He retorted. I was crying uncontrollably now. I couldn't believe he could think that about anyone let alone me.

'Most of what people are saying there is untrue and I shall prove that.'

'That's fine. That's what we're supposed to do in life. That's the idea of it. That's the very reason I wanted to talk to you as an individual and not with all this witness business, I don't want all that'

'Unfortunately it's going to end up like that because they'll turn it into that. Instead of being dealt with in a completely different way.' I argued.

'You see, you're pre-judging immediately again.'

I couldn't believe I was the one accused of pre-judging.

'There are one or two alternatives, Matt. Either, you could resign from the whip and you can put it down to pressure of work or whatever, I don't mind. That's a way of doing it so as no dirty linen is aired in public or I would turn round and say there would be indefinite suspension. You would then have the right to appeal and stand up and say that's not right or whatever, but in doing so other things could come to light as well that may not be to your advantage. That could be a danger. That is entirely up to you. On the indefinite suspension, hopefully you can clear it. Hopefully, after a period of time, you can come back and make your mark in society because I think you have a got a damn good chance in life if you would look at it in a proper manner and you're not looking at it in a proper...'

Angrily, I interrupted him.

'Some of these people are lying and I don't care what you say, that is not the proper way to behave, Len. You putting it all on to me is not right.'

'I am not putting it all on to you, at all. I am saying to you that there is a lot at stake for people, for the authority. You should never allow yourself, as a responsible person, especially standing as a Councillor, to get yourself into the difficulty that you have done and if you carry on like that you are going to get into worse difficulty.'

'I am not carrying on like that. I don't.'

'I am trying to help you. Other people are trying to help you'. A scary thought dawned on me at that moment – that Len sincerely believed he was trying to help me by what he was doing. He couldn't realise that asking for my resignation or suspending me based on something I hadn't had the chance to refute was just wrong, no matter the severity of the charges.

'I will not resign for the reason that these are half-truths and lies and I have not had the opportunity to answer these. You cannot ask me to resign before I have had the opportunity to answer these'. He then just repeated his offers.

'I told you when we first started, Matt, this is the worst job I have ever had to do in all my life, in seventy three years.'

'There are people in this dossier who were my friends. Soraya Mentoor, we worked together for three years, I mean we were the best of friends. I spoke to her last week. There are people in here that can back me up.'

'Fine, if you have got people who can back you up that's exactly what I am trying to tell you. If you can't then that's it. But, in the meantime, I can't leave it untidy. I cannot leave it untidy because the talk goes on and on. It will go from bad to worse, for whatever reason and I can tell you this, that these people who have opened their mouths, I will be having a word with them also, make no mistake about it. But, you see, I can't be responsible for other people. If they go around tittle-tattling, they are supposed to be mature, sensible people and it seems to me that they need a lesson also and I think you are getting a lesson and that is a hard one in life and you are one of the last people I would want that to happen to. I once said to you that I would be proud to have you as a son and if you prove yourself here, Matt, then I would still be proud. But, in the meantime, I have a job to do. I cannot leave it like it is. Can I? I will not, I love the party, I love the people too much for that.'

I was angry at his sense of justice. How could he think this was justice? I had just been presented with a dossier of accusations, two-thirds of which were downright lies. He hadn't given me any time to respond or to obtain evidence to counter the claims. How was that in the interest of the party he loved?

'What happens now? You know *The Barking and Dagenham Post* already have this information? Do you know that?'

'I don't know'. He said.

'They do' I didn't know for sure then. I just knew how this game was being played now. I wouldn't be giving the press the information, but I was sure that the way this had been set up I was bound to get a call later to ask for a comment on my suspension.

'I never get involved with the papers, Matt. I don't think there's a need to, I really don't. When the papers have ever got on to me I have turned round and said, 'well they don't run the authority'. I have always said that and I mean that. The Editor of the local paper will tell you that and that is my way. I am hoping sincerely that one day, because I am not going to stand for much longer, at my age, now 73, I was hoping people like you could take over. It has been my thing to get young people involved, the party knows that. It was my thing and I would love to have you taking my place representing Eastbrook Ward when I retire. I would love that, once it is clear; but you have got to do it yourself. You have got to clear it. You have got to get out of this mess'. I couldn't believe he was asking me to get out of a mess that I hadn't created.

'I will do. So I am no longer a Labour Councillor?'

'That's right. I will send it to you in writing.'

'I am still a Councillor. You realise that?'

'You are suspended indefinitely'

'But, I am still a Councillor?'

'You are still a Councillor yes. But it takes effect as from now, Matt. I will still have to do it the correct way and report back to the Labour group. As far as it goes now, I have done all that I felt it is right to do, Matt, in my job.'

We turned the tape off and, as I waited for the papers to be copied with Len in front of me, I started to cry. I felt humiliated, bullied and defeated. I had been stitched up and I regretted not having Alan or anyone else there to help me fight back.

'All I have done, Len, since I left care with nothing, is build a life for myself. I'm not saying I haven't made mistakes, I have, but nothing like on the scale of what I'm accused of here. I have just tried to present a positive image of care leavers by going there and talking about it. I have never spoken about my experience of children's homes here. If you knew what happened in those homes.'

'I do know Matt, I used to go and visit the children at times. I cared deeply about the children.'

'You don't know what happened. They were horrible places. But despite all that I got through it and this is how I am treated'. At that moment I started to think about giving up. Just as the thought entered my head it was interrupted by the person bringing back the copies of the paperwork. I left Len and went straight to the emergency ward meeting we had called at Bob Tappin's house, where Alan, Jeff and other ward members were waiting to hear the news. On my way, as I had predicted, I got a phone call from a journalist at the *Barking and Dagenham Recorder*.

'Councillor Huggins, have you just been in a meeting with the Chief Whip?'

'How do you know about that?'

'That doesn't matter. We have been told you have been suspended. Do you have any comment to make?'

'No comment'. I put down the phone. Despite my anger I knew that if I started talking to the papers now I would lose the high ground when I proved the dossier to be what it was; a long list of lies. The story was already written anyway. The front page that week read 'Councillor Booted Out.'

The website for the book has full transcript of this encounter and of the dossier.

After spending a few hours reading through the dossier line and by line, and hearing my responses as to what was not true and what I could prove to be not true in time, the anger from my Ward members spilled out. Alan was angry he hadn't insisted on coming to the meeting with me. Others were angry that something like this could happen; a process by which someone was first proved guilty and then had to prove themselves innocent after the punishment had been delivered. What got them most was the section that referred to my mental health and calling for me to seek treatment.

'This is like the bloody Nazis in wartime Germany.' Jeff said. I looked around the room at them all. I wasn't sure what I was going to do next. I was supposed to do what? Prove I was sane? I have subsequently learned that in Communist Russia people could go to their GP to get a certificate of sanity. Or was I supposed to prove I was innocent? Or was I meant to be put in the quiet room as I'd been in care and beg forgiveness from the adults who knew best?

'I'm sorry about all this.' I said with my head down.

'You have nothing to be sorry about, Matt. This is them. As you have said, most of this isn't true. I can't see what the problem is with the bits that you have admitted.' Alan had always been a huge support to me.

'If you give me time I will prove everything in here is wrong. You have to decide what the ward wants to do.'

'We can only do the right thing and that is to support you. As Alan says, as far as we can tell, you haven't done anything wrong. This is like a witch hunt'. Bob Tappin told me what I needed to hear and, after the morning I had had with Len, I started to feel like I wasn't going crazy.

After the ward meeting I went to meet Cameron and Bryan to show them the dossier. Both had always supported me, but when I showed them the dossier Cameron started to take a different tone. He was questioning me on each charge and after answering he would question me further. In the end I lost it.

'Cameron, are you saying you believe this? I thought we were friends.'

'We are friends, Matt, but there are serious charges in this dossier. We need to be able to answer them and you need to prove to me that they aren't true for me to help you.' I felt I didn't deserve this. Now, even my friends were questioning me. I was determined to do as much as possible to prove my case.

The first section in the dossier I wanted to deal with concerned Caldecott and the 'statements' made by the Chief Executive, Derek Marshall. I knew Derek well by now and respected him. I didn't believe he would make such statements and doubted whether he actually met Bob Little. However, when I spoke to him on the phone, I was shocked to hear he had indeed met Bob little; he said he thought it was the right thing to do given the circumstances Bob presented. I met Derek in a cafe at Victoria Station and took him through the dossier.

'I can tell you now this is not true and I cannot explain how angry I am, Matthew.'

'So what actually happened?' He said his office had been called by someone claiming to be from Jon Cruddas's office to answer an enquiry as to whether or not I was a Trustee of Caldecott. Although I was considering this, nothing was certain and I had never told anybody I was. Derek had told them he needed the request in writing and a letter was faxed through, with Jon Cruddas' signature on it, asking the same question. Derek responded directly to the House of Commons Office, confirming I wasn't a Trustee. He was surprised to receive a call from Bob Little. He asked to discuss the matter further and hinted that there was, at best, some confusion about me 'claiming' to be a Caldecott Trustee. On the basis of clarifying this issue, Derek agreed to meet him, something he now said he regretted.

When they met, Bob Little told Derek that I was being investigated by Barking and Dagenham Labour Party regarding irregularities in my submission of paperwork. He also tried to talk through a wider range of difficulties, but Derek responded that it was not their place to interfere, pass judgement, or do other than support anyone who had been in their care.. He emphasised to me that, at no point, did he intimate to Bob any opinion regarding my stay at Caldecott,. He also told me he had not made any comment on the 'facts' that Bob presented. Derek told me he had the impression that Bob was driven by pastoral concern for 'a young man in trouble facing up to new responsibilities as a Councillor'. Derek said it was nice to see politics have a human face. We laughed at this, now knowing what we knew.

Derek did say to Bob that if I sought their assistance or support they would be pleased to be of service to me, but, that I was a free agent. Derek said the comment in the dossier, where Bob implied clearly that I needed help with my mental health and that Caldecott concurred, was completely made up and a slur both against me and Caldecott. He did not, and would not, enter into any discussion regarding my so-called sanity, but was prepared to clarify, which he later did in writing, that he had no suspicion, nor knowledge that I now, or had ever, required psychiatric or counseling help, as the dossier claimed.

Next came something of a surprise, after I thought nothing else could surprise me. In his meeting with Derek, Bob claimed that the Labour Party was seriously concerned with this matter, not least because of my 'apparent close "relationship" with Stephen Twigg MP'. Bob made clear that this relationship would be considered an 'inappropriate relationship'. Derek was smiling as he told me this. It took me several minutes to work out why he was smiling.

'Are they saying I'm gay and in a relationship with Stephen Twigg?'

'That is what I believe he was implying.' I had a quick think about how they could come to think that about someone whom I'd met, but only a few times. Then I realised.

'Well, I did go to a gay club with Stephen and some others for his birthday. But, that was a group of us and I am certainly not gay.' Later, when Charlie Fairbrass, the Leader of the Council, was asked why he thought I was gay he said 'well, he went to a gay club didn't he. Why would he go there if he wasn't gay?' When Stephen Twigg was faxed a copy of the dossier, his response was 'I thought Matt was straight'. I was. But I decided then that I wasn't going to answer questions about my sexuality and the Labour Party is not supposed to discriminate. Cameron and I argued often over this position, him pushing me to just correct the record and say I was straight. Cameron later had a taste of this when a Councillor tried to spread rumours that Cameron was only supporting me because we were in a gay relationship with each other! I think it was then that Cameron got my point.

Derek said in the café, 'I just can't believe what they have written, Matthew. And I am sorry I ever met him. He came under the pretence it was on behalf of Jon Cruddas MP and I didn't really know how to handle it best, as we hadn't heard from you for some time. I wish I had spoken to you first. But I can assure you that nothing they have quoted as me saying in the dossier is true'. We parted on good terms, although I was still angry that Derek had allowed such an intrusion into my childhood. Derek stuck to his word and fired off a detailed letter to all the people concerned, including a complaint to David Triesman (now Lord Triesman), then General Secretary of the Labour Party, threatening to take legal action. He emailed David Triesman and got a response.

'The whole matter is a complete mystery to me. I will ensure I get copied into the loop, but hope you will excuse me if I start by asking my PA to get me in the picture. I am involved in a difficult national political matter, I am not in a position to say more, that requires urgent attention and has very broad implications. Please do not think this is dismissive in any way, but I would appreciate it if you discussed matters first with my PA.' He then briefed Triesman's PA and waited several weeks, but had no contact from the party. Then he received a very strange and disjointed voice mail from Bob Little on his answer phone.

'Hello Derek, this is Bob Little, from Jon Cruddas's office. What it is about, actually Derek, just very briefly, is I had information back, basically from the Chief Executive's office of the borough, is that apparently he said you were livid and that is all I have got at the moment Derek. I am obviously very concerned that, sometimes, in my possible kind of reactions, or something like that, I may have, whether I caused an embarrassment to you or your organisation. If I have, if you can let me know and I can then put you in the picture. Obviously Jon Cruddas has been fully aware of what has been going on, but officially, of course, we take the line that he does not know anything about it. But, as I say if you could come back to me, I was very concerned obviously to hear that, I do not know what it relates to and hopefully if it is in my area of responsibility then, of course, I will try and make amends for that, or I will try to answer your concerns. Thank you. Bye.'

Shortly afterwards I was due to face the Labour Group to the charges against me and Derek could no longer wait for a response from the Labour Party. He telephoned Bob Little and informed him he was on speaker phone and had a witness present. Bob said that whatever happened was his personal responsibility, but gave no answer as to whether Jon Cruddas either knew, approved or instructed these actions against me. When Derek reminded him that he had a tape recording of him assuring that Jon Cruddas knew all about this; he just responded 'I will discuss that with Jon'. Bob never contacted Derek again, so Derek wrote a long letter detailing his complaint to the Labour Party and confirmed that the statements in the dossier attributed to him or Caldecott were false. He then sent me a letter thanking me for the contributions I had made to their children's understanding, particularly in the school. 'The benefit of your experience has helped to assure them that there is indeed a positive life beyond care, full of trials, tribulations and challenges as for any young person, but full of opportunity also'. He then went on to apologise about the meeting with Bob and confirmed he would take this to the highest level to get it rectified. I was just relieved that Caldecott hadn't said those things and it also made me feel less 'crazy' than I felt when I read the dossier. Sometimes, if so many people say you are, you begin to believe you might be.

The next person I went to see was Andrew Winton, who had also been quoted in the dossier. He was appalled at what he read and, what's more, had never even met or spoken to Bob Little. He wrote a statement in response to the dossier, which highlighted my strengths and weaknesses, confirmed the work I had done at the Council and said he had been happy to work on several projects since in partnership with Inter-Action Trust, my new employers. He has even recommended me for a project since working with the Council. Two of the main witnesses in the dossier were completely denying the statements attributed to them. What's more, one of those people, Andrew, had never spoken to, met or even heard of Bob Little until he saw the dossier.

The most difficult charges to refute were Ed Berman's. They pertained mainly to my character and I couldn't make Ed see what I believed Bob Little's agenda was. When I heard from the CLA that they had talked with Ed Berman and Bob Little, but still knew nothing about the dossier or its contents back in August 2002, I rang Ed to confront him and ask what he had said. He refused to talk to me and then emailed Charles Fairbrass. I might as well record the evidence against me.

'I personally believe that MH is a dangerous and loose cannon. I have written evidence that he has slandered me/us' (evidence he never produced). 'I would be most grateful for a guarantee of some kind, drawn up by our solicitor, that anything provided to you leaves us and others both personally and institutionally firewalled against this loose cannon. I asked him which union he belonged to and he refused to answer. I asked him about his real name and why he had not given us his NI number; he claimed not to know what I was speaking about. I have asked two other agencies to join. They will want the same kind of guarantee; is it possible that your Council solicitor can both draw up a document and be present at the meeting? This matter is perhaps more serious for you folks, as a statutory body, than for us who are in his past. Do you have evidence of his real name and his NI number under that name? As I have said, I personally have no problem meeting with you, but a call to ACAS and your solicitor wouldn't go amiss, if you don't mind my suggestions. I am still willing to meet with you, but to obtain a full picture, the others would find this very useful indeed and they are less experienced and more frightened. I would have hoped that you can send a letter/document to me to forward which will indemnify everyone against retribution. The Council is big enough to look after itself. The others are afraid. I'm sure you see the predicament.'

It still makes me laugh when I read this email today. It is a typical Ed Berman email.

Despite his claim that I remained a problem for him and did little work, I had several references from people who had worked with me on projects I had led on in Jamaica and South Africa.

As the support flowed in from people like Wayne and Sydney from Jamaica, I started to believe in myself once more. Years in and out of care do leave you feeling guilty and inadequate. The dossier wasn't just a set of lies but it wormed away whatever self-confidence I'd acquired. When I first read it I thought that if so many people think those things about me then there must be some truth to it. But the more support I got, the more I knew it was a trash document with its own nasty agenda. If I was a 'loony loose cannon', how come many people, who had worked with me on projects whilst at Inter-Action Trust, had such a very positive and consistent view of me? Eventually, though, it comes down to who they choose to believe; and they chose Ed Berman partly because he came with the appearance of credibility and status but mostly because his version matched the version they had already written; that I was a dangerous, mentally ill loose cannon that needed to be stopped.

Other smaller charges were easy to deal with. The issue of my name was a surprise to me because it had never come up before. My Mum had simply given the surname of the person I had thought to be my Dad to me when she got married to him after my birth. My birth certificate said Huggins and when I was sixteen, applying for a passport, I was told I could only get one in the name of Huggins. I never liked my other name and, also, didn't have any contact with my 'Dad' any more so I accepted the change thinking nothing of it. They had found out I had grown up under a different name and immediately assumed I was using Huggins as a decoy name, like some kind of conman. But nobody ever thought to ask me about it. Seven years later I still hear from people who tell me they were told that Matthew Huggins isn't my real name.

The one charge that was most difficult to refute was about my mental health. By that time in my life I knew I got depressed in periods, but I never told anyone about it. I didn't see the need and certainly didn't think it affected my work. Besides, the type of mental illness they were talking about was far worse; although they never explicitly said it, they were referring to someone who had a major personality disorder. I remember one argument with Cameron, where he suggested I should get checked out and provide evidence that I wasn't mentally ill. I was livid. Why should I have to prove I am not mentally ill? As they used to do in the Soviet Union.

I was getting angry at the wrong person, however. Cameron just wanted to beat them; he had initially been concerned, after first reading the dossier, for my welfare, as it looked like I was some kind of lunatic. He had phoned Labour Party Central Office for advice about how to handle it and they had said that 'they would take a very dim view' about anyone with such problems been treated this way; it would be seen as a welfare issue, quite rightly. (It has been since suggested that all MPs should be tested for their mental health but they don't seem likely to vote for it.)

Whilst I wasn't prepared to see a medical professional to certify that I was not mentally ill, in the way that they described, I was prepared to seek character references from people who had known me a long time and could vouch for my mental health. Hugh Pelham wrote a statement in support of me, as did Maggie Mulverhill, writing in her capacity as a qualified and experienced child protection social worker.

For a loose cannon, I didn't fire many balls. Alex was advising me to go 'nuclear' at the time, thinking it would help reform Dagenham Labour Party. But I didn't want to be put down as a troublemaker and just thought that this would make Labour Party central office and Dagenham close ranks against me. I hadn't realised they already had. Alan and several of my ward members also thought we should fight back harder. But Jeff and Cameron persuaded us the only way to go was with the formal process and we had to wait until the next Labour Group meeting to present my defence.

A lot of lobbying was going on to try and get the case a fair hearing. Both Hilton Dawson MP and Margaret Hodge, the MP for Barking, spoke to David Treisman, who told them it was a local matter and needed to go through the due process. I phoned to complain to Hillary Perrin, the London Regional Coordinator, but she didn't want to talk about it with me

But I had put the hard work in and everything in the dossier was now refuted. I was as prepared as I could be for the hearing. Then on the Friday before, I was informed in writing that they had pulled the dossier and instead put a set of five other charges against me. I only had two days to refute them and at a weekend!

I was livid. And so were my supporters.

The meeting was tense; out of about sixty people I could count the number of supporters I knew I had on both hands. Of course, if I were to believe the people that told me they were supporting me it would have been double that, but many in the Labour Group were playing both sides. There were those who knew what was happening to me was wrong, even if they didn't know for sure what was true and what wasn't, but chose to go with the flow because of fear about the own political careers; many of these people had roles in the Council's cabinet or other paid roles in the non-executive functions. Most of them had heard so many rumours and accusations about me over the previous six months so that it was difficult, without seeing any contrary evidence, for them to see me as anything other than what I was presented as, a dangerous con artist.

The five charges against me included the rent arrears, the accusation that I had lied to a reporter about the rent arrears, an accusation that I had 'bullied' a Council officer (who was also secretary of the Local Government Committee, which had recommended my suspension and medical treatment), the HMS President Bill and that I had flirted with a female member of the Council's staff. It was true that I had chatted up a press officer at a Council function. I didn't see anything wrong in it, as I was her age and certainly didn't consider it as harassment.

A few weeks later when Graham met me, he told me he had received a complaint about the incident. I was flabbergasted; it was never my intention to make her feel uncomfortable. I immediately offered to apologise but he said that was not necessary and that it was unwise, though he would pass on my apology. As far as he was concerned the matter was closed. However, now, months later, the charge resurfaced without any formal complaint from the individual concerned. The 'bullying' of the Council officer referred to a conversation I had had with her when I heard that the Local Government Committee in Barking and Dagenham were sending out meeting letters to discuss my 'case'. I was angry and abrupt, but given we were in an office opposite the Chief Executive's, I didn't raise my voice, as was suggested, or swear at her. The accusation that I had lied to a reporter was laughable; it was the same reporter who had previously asked me to leak him the Social Services Inspection report before the embargo date; he had banked on my previous experience of care being my motive in releasing the report. I refused. And now I was stuck with a false charge, again with no evidence either way, that I had lied to the reporter about my rent arrears.

I read a statement refuting the charges and whilst I referred to the dossier I was not allowed to go into any of the details of the accusations, even though many of the people present had read them or been told about them. Various people asked questions that related to accusations in the dossier, including about my mental health, but each time the chair would stop them and say it wasn't relevant to this discussion. I actually wanted to answer the questions; it was so frustrating to have everyone know the accusations but not my response. My supporters were steadfast in their defence of me; Alan, Cameron and Bryan refused to hold back their anger and amazement. Cameron ended the meeting with a long summary, the most accurate I had heard throughout the whole case, pleading for the Labour Group to see sense. But, as the votes were counted I could see by the looks on people's faces that I had lost. The vote

254

came back; 50 for my suspension from the group and 11 against. As soon as the vote was announced, Len came over and handed me a letter confirming my suspension. It must have been written already. He had a smile on his face that said 'you shouldn't have fought this.'

We saw an appeals panel within a month at the London Labour Party. Again, we were not allowed to mention the dossier, so it was difficult to explain the background to the case. At some point with Cameron by my side, I realised that I was going to lose the appeal. It was disheartening as we had been so convinced that London Labour would dismiss the case. Cameron even thought they would intervene to sort the local party out. But, now we sat here with Charlie Fairbrass convincing the panel that it was 'only a six month suspension and if he behaves we will let him back'. I really could have been back in care. They upheld the decision. One member of the panel later told Alex it was one of the worst decisions he had made in his career; it was just there was so much mess to look through in the case that, given I would only be suspended for six months, it seemed the easiest decision. The member was appalled when Cameron told him that Dagenham Labour Party were now talking of having me expelled.

I didn't end up on a bridge this time trying to throw myself off. I got on with my life. My career outside the borough was taking off My first major conference was as a key note to the Local Government Information Unit conference on Corporate Parenting to around five hundred Councillors and officers. I felt passionate about the need for politicians to take the issues around children in care seriously, despite Len Collins saying I should really put this care leaver stuff to the side.

At the end of one of my speeches a Barking and Dagenham

Councillor, who was at the conference, congratulated Cameron on the speech.

'I suppose you wrote that for Huggins.'

'No actually, I helped a little bit, but mostly it was Matt's work.'

'He didn't write that'. I realised that no matter what I was to do outside the authority, no matter how successful I became, the elderly white men would still think I was a fraud.

Around the same time I met someone who was going to transform my life beyond recognition. Jo Cleary was speaking at a conference alongside me and we hadn't seen each other for a year or so. Afterwards she suggested I meet a friend of hers, Mike Reid, who published a magazine in the care sector, *Care and Health*. Several days later Mike called and asked if he could do a feature interview. I was privileged to be asked and excited to be doing my first big interview. We talked about my life in care and discussed the issues that the care sector faced. Mike did me proud – the feature was a lot bigger than I expected; four pages including photos of me standing outside the House of Commons. I looked every bit the politician, despite my youth.

It quickly became clear that the Labour Group had no intention of allowing me back after six months. They had begun to prepare a case to the National Executive Committee for my expulsion. I attended an interview with Dagenham Labour Party investigating whether they should seek expulsion, as a show of good faith, with Alan as my witness. We tried to present the evidence in response to the dossier but they didn't accept any of it. They kept asking me questions about my family, implying each time that I had made up the fact that I had grown up in care. In their care!! When it became clear that they were set with their views, we left. A few months later we sat before the National Constitutional Committee of the Labour Party to try again to prove my innocence.

Hilton Dawson MP acted as my advocate with about six other witnesses who would refute each allegation. This panel was different in that we could bring the dossier into the proceedings; in my bundle of evidence submitted I included all paperwork from both sides; their dossier, my response and all the supported statements. Any sensible person would have read it and seen what a mess this whole thing was. After more than four hours at the hearing, when they had presented their case and we had questioned the other side and systematically exposed each of their claims as false or driven by other motivations, Hilton pushed for me to present a 'no case to answer' plea. Although I was keen to present my case, I didn't want to spurn his advice. I presented the plea and the panel chucked the case out, one of them calling it a 'witch hunt'. George Brooker, who was presenting the case from the other side, got into a verbal scuffle with one of the panel members, which ended with them threatening to remove George from the room if he didn't leave. Although I had won, I didn't feel a sense of victory.

The local press carried a short piece way into the pages of the paper reporting that I had been cleared, which I was angry about, given the one-sided story about me that had been plastered all over the front pages and on the billboards.

Shortly after the 'victory' we went back to the Labour Group to ask for my re admittance into the Group. It was the last time we would be allowed to do so. I presented my case in a conciliatory way; accepting I had got things wrong and that I had learnt my lesson. It stuck in my throat, given everything they had done to me, but it wouldn't help for me to be angry or defensive. A few questions were asked, but no one said much. I was asked to leave while they voted.

Once I left Charlie Fairbrass made a damning speech against my re-admittance. He claimed there was a lot that the group didn't know and they couldn't say, but it was clear that I hadn't changed and would be a danger to the Group. We didn't know what he was referring to at the time, but Cameron had had a call around that time from another Councillor who had begged him to stop supporting me. He told him that they had found out that when I was a child I had killed my parents in a fire and later trashed the civic centre. Neither was true, although if they had had access to my social work files or discussed my past with a social worker in the know then they could have twisted the incident with Kevin and the sofa and the altercation with the Security Manager when I was sixteen. Whatever the reason, the Labour Group took the Leader's advice and voted for my permanent expulsion. This time I had even fewer supporters, which only went to show how much energy they had put into trashing my credibility in whatever way they could. Alan was furious and immediately resigned from the Group. I was touched; he didn't need to do that nor did I want him too. But a man of integrity and uncompromising values, he couldn't be part of what they had done.

My ward met several days later and most resigned from the party. Brian Speake was so angry that 'they have tried to destroy this young man and his career'.

Just as they had done all they could, so had I, and I didn't have the energy to fight, nor did I believe that it would make any difference. I decided that I would focus on work and resign from the Council. I was sad not to complete my full term and ashamed I hadn't kept my promise to my constituents to serve them. I just couldn't face those people, who were supposed to be my colleagues and even my 'comrades' any more, which is why I stopped going to the meetings.

Cameron argued long and hard against my resigning, fearing that calling an unnecessary by-election at a time when the British National Party was on the rise would make my remaining supporters look bad. He knew that neither Alan or I had any future locally and was starting to question whether or not he would carry on as Deputy Leader or stand at the next set of elections, but he was concerned at the grief the 'powers that be' might give to others, not least Bryan.

Whilst I agreed to at least delay my decision to quit I couldn't face the meetings so intended to attend the bare minimum. A Councillor must go to at least one meeting within a six month period or face disqualification.

I was not looking forward to the meeting I had to attend to avoid this fate. A few days before it was due to be held I received a 'phone call from the local press. They informed me that the meeting was going to be cancelled and that therefore I would be disqualified. I contacted Cameron, who airily assured me that it must be a cock-up. 'They are not stupid enough to deliberately disqualify a Labour Councillor to fight an unnecessary and potentially difficult by-election at a time when the BNP are doing well.' He had a meeting that day with Graham Farrant and assumed he would be able to sort it out.

Cameron and Graham and discussed the legal position. This was clear. Unless there was some other meeting called for me to attend then I would be disqualified. At this stage

Cameron had said to Graham that one of them was going to have to explain the mess to Charlie so that a meeting could be arranged. Cameron said that for the first time since he'd met Graham, the latter was briefly lost for words. Then he explained that the people who had cancelled the meeting had known exactly what the consequences would be. Indeed, Graham had even received complaints from staff about the shouts of 'We've got the bastard!' echoing down the corridors in the Civic Centre.

In truth, I should have resigned sooner but was struggling with the fact that I didn't want to give in to them. My leaving Barking and Dagenham Council spelt the end of my political career and any belief that I had a future in politics. But, it also ended my relationship with the Council that had looked after me as a child and later attacked me as an adult. I became estranged from them just as I had been from my parents.

When the dust settled it seemed sensible to try to analyse what went wrong.

One of the more supportive Councillors suggested that I'd just upset The Leader. Avoiding debt and being truthful were central to his moral values. I was in debt, and he didn't believe the claims I'd made about my years in care. But I had the debts cleared, and why didn't he discuss his doubts with me after he had been initially so supportive?

Cameron was told by Liam Smith, who is now the Council Leader, that Charlie Fairbrass largely turned against me after someone in a pub had said that I had deliberately set fire to my flat in Kent in order to be moved back to the area. Liam had concluded, therefore, that I was a threat to the good reputation of the Party and so 'something had to be done'.

They didn't mind that I was young or had been in care. But they did seem concerned when they'd persuaded themselves that I might be gay when combined with the earlier two factors. I lost the support of some influential people and then I seemed to incur their hatred. Whilst Cameron kept maintaining that the issues would be judged on their merits, Jeff kept warning that what would decide matters would be 'bums on seats'. And Liam was very good at getting bums on seats.

By the end of it all the actual details of Bob's dossier didn't seem to be important to anyone, except perhaps to Bob and, of course, to me. When friends challenged my detractors about these matters they were confronted with noses being tapped knowingly and observations that, 'Bob knows loads more stuff!' Bob Little is now deputy leader of Barking and Dagenham Council.

13

Aged Twenty-Six – Breakdown

I was no longer a Councillor but I did have a job. Mike Reid and I met for dinner several times. We clicked instantly; he had an amazing mind that flitted from one subject to another, demonstrating an intimate understanding of each, refusing to dumb it down for me. The first time we met he promised to send me a few books; I didn't think much of it at the time. But the next day his PA sent me over the two books, *Atlas Shrugged*, by the controversial Ayn Rand, and *The Lyndon Johnson Years*. He gave me the intellectual stimulation I'd been craving – and offered me a job in business development in his therapeutic care home company in Scotland. I divided my week between London and Scotland, which was a struggle to say the least.

That was the first job in which I really felt like a professional; I had an amazing boss, a gruff South African, Martin Evans, who taught me the basics of business development. My job was to open the North West England region and I felt like a fish out of water, having never dealt with the logistics of opening children's homes. It was surreal, when I thought about it, going to look at potential homes and coordinating the design and building works. Only six years earlier I had lived in a similar home.

I wasn't ready for the job, at only 22, and struggled to manage the implementation of the plan; primarily because it was too ambitious and underfunded. The senior team were not on board either and there were confused messages. By the time our expansion plans started to fail, my relationship with the senior management team was tense. I had been doing the dirty work of the boss for so long that I was the one they disliked, not him. Being as ambitious and eager to please Mike as I was I didn't think about the position I had put myself in.

Having a job meant I could take my girlfriend on holiday.

Venice was the most beautiful city I had ever been to and I was there with the most beautiful woman I knew. Caroline was as unique, creative and gorgeous as the streets we meandered through hand in hand. I was in love with her, and realised I had never truly loved before. She was everything I wasn't. She had a first class education and a loving successful family. She didn't care what I did, what mistakes I made or how difficult I became. She was always able to see beyond that. I didn't realise how much I would need this – and soon.

Venice was hot and the streets were busy. Our hotel was on a small island west of St Mark's Square. Boats glided and chugged across the muddied waters past grand buildings that had stood for hundreds of years. I was inspired. We went up to get changed for dinner. I checked my phone; there was a voicemail message.

'Matthew, it's your Grandad. Give me a call, it's about your father.' My father? My father? I knew exactly who he meant by that word – father. How could he be a Dad? Dads take their sons to football. Dads buy their sons their first pint. Dads put their sons straight when they are going the wrong way in life. My father had left before I was born and I hadn't seen him since. So he never was a Dad to me. Strangely everyone else referred to him as my 'father', not my 'dad', so I figured they must have thought the same.

I had spent many hours dreaming about seeing my father, rationalising and romanticising in equal vein. Over the years I had asked questions but nobody told me much, mostly, they said, because they didn't know much. This is what I did know. He had met my Mum at a party when she was fifteen and he was in his early twenties. They fell in love; he was her first real boyfriend. My Grandad thinks he knows the night I was conceived – my uncle, who was a lot older, came home to find my Mum and her older man in one bed in the house and her brother and his older woman in another bed. Weeks later she was pregnant: a few weeks after that my father was gone. The most romantic part of the story was that he had turned up on my grandparents' doorstep on Valentine's day, the date I was due to be born, with a bunch of flowers. Nobody ever saw him again.

She met Paul about a year later and they decided to bring me up as if he was my Dad. She was young and naïve, just seventeen, and they married quickly. They had my brothers in quick succession, John two years after me and Danny three years after John. When they had told me that Paul wasn't my real father I couldn't quite believe it. I didn't know how to feel at that moment. I felt numb; except for small tears that tore down my face. I wasn't angry or disappointed. It was as if I had known – like it all made sense. That was why he didn't want to take care of me. I *wasn't* his son, so he didn't need to show as much love for me as for my brothers. His promise to be my Dad always was made in front of everyone I cared about; he'd said that he would never leave me. But by then, he'd already been gone since my birth.

265

So I knew who my Grandad meant when he said 'father'. He meant Brian. My heart filled with hope, my head with the fantasies I'd clung to for years. I needed to get to a phone now; I didn't have time to explain to Caroline and, anyway, I needed to make this call on my own. I raced down the stairs to the hotel reception. A dozen thoughts went through my head all at once. Did he want to see me? Would he love me? Why was he in touch? I had waited for this moment and played out our first meeting, preparing for every eventuality. In my wildest dreams he would greet me at the door of his nice house with the warmest, hardest hug I had ever had, telling me how much he had always loved me. Now it was happening.

'Grandad, it's Matthew,' I said. The tone of my voice was clear. *Tell me what my father wanted.*

'Oh, hello. How are you?'

He really didn't seem to have picked up on my tone. I had to be clearer.

'You left a message about my father. I need to know.'

'I'm sorry. He's dead.'

I had prepared myself for every eventuality: except *that* one. I slumped to the floor; I felt like I had been running freely in a field of hope that went on forever and then, all of a sudden, hit a brick wall, head on. I was winded, my heart punctured. My hopes and dreams about my father, all gone, dashed, at once.

I had been planning to find my father for years. I was sixteen when I finally built up the courage to ask my Mum. She recalled some strange tale about how the last time she'd seen him had been a few years before, giving evidence for a court trial before the local magistrates. On the court list for that day she came across the name Brian Phillips. How strange, she thought, what a coincidence! She investigated further and, on entering the court, she saw my father being sentenced and led away by police. She couldn't remember what he was sentenced for, but, she added for dramatic effect, she gave him a wave and smile as he was led away. It didn't take long for me to realise this wasn't true, and I always wondered why she didn't want me to find him.

Despite my fears about who he might have been, I needed to know where I'd come from. I was ready to deal with rejection or the pain of learning my father was a bad man. Who knows, I reasoned, maybe he would be different than I thought? Years later, when Mum and I no longer spoke, I asked my grandparents for help. She told them when she fell pregnant he was 36 – not in his early twenties. This changed things for me. What kind of 36-year-old gets a 15-year-old girl pregnant? I wasn't so sure any more I wanted to find such a man.

But there is something deep in the core of people who have few or no blood relatives, a need to find out who they are. I've talked to people who have been adopted, and they feel it even more. It is like a piece of your body is missing and until you find it you will never feel quite complete. I had one photo of my father and we looked identical. It is a strange feeling to look at someone you have never met and know nothing about and yet be linked in that physical way. I had thought endlessly about what I would say to him, and wondered if he had other children.

Now, in the phone box in Venice, I was about to speak to his mother for the first time. My grandmother! I didn't stop to think about it. What was I going to say to her? My heart raced so fast I thought it was going to explode, but I had to speak to her now. I wanted to hug her tightly, this woman I didn't even know.

'Hello.'

This sweet, old woman came on the line with a thick northern accent. I had no idea where I was calling and it was then that I realised that I had no idea *who* I was calling.

'Is this Mrs Phillips?' I figured that would be her second name.

'Matthew?'

How did she know my name?

'Am so, so happy to hear from ya.'

I couldn't control myself. I cried; I felt deep sadness that I had lost someone so close to my heart, someone I never knew. But I also felt that lost piece of me had been completed – a bit of my body filled in – I had an answer about the missing person I'd longed to know for so long. I felt regret that I would never meet or know him and was drained of hope. Strangely, the one thing I didn't feel was anger – anger for leaving me as a baby and never coming back.

My real grandmother sounded like a shattered woman, consumed by grief, as she told me how he 'passed away peacefully one night' with a heart attack. They had found him in the morning in an armchair with a sock in one hand – he had been trying to take his socks off. He died living with his mother and her husband without any relationship of his own, no serious friends or other children. Even then it struck me just how sad that sounded. He was 46 years old, with no significant career achievements, no relationship, no friends to speak of and no other children. Nothing except me – and he had spent all his life staying away from me.

I don't remember the rest of the conversation, but we agreed to meet up. She did say two things that would play on my mind for some time. First, he was only 46 when he died, so Mum had lied about his age. Secondly, she explained he had a heart murmur, which caused the heart attack. Then, as if realising what she said, she quickly reassured me that I wouldn't have to worry. Why? Surely it might be hereditary – no, really I shouldn't worry, she assured again. That was when I first knew there was more to this story.

As we took the taxi back from the airport I sat in the darkness holding Caroline's hand. Over the radio 'Cold Water' by Damien Rice came on; I started to cry. Caroline squeezed my hand, but I couldn't stop. Venice is a special place to me. You might think that strange given the circumstances. But that weekend I found my heart with Caroline and lost it with my father.

As we sat on the train to Newcastle I looked across at Caroline, reading her book. Having her there put me at ease; I didn't know what to expect when I first saw Anne, my father's mother. Should I hug her? Having Caroline there didn't provide any answers but it meant I wasn't on my own. I knew that whatever happened I would have her afterwards and that made me feel safe. I looked out of the window at the passing fields dotted with small lakes, beautiful cottages and acres of woodland. I had always enjoyed travelling because it gave me a chance to think about things. It was the only time when I could sort out the mass of clutter in my head and put it into some kind of order. As I looked out of the window today I contemplated my life back in London. I thought just how far I'd come from my dreams of changing the world.

Since moving back to London to work for Mike's other company, *Care and Health*, I had successfully reinvented myself as an asset to Mike's senior team. I was now heading up a department called Knowledge Services. The three business units, conferencing, training and a news and information website all provided knowledge services to senior management in social care and health services. I was burned by my experience at CareVisions (Mike's other company), more than I knew at the time. There was no time to think about what had happened. All I really knew was that my mistake had been to put myself in the position of leader without having the necessary skills. Now, eight months into my start with *Care and Health*, the news and information website had been successfully launched and we had just completed the acquisition of a small training provider in Harrogate.

I didn't realise the toll my time at the children's home company – the seven-day, eighty hour plus working weeks, the failure of the business plan, and the redundancies of the staff – had on me. I felt an immense pressure to perform for Mike. I owed it to him because of the opportunity he had given me when I had so little experience of the business world. But also because I saw this as my only option; I thought that if I didn't have my job with Mike, then I wouldn't be able to get a job anywhere else. I was determined not to go back to Burger King.

I had the appearance of being successful financially and professionally: I was earning a lot of money. Success at work was the core of my self confidence; the only way I had learnt to love myself was through being successful. So the idea that I could lose that left me feeling squeezed, as if my head was about to explode. Much as I loved working for Mike, continuity of management style was not one of his qualities. Some days he would be ecstatic with my work, thinking I was the best thing since sliced bread; other days he would be so angry he wouldn't even talk to me.

I started to drink heavily. I didn't notice it at first. It started off as binge drinking on weekends where I would really let my hair down to de-stress. The first time I noticed I might have a problem was when I found myself sitting in a police cell with my head in my hands, wondering how on earth I had got there.

I had got through several bottles of wine and over a dozen shots that night. I was out with Rob in Romford and we had been refused entry to a night club for being too drunk. I don't remember all the details, and neither does Rob, but we had got into trouble with some loutish lads who had blood on their faces. Scared, and the wimp that I am, I ran off, not realising, until I got some distance away, that Rob was still in what appeared to be a tussle with the lads. There had been some nasty attacks reported in Romford recently that had resulted in death so I immediately called the police, begging them to come.

'Calm down, Sir, we won't be able to come right away, we don't have officers available' the operator replied.

'What do you mean you can't come? My friend's been attacked! You would come quicker if you knew there was a bomb here.'

Why I said that I don't know.

'Sir, are you saying there is a bomb?' I thought for a moment. Now was my chance to get out of this situation.

'I'm not saying there isn't a bomb and I'm not saying there is one. Just get here quickly.' I hung up the phone. I had made the situation worse. After what seemed like five minutes, but was actually only a minute or so, I rang again.

'I just called saying there is a bomb. I got this wrong.'

'Are you saying there is no bomb sir?'

Another chance to get out of this hole.

'It depends if you are going to come quicker and help my friend?'

No, I was going to dig deeper.

'Sir, I need to be clear. Can you confirm there is not a bomb?'

'I can't say if there is or isn't until you come,' with that last giant dig I hung up again.

I couldn't find Rob so I went back to his flat where I waited in the car. Eventually he turned up at the window just like in those horror films where the bloodstained victim bangs his hands against the glass. He couldn't remember a thing, but thought he had been mugged on the way home as he didn't have his wallet or keys. In my heavily drunken state, stupidly thinking I had done nothing wrong in my earlier phone call with the police, I went with Rob to phone the police and report the mugging. I gave them my name, which I had also done earlier, and told them where we would wait, outside Rob's flat. We waited in the car with the engine on as it was freezing cold outside. Then a police car and a police van came up the road and in my panic I realised they might think I was driving the car. Instead of explaining, I stupidly threw the keys into the garden. Several senior looking officers came towards me.

'Are you the bloke that's been calling a bomb threat?'

'Yes, but only to get you to come quicker!'

I still thought I had done nothing wrong. In minutes I was handcuffed and in the back of the police van. Rob had no clue as to what was going on and, amazingly, given his link with me, he was not arrested. It was only in the police van on my way to the station that I realised exactly how stupid and dangerous I had been. What on earth had possessed me? You often hear people blaming drink and think it's a bad excuse. But it is the only excuse I have.

Once at the station I begged them to believe that this was something I never intended to do and that something had gone horribly wrong. Despite my pleas I spent the night in the cells arrested on Terrorism charges and was told I was lucky I wasn't being handed over to Special Branch. I thought about all the stories I had read of people making jokes about bombs and being sent to prison as an example. I cried all night as I convinced myself that I was going to prison. As I sat on the cold hard blue mat of the cell wondering what would become of my career and my life I was angry that I had come to this point. It was the first time I realised something was wrong with me.

The next day, as the Detective interviewed me and read back the transcript of my calls, I pleaded my regret and guilt over the incident. My remorse was my saving grace.

After waiting on bail for almost a year, due to the detective being on sick leave, I was finally cautioned. But it is still an embarrassing scar on my character and every Criminal Records check I have to complete for work is a reminder of how drink can cause disaster. I was banned from several political party conferences and it was only in 2008 that, after representation to the Chief Inspectors in charge of security, I was allowed back into party conferences.

But I still continued to drink heavily. As I got into a desperate cycle of irrational paranoia and depression, I turned to drugs to cope. The first time I smoked cannabis I felt all my worries about life and what people thought of me evaporate. I loved the instant relief it gave me from life. When I was high, I didn't care what people thought of me or my failings.

But as with any drug, the positive effects of social cannabis use wore off and I became a daily user. At the start of 2007 I had a breakdown; not a nervous one. I was hospitalised with severe pneumonia and had an anaphylactic shock in reaction to iodine. A nurse who called my grandparents, told them to come to the hospital quick. I'd never been so relieved to see two people. My grandma looked as though she was going to cry and I can only imagine how panicked she must have been. The pace at which I had been going, combined with the stress of my current way of life had brought on pneumonia; although no doubt the drugs and drink contributed.

Then about three weeks after leaving hospital, I came down with acute appendicitis. This wasn't just bad luck. It was my body trying to tell me that if I carried on like this I could end up killing myself before I was thirty. I knew I had to change things, but I had no idea how or where to start. So once out of hospital I just blindly carried on; taking on more work and more drink and drugs to support it.

Mike Reid, my boss, had become a father figure to me. I admired and respected him; I loved him. In my eyes he was the person who had given me an opportunity that no one else would have. My work every day wasn't about making me a success; it became a way of getting Mike to love me. When I got his love I felt at ease with the world and my place within it; when I didn't, or, worse, when he was angry with me, it was as if my world was going to explode.

I look back on this time and sometimes wonder whether he knew that about me. I wonder if he played on it to get the best out of me. He knew exactly how to bring me down and build me up. Just like a drug, I needed that affirmation from him. If he turned off that supply or raised the price, I would do anything to get my fix.

At times we were the closest of friends. We'd sit until the early hours of the morning smoking and drinking together, solving the world problems. Mike always had big plans for himself, the company and me with it and I loved nothing more than to talk in this 'blue sky', can-do kind of way. At these times he would phone me daily to run a new idea past me. Then I could do no wrong and he would sing my praise. But at other times he'd cut me off, not speak to me for days or treat me as if he were about to sack me.

At these times I felt dumped, just like my Mum had dumped me for Kevin. That scuppered every ounce of self-respect and confidence I had. This inconsistency in our relationship, a relationship that meant so much to me, just fuelled my paranoia and depression.

Many members of my team also didn't like me. Several times I found out that they had had staff nights out and leaving parties and not invited me. This hurt a lot, more than it should have done given that I was their manager. I didn't get on with my deputy too well either and she would challenge me in the staff meetings, one time rolling her eyes as I spoke. I felt personally wounded and would often go home in tears.

Caroline would try to rationalise with me that it wasn't my fault and I shouldn't worry so much about it; 'they don't really know you'. But nothing I was feeling was rational. So each night, instead of crying and hating myself I would light up spliff after spliff and smoke my worries into oblivion.

My biological father

When I left hospital, I went to visit my grandmother.

She began to tell me the story of my father's life. He had been a Royal Marine based in Plymouth until his father

275

died. He had left to come and take care of his mother. She spoke proudly of his doing that. Then he had got a job in Dagenham at the Ford plant. He had met my Mum at the local church and had fallen in love with her. Of course, they would tell me that, but she described it with such passion that I like to believe that she was telling the truth. She clearly believed it to be so. Everything was going well until near the birth, when my Mum decided she no longer wanted to be with Brian.

After I was born he tried to see me many times and they were all so desperate to see me. Mum always refused and returned their letters with sneering replies telling them to stay out of my life. They eventually decided it was the best thing for me. A few years later he had found another woman and a flat in Dagenham.

One day, when he came back from work sick, he found his partner having sex with another man in their bed. Beyond distraught, he was emotionally numb. For several years he disappeared and they didn't know where to find him. Eventually he came home to his mother in Sunderland and she gave her job up to look after him. By now he was ill and spent the rest of his life in and out of psychiatric hospitals. He never formed another relationship. One morning Anne found Brian slumped in the lounge armchair in their tiny council flat, dead. Here is where the story got muddled. Anne's belief about his death is that he had a heart attack caused by his medication. This is not so bizarre a belief. At least two psychiatric patients a week die in the UK from unexplained reasons while on psychiatric medication. However, she admitted that the doctors had a different story; they were adamant that he had killed himself. I didn't know what to believe; part of me wanted to believe the former, but that would mean believing there was a conspiracy amongst the doctors, which is also difficult for me to accept. It didn't help Anne in her grief that the cause of death was recorded as an Open Verdict.

As soon as I was back in London I returned to work. I didn't take time to grieve. At times I felt like I didn't have a right to grieve; I never knew the man, so why would I be so upset that he died? But was a piece of him. Not just in flesh and blood, but in mind and spirit. He had lived as part of my dreams and hopes for so many years and now that they were gone I was left with a feeling of emptiness. I was suddenly lost, which seemed silly, given that he'd never been there as my compass. It was more likely that I had been lost for a while, but this had brought things to a head.

At work, although Mike and a few others knew about it, no one asked about how I felt. My Mum didn't bother phoning me either, not that I ever expected her to. But I was angry that she didn't care how I might feel about my own father dying. As for Anne, I didn't speak to her until a year later. I just couldn't bear building a relationship from scratch like that with such intensity; every time I looked in her eyes I could see how distressed she was.

I got through the end of 2007 by taking more drugs and drinking. I was becoming more paranoid than ever. It wasn't only my staff and colleagues that I thought were talking behind my back – which was probably true – but also my closest friends. I would sometimes get ideas into my head that I had done something to upset one of them and it would drive me crazy until I spoke to them about it. Caroline got the worst of my paranoia; I began to think that she was leaving me for every guy who texted her. She always understood but I knew it put great pressure on her and I hated myself for it. It was a vicious cycle; the more paranoid I became, the more I hated myself and took drugs, which made me more paranoid.

The last 'calamity' that year was the loss of the final hope I had of reconciliation with Danny, my youngest brother. It had been eight years since I saw him. My grandparents found out where he was working and gave me his number. It was a pub in King's Cross and I was startled to think he was just around the corner from me. I phoned him immediately; a man answered.

'Is Danny there, it's his brother, Matthew.'

'Yeah, I'll just get him for you'. I waited for what seemed like five minutes, my heart pumping fast, trying to think of what I might say to him.

'Err. I'm sorry mate; I don't know how to say this. He doesn't want to speak to you. Look, I'll see what I can do and talk to him.'

I put the phone down. Later that night I got a text from Danny.

'Please don't contact me again. I don't want to speak to you. I can't risk you ruining my family again.'

I felt like I had been stabbed through the heart. It was the one word in his text that made it so painful – 'my' family – as if to say *I* didn't have a family. It was then that I understood the reality of my situation; I didn't just have to come to terms with the loss of my father, I also had to come to terms with the loss of mother and brothers. They were never going to come back to me.

After I had barely got through Christmas, it got to the point where I just couldn't function day-to-day without drugs. I was physically unable to get to work some days and would often turn up late, if at all. My relationship with Mike was at its lowest ebb as he felt the only way to help me through this and make me perform was to bash me over the head as hard as possible until I got better. It had just the opposite effect. It was difficult to know what he really thought because when I tried to leave he did everything to make me stay, from telling me that I couldn't get a job anywhere else to reasoning that this was my only real opportunity to make a success of myself and that he genuinely cared about me. That was why, he said, he had been so harsh with me.

But I just couldn't cope with it any more. One night I got home from work and had to prepare a presentation for the future of my business stream the next day. I was physically sick with the idea of facing all my colleagues. I phoned Mike in tears.

'I just can't do this any more, Mike. I really tried hard but I can't make it work. I want to leave' He paused for a moment.

'I know, Matt. I know you have tried, I can see that. But if you want to leave I'm not going to stop you.'

He seemed genuinely sorry that it had come to this. I was just relieved not to have to face everyone again. Several weeks later I made my final speech to a *Care and Health* conference on Corporate Parenting. I'd been high the night before and, although I delivered the speech sober, I was still suffering from the effects of the drugs. It was my most personal and emotional speech. At the end I said I couldn't do this any more, giving a piece of myself and my history each time I made a speech. I needed to live a life where I followed my own dreams. A sad indictment of the care system is that a lot of successful care leavers end up making their success in the very system they were so desperate to leave. I was now leaving. As I closed my speech I felt myself breaking up.

As soon as I came off the stage, I went downstairs and lit up a spliff. Inside the senior managers from Children's Services were continuing their discussion on how to improve the life chances of children in care. Outside, one of their care leavers was a broken man, high on drugs, crying, his head in his hands. The irony was painful.

Caroline was the only good thing left in my life and I was still amazed that she stuck by me through this. She had been the one true love of my life. She had offered me unconditional love and in return I had offered as much resistance to that love as possible. Each time I pushed back, she clung on. She understood why I felt the way I did and I loved that about her. When we – rarely – talked about the drugs, she would simply say that I needed to give up when I was ready and it had to be my decision. But underneath all that, I knew the state I was getting myself into disappointed, and, most of all, worried her.

On my birthday we went to a hotel for the weekend. Birthdays have always been a difficult time and a painful reminder of the people missing in my life; my Mum, my brothers, my father. As we sat in a restaurant eating dinner the table opposite us had a birthday cake come out as they all sang 'Happy Birthday'. Something inside me just clicked and I started to cry. Already depressed at this time of year, compounded by the drugs, the birthday song and the happiness of the crowd just made me so sad. As I cried so did Caroline, and she lovingly took my hand in hers.

But drugs can cause you to be very selfish. The more I took to cope, the more selfish I became. I kept cancelling weekend arrangements to go and visit her as I spent the time hiding away in my room stoned. Much as I loved her, I loved drugs more.

Shortly after quitting *Care and Health* I decided to break

up with Caroline. It happened quickly in a phone call; she was as understanding as ever, which made it even worse. I wanted her to be angry at me. She had a right to be angry at me. I didn't realise it then, but later I would regret this decision more than any I had made in my life. We never saw each other again.

With no job, no girlfriend and no future prospects, I simply shut myself away from the world. It wasn't immediate; for about a month after leaving *Care and Health* I went back and forth to Germany on a whirlwind, rebound relationship with a woman who managed to mess my head still more. Once that was over, I shut down completely. I locked myself away from everybody that cared about me. The only thing I cared about was drugs. It may seem strange to people who have never been addicted, but the addiction itself is like a relationship. I needed drugs to function. In order to eat or sleep I needed drugs; to stay awake and be calm I needed drugs; to be happy and laugh I needed drugs. So I didn't need anyone else around me. I also couldn't bear to see anyone who would remind me of how I used to be. If I saw my friends I would just feel ashamed of the person I'd become. On my own, I could hide away in my private world where all that mattered was me and my drugs. It was a long fall from where I'd been as a Councillor, shadowing the police on the streets to now traipsing these same streets desperately seeking drugs.

I didn't know what to do and I wasn't letting anybody help me. Several people tried. Rob kept calling and turned up on my doorstep one day. Once I let him in, I explained what was happening to me and how dark I felt inside. He simply listened and, surprisingly, didn't tell me to stop taking the drugs. I think he knew that any attempt would have been a waste of time, and might have resulted in me shutting him out completely.

Instead he told me to call him if I needed to talk; or even if I wanted to sit and get stoned. It was better than being on my own all the time, he said. Harvey Gallagher, who I had worked with professionally through a partnership with the British Association of Adoption and Fostering, where he was Director, kept calling me. I always thought he saw me as a pompous, arrogant twit. But he kept calling and wouldn't stop until one day I answered. I broke down and told him that I was on drugs every day and didn't know what to do.

We met for a coffee. He was only the second person I had been out to see in weeks and I was paranoid that everyone around me was staring. I was high, but panicky as I was waiting for a dealer to contact me to deliver my next batch as I had run out. I always got panicky when I didn't have any drugs left. Again he just listened and I just cried, openly in the coffee shop. He didn't offer any solutions, knowing that wasn't what I needed, or could for that matter, hear. He just told me over and over again I would get through this. He would be there if I needed to talk. I remember being so touched that he cared enough to persist.

In that final week I sank to the lowest I had ever been in my life. I was smoking non-stop now from the moment I woke up until the moment I crashed; I was using about £30 to £40 worth of White Widow (strong skunk), and several hundred pounds of crack cocaine and ecstasy a day. My money was quickly running out and very soon I would not have a penny to my name. I knew that would be the end for me. I kept thinking about the life that I had and played out all the bad things that had ever been done to me or said about me. I wondered whether they had all been true and what they would all think if I died. Would they even care? Would they come to my funeral? Would Mum?

I thought of my father and told myself I couldn't live a life like his. I decided that when my drugs and money ran out the only thing for me to do was to kill myself.

I had thought a lot over the last few years about how to do it; it was always the option of last resort should things go wrong, as I always believed they would.

As I got more depressed, I would find myself standing at the tube station watching intently as the train zoomed into the platform, tempting myself to jump. I would play out the moment of jumping mentally. Would it hurt? Would people care? That was the question that always made me stop. I knew I could jump if it wasn't for the fact I still had people in my life who loved me. I knew it would tear them apart if I ended it like that. I couldn't do that to my friends and my grandparents. The only thing that stopped me killing myself was that final thought. But now I was slowly detaching myself from all that. I was closing all those relationships down. My cowardice in not wanting to take responsibility for my own death meant I chose to slowly kill myself with drugs.

It all ended and began at the very same time when I took a monumental amount of drugs. Rob had convinced me to go to a comedy night with him and some of his friends. I had drugged myself up to the eyeballs with crack cocaine, dope, ecstasy and whisky. By the time I got to the club, several hours late, I was out of my mind and sweating like crazy. After the comedy there was dancing and I took up the whole floor and danced the craziest, wildest dances of my life, making a complete fool of myself. Only Rob knew I was on drugs, and even he did not know how much.

I had spent the last few days without any sleep, living on crack cocaine and cheap ecstasy. I would get through the crack cocaine quickly and tried to lengthen the periods of taking it by smoking dope. Every hour or so, I would receive a call from my dealer asking me if I needed more and offering to bring it straight round. A drug user doesn't need persuading; after they passed on the tiny balls of solid white rocks wrapped in clingfilm and covered in saliva they would say: 'don't worry mate, we here for you, init? Just call us and we be round for you, just like that, anything you need bro.'

That night to keep my dose up I broke some rocks into several spliffs and kept going outside to smoke them. Amazingly, the bouncers never stopped me coming in, though I'm sure they must have smelt it on me. Towards the end of the night Rob gave me a hug and asked me if I was alright. I told him I was now doing crack and he looked at me, shocked. I went home that night more ashamed of myself than I ever had been and knew that I had one of two options; either get on and kill myself or get some help.

At about five in the morning, with no drugs left, I decided that the only thing for me to do was get help. I just wasn't brave enough to go through with suicide, as much as I wanted to end it. It is such a horrifying and hopeless place to be when you desperately feel like you want to die, but you can't do it. It's a complete jam with nowhere to go. Even as I walked to the hospital I thought about the passing cars and whether I could just step in front of one of them. But I didn't. The next day Rob sent me an email saying I needed to get help or he was going to make me. I already lay in a hospital bed. He pleaded with me 'as your brother, get some help.'

I didn't want to leave hospital because I was scared of what I might do if I was left by myself again. So I begged the doctors to section me so that I could be protected from myself; it was the only way I saw out of this mess. The doctors spent the day talking through the problems of the past few years. I told them about my difficult childhood and everything I have written about. Most of all, we spoke about my feelings and the rollercoaster of emotions I felt, from an extreme sense of optimism and hope to the depths of pessimism and depression. Eventually they told me they knew what was wrong with me. I had bipolar disorder. I wasn't surprised; I had feared that since learning about my real Dad and mental health problems.

At first I was relieved. Finally, I had an answer as to why I had been feeling all these things ever since I was a child. It wasn't because I was a bad person and it wasn't simply because bad things had happened to me, although that was no doubt a trigger for the disease. They explained that it wasn't my fault; the drugs had been my way of coping when things got tough but, over time, it had just got too much and I'd had a nervous breakdown. I was lucky I had come to the hospital for help, they said. Although I seriously considered sectioning myself, the doctors spent a lot of time talking me out of it. First, the argued that my experiences of institutions as a child would bring back bad memories. Secondly, the psychiatric hospital was no place to rest; there were some severely ill people there and the facilities were not those of the Priory. I would be handing over control of my life to someone else. The fact that I had sought help and not gone through with any suicide attempt was a sign that I could be treated on a voluntary basis.

An emergency team would come and visit me several times a day for the next few weeks to provide medication and support in the withdrawal phase of my drug use.

After thinking about it I realised that this was a better option than hospital; I still didn't trust myself, but knew now that my friends would not simply let me go back to what I was doing before and, with the hospital's support and medication, I could come off the drugs in the safety of a metaphorical padded room, rather than an actual one.

In the weeks that followed I stuck to my medication routine rigidly and went cold turkey on the street drugs. It was a difficult time. I had to come to terms with what I had done to my life and the people around me. As I said, when you are on drugs you become completely self-centred. So the first thing that happens when you get clean is that you are hit with the cold reality of what you have done and the natural emotions of empathy, understanding and love, previously suppressed by the drugs, return. It took a long time to get over my shame. What made it worse was how understanding my friends were; Rob read up on my disease and took the time to talk to me about what I was going through. Another friend, Stu, insisted on calling me every day to check I was okay. Rob even attended several meetings with doctors so that he could understand bipolar disorder more.

I also had to get work, quickly. I met with Kevin Williams, who was Chief Executive of The Adolescent and Children's Trust. We had a good relationship. I just told him I needed work, and, without a second's thought he opened his diary and said, 'when do you want to start?'

It was a tremendous act of compassion and one that helped me to rebuild my life over the next eighteen months. I was relieved that I finally understood what was wrong with me. But that understanding wasn't enough. It would take a while, with a few setbacks, for me to work out how to live my life, managing my disease and staying drug and alcohol free.

This time, though, I was starting on the basis of honesty about who I was, where I came from and how I wanted to live the rest of my life. I was beginning to feel free; the kind of freedom you get from within, the only kind of freedom that is worth anything. In the words of Bob Marley, I was, at long last, 'emancipating myself from mental slavery.'

Epilogue

The turning point was my breakdown. Once I'd accepted I had bi-polar disorder I began scrutinising my past intensely. Had all those people who'd blamed me for the things that went wrong with my life been right? Was I mad? It wasn't that simple. As a child, I had been depressed from a very early age. Had I not been depressed I might have been able to navigate those family troubles, as my brothers seemed to, but I can't know for sure. My time in care probably compounded the depression: which is a telling comment on the brilliance of child shrinks. The state spent almost £500,000 on caring for me, which 'care' included more psychiatric assessments that you could possibly imagine: yet no-one, in all those interviews, ever identified the causes of my depression. Contemporary children's mental health services are not much better.

Statistics claim that one child in ten has a mental health disorder and this number increases to five in ten for children in care. Many children go undiagnosed, misdiagnosed or, even if diagnosed correctly, don't get the care they need. Parents, carers, children and young people will line up to complain that getting support for mental health problems is a battle.

After my breakdown and my self-destructive period, I had to start again. One of the first things that helped me get back on track was the opportunity Kevin Williams, Chief Executive of The Adolescent and Children's Trust, gave me to get back to work. I needed constant assurances from Kevin that I was doing a good job, sometimes three or four times a day. Anyone else would have given up, but he was steadfast and stood by me.

Bi-polar disorder doesn't get sorted fast. It's not that you take the medication and, then, everything switches to normal again. The medication is a cocktail that has to be balanced correctly, as everyone's mind is different. It often takes months to get the balance right. In the meantime your body is subjected to side effects, emotional ups and downs, fatigue, weight gain and paranoia. But medication, which is something I will probably take for the rest of my life, is only one part of the treatment. 'Talking therapies', central amongst them is Cognitive Behaviour Therapy (CBT), are at least as important. CBT teaches you coping mechanisms and strategies to cope with, combat, the troubling feelings bi-polar disorder causes. Mental health services for adults are poor too. Those in crisis get good support. Afterwards, though, it is usually medication and waiting to get some sessions of counselling. Meanwhile you are left to cope pretty much by yourself, outside of support meetings with your mental health worker – every three months.

As I returned to work, took my medication and stopped the drugs and drink completely, I began to think about my future. I was torn between two lives; one that had led to my self-destruction, working all hours of the day to make a success of myself, the other taking things slowly, working and having fun. I tried the second and after about a year I realised that wasn't the life I wanted. Pushing myself might put my mental health at risk but I couldn't be happy with not trying my hardest. I wanted to live and do all the things I'd dreamed of for so long; be my own boss, change things for the better, maybe become a politician, write this book. It didn't seem fair that I couldn't do those things because of my bi-polar disorder.

I needed to be my own man. I was starting to feel depressed again and taking more time off sick.

One day, with very little time to think about it, I decided I had to risk taking my own path. I didn't want to ask myself when I was forty, 'what if' I'd had the courage.

I rarely look back now on that lost young boy shivering, clinging on to the side of Southend Pier. When I do, I often struggle to recognise him. In writing this book I had to explore that boy in detail, his despair and his loneliness. I had spent so many years with a comfortable, albeit painful, narrative about my childhood. My mother and Social Services were to blame. That version controlled my pain to some extent, but I forgot the boy in the middle of it; I forgot that the child I often talked about was me. Writing helped me rediscover that boy and claim him as myself: I also began to understand my childhood problems were so complex I couldn't continue blaming anyone.

My memories of life in care will always be harrowing. These memories will stay with me forever. My feelings about Social Services are mixed. I now know how difficult job of social workers is and how dedicated many of them are to changing children's lives. It is difficult for me to reconcile knowing that with the feeling I had of being let down, totally abandoned.

People often ask me about my Mum and whether we will ever speak again. It is a difficult subject for me, one that will probably never be resolved. It is like a cycle of grief where I go through the wheels of denial, anger, acceptance and then just when I have come to the last phase something happens, a birthday or Mother's Day, and I go back to the start of the cycle again.

I have seen my mother once, and spoken to her once, in the last ten years. Both were unexpected and both helped me on my way to a conclusion about our relationship that I can just about live with. The first time was when I was twenty-two and on my way, very happily, hand in hand with my then-girlfriend, to the theatre in London's West End. As we passed a pub I saw my mother standing outside alone. My heart was thumping, but I carried on walking. I glanced back to check it really was her and saw her looking solemnly down at the ground in thought. I wondered what she was thinking. I always imagined she thought I was manipulative, difficult and disturbed. I imagined her view hadn't changed.

Several years later, after being in hospital, I had a call from her. Nothing had changed. Mum blamed me for everything. But I chose to listen and not argue, for the first time in my life. She really didn't understand what I had gone through and I realised then that she had no clue as to what had happened to me whilst I was in care. Then she said something strange, but revealing.

'Well, Matthew, you have obviously done very well for yourself. What do you do now?'

I explained I was a senior manager for a residential care provider.

'I always knew you would do well. You've always been good at manipulating people. You were always going to get what you want,' she said, with great bitterness. Somehow it no longer hurt me. It just made me feel sorry for her. As she ranted at me I listened and spoke calmly, something I'd never tried before.

'Why are you using all these big words with me?' she

said, 'you've always been articulate, Matthew, but you can't get round me like that'. Big words? That was just how I spoke. She hadn't seen me for six years and I had done a lot of growing up in that time. She couldn't reconcile the vulnerable child who found it difficult to communicate his feelings and with the ... well, how should I describe myself? I can put two words together and cope without going into a rage. I was calm and, I believe, adult. That was the last time we ever spoke.

I felt some kind of closure. In writing about my mother I have tried to give as balanced a view of her as I could, which may not be all that balanced. But I do feel, at this time in my life, that she is not an evil person or, by any means, a failure. She is an ambitious and talented woman who I have always admired from afar. She has no qualifications but now runs her own very successful company. I know she didn't set out to be a bad mother to me.

My experiences in care (or 'uncare' or 'miscare'), made me see that in some ways, I'd been very lucky in my childhood. I didn't have to go through some of the horrifying experiences that many of the other children in care had suffered. I met some fantastic and inspirational adults in my childhood, who gave me hope and courage. In adult life, I found great mentors and friends who gave me solace, love and opportunities, allowing me to achieve. Many children and care leavers have not had such good fortune.

A close friend of mine, Stephen Sloss, who is a Director of Social Services, once said to me that there is a thin line between him or me and the beggar on the street. We could cross that line anytime, he said. I know through tempting fate, with drugs and suicide attempts, that he's quite right about this. Despite several billions a year being spent on children in care, many leave care in dire circumstances.

Most leave with few qualifications, and only 12% achieve five good GCSE grades, compared to 57% of all children. It is estimated that a third of the prison population was in care. More turn to drugs, become long term unemployed or have mental health issues; some commit suicide. So I consider myself very fortunate.

Most people assume, or at least they did until the publicity over recent years on issues like Victoria Climbie and Baby P, that children are in care because they've been bad, and deserve to be institutionalised. Mr Taylor, my teacher from junior school, used to tell my younger brother when he got into trouble 'if you carry on like that you will end up in care like your brother.'In fact, only one in ten children in care end up there because of 'bad' behaviour. Most are there through no fault of their own and have suffered severe trauma and neglect. But most people assume children in care have committed crimes or been uncontrollable, just like most of the Barking and Dagenham Councillors did when they produced the infamous dossier.

Once I thought I had proved myself professionally I unexpectedly came face to face with that prejudice again. One of my jobs was to set up new children's homes in Greater Manchester. As the local community discovered our plans to open the homes, expected to house between two and four children in each, a vile and despicable campaign of abuse began. Residents' meetings were called; politicians waded in with 'not in my back yard'; the front page of one of the many local papers that fuelled the outrage ran the headline 'House of Horrors – home for ASBO children'. Residents wrote to the paper, saying that they would be scared to let their young children out on their own with a children's home nearby.

I was incensed, and to this day I feel more anger about

that than any other thing that has happened in my life. Those parents who wrote to the paper were talking about the children that I had grown up with. They were talking about me. When I met the editor of the local paper she looked at me coldly and said 'is this supposed to change my mind?' I would like to say that the shocking NSPCC adverts that many of us turn our heads from, or the Victoria Climbie and Baby P deaths which stirred up such public anger have changed those people's minds. Sadly, I think that unlikely and it still remains difficult to open children's homes. One ten-year-old told me recently that her friends had stopped playing with her when their parents found out she was in care. She looked heartbroken.

Now, either the prejudices about my past have diminished, or else I have come to naturally ignore them. I think it's a bit of both. I'm still sensitive to being judged as a care kid, and I don't like to think that I am been done any favours because of my childhood. I had a boss once who regularly told people he had given me a job and supported me because I am a care leaver and he believed in helping this vulnerable group. I don't question his values, nor was I ungrateful for the support he gave me. However, I resented, and still do, his discussing my past with other people, who I wanted their professional respect not their pity.

Like all care leavers, I have a huge amount to offer despite – and because of – my experiences in case. I consider myself to be a professional first and a care leaver second. My difficulty has been freeing myself from the shackles of having my life run by social workers and others who assumed they knew better than me. What has made that worse is always needing the assurance of adults to feel good about myself. An example is my relationships with bosses. I colluded with those bosses who chose to either exploit this to get more out of me or saw their role as that of supporting a vulnerable person. A great mentor, friend and colleague who has over thirty years experience in child care services, Susanna Cheal, summed it up nicely by saying that the problem for care-leavers is they don't always know how to separate work from their personal feelings and problems; the system they had grown up in taught them that if someone asked you how you were, you had to give them a full and honest answer. In the real world, if someone asks you that – they don't want to know how you *really* are. To say you are suffering lumbago and depression is a good way of losing friends. For some care leavers, particularly those from more therapeutic homes such as Caldecott, find it hard to learn the masks society makes us wear.

With a bit of luck, support and hard work, I have begun laying the groundwork for a happier future. As I finished this book I started my own company, Care Matters Partnership, working to change children's lives by influencing policy and enabling its implementation at a strategic and frontline level. I was now empowered to try out my own ideas and solutions to many of the issues I had spent years of my childhood living through, and years of my adulthood battling against professionally. My company is now working with Local Authorities and is involved with many national projects run by governments and non-governmental organisations.

Being my own boss changed my life dramatically in that I was the one calling the shots and the only reassurance I needed was the success of getting things right. It doesn't matter to me now what my boss thinks because I am my own boss; I control my own destiny. Of course it matters what others think, such as my clients and staff, but I focus on delivering the best service I can and being a leader to my staff. The better I do that job, the better I feel about myself – it is no longer the other way around, where I needed *them* to feel good about me for me to do a good job.

Life is a journey and in writing this book it staggered me just how many people I had met; the children I had grown up with, the staff, the social workers, the people I had worked with from Burger King to being a Councillor and the family and friends I had made. Every one of those people and all of those experiences has contributed to my becoming the person I am today. People often say that if they could change anything about their lives, they wouldn't change a thing. I always thought that to be strange. Of course you would change things wouldn't you? Everyone has their regrets. But I now know for sure that I wouldn't change a thing. I can't imagine what my life would be like without the friends I have or the people I work with. I would be a different person and I suspect a more vulnerable one.

But whilst I wouldn't change anything, I will always remember the children that I grew up with. Some are doing okay, some very well, but a lot of them ended up either in prison, unemployed or worse. I remember those children every day in one way or another. I remember Louis most of all. Louis and I were friends at Caldecott – he was the boy who taught me about girls, and the person I could share my complaints about Caldecott with, as the place sometimes drove him every bit as crazy as it made me feel. We left at about the same time; he went his way and I went mine. Perhaps we didn't keep in touch because we just forgot about each other, but I think it was more that we were so consumed by our lives after care, and eager to keep the past buried so that we could be 'normal again'. Louis took a very different journey from mine. One night, when he was just eighteen, he ended up taking a drug overdose and died. No one thought to tell me or the other children he grew up with and it was only several years later that I learned of his death. I knew the statistics about care leavers, drugs and suicide by then but this was not just a statistic; Louis was my friend and someone I had shared many experiences with. I felt like I had let him down by not keeping in touch. I felt angry that nobody seemed to have supported him after he left Caldecott. But most of all I felt angry that the very people Louis grown up with didn't get the opportunity to say goodbye. I think about him every day, and it is always a stark reminder of why I do the work I do.

Oscar Wilde wrote 'To love oneself is the beginning of a lifelong romance': an inspirational notion, but a difficult one to live by. Throughout my life, I had struggled to love myself. In the absence of the only unconditional love available to a person, that of their parents or children, I desperately searched for it, everywhere I could. I begged girlfriends, pleaded with friends and colleagues and harangued bosses for it. Just like my addiction to drugs, where I lived for the next high, I lived for the next dose of reassurance or morsel of love and attention. In the last few years I had a breakthrough, the most powerful one of my life. I was searching for something that wasn't available. The only people I could get that unconditional love I craved didn't want to, or couldn't, give it to me.

My Dad was now dead and he would never say what I had always longed to hear; *I love you son.* My Mum was never going to turn up and say the words I had dreamt about; *I am proud of you son.* And that wasn't my fault. Once I came to that conclusion my life began to change for the better. I became an easier person to be with, because

I was easier within myself. I became a much more supportive and giving friend and colleague; because I was supporting myself. But most importantly I could feel proud of myself. I no longer needed to seek that unconditional love. I was happy enough with the love and support that was around from my friends and colleagues.

Almost all of the time now, I love myself. And there's no 'if' about it.

A Note on Bipolar Disorder

Bipolar disorder, previously known as manic depression, is a psychiatric diagnosis referring to what might be described as an 'extreme emotional see-saw.' Bipolar patients experience periods of euphoria often compared in clinical literature to amphetamine or cocaine intoxication. In this euphoric state, bipolar patients typically suffer from impaired judgement that can manifest in spending sprees, promiscuity, enhanced productivity, sleeplessness and, in the most extreme cases, psychosis and hallucinations.

This euphoria or *hypomania* alternates, in bipolar patients, with pronounced and often life-threatening depressions, in which suicide attempts are common. Some patients experience periods of relatively 'normal' mood between manic and depressive states, while others alternate constantly between euphoria and depression – this latter is known as 'rapid cycling'. Considered to be one of the best-documented of psychiatric diagnoses, bipolar disorder is quite common, said by statistics to afflict, for example 1–1.5% of the adult population in the United States. It generally manifests in late adolescence or early adulthood.

A variety of drugs are used to treat bipolar disorder – famously, lithium carbonate was the treatment of preference for generations, though its toxicity and side-effects led many patients to refuse to take it. A new generation of drugs used in treatment of bipolar disorder are said to be less toxic, and chemical therapies are generally used in conjunction with psychotherapy of various kinds.

Although bipolar disorder can in many ways be crippling, high-achieving bipolar patients are not by any means uncommon – indeed, the euphoric phase of hypomania can lead to extraordinary, almost superhuman accomplishments on the part of some bipolar patients. Winston Churchill is one example of a bipolar high achiever, and others include Kurt Cobain, Charles Baudelaire, and Kay Redfield Jamison, a clinical psychologist and Professor of Psychiatry at the Johns Hopkins University School of Medicine. Professor Jamison wrote of her own bipolar disorder in her memoir *An Unquiet Mind* (1995), and claimed that a connection exists between bipolar disorder and artistic creativity in her 1993 book, *Touched with Fire*. Perhaps the best-known study of bipolar disorder by a psychologist in the UK is *Breakdown* (1976, 1995), by the late Professor Stuart Sutherland, who developed bipolar disorder in his forties, and wrote a singularly engaging and likeable memoir on the subject.

While many treatments are available, as with all psychiatric measures, they are far from reliable in each individual case, and finding the right balance of medications for a given patient can be a difficult and lengthy business. Finally, there is no such thing as a 'cure' for bipolar disorder – a condition that Matt Huggins and many others will always have to live with.

The author is donating part of the royalties from this book to the Mental Health charity MIND

Thanks

I always used to read the author's 'thank you' page and feel a bit like I was reading a Kate Winslet Oscar acceptance speech. I do not apologise to the reader for doing the same; the journey through this book has been my life and I am who I am because of the people who helped me along the way. Capturing all these people would be impossible in this book – and it is no reflection on their significance on me and my journey if I have not been able to include them.

A lot of people ask me how I survived given my background. I can only answer that it was in no small part due to my grandparents. They adopted my mother without a second thought, when she was only a few months old, giving her a better chance in life. They never gave up on her. To all intents and purposes they are my parents and I thank them for the love and grounding they have given me. I hope they know just how much I love them.

I want to thank Julia Ross, her integrity, powerful intellect and passion. She was immensely helpful in writing the book. Without her support in my late teens, I might not have had much hope of developing my potential – whatever that might be.

I would like to thank the many others who gave me the encouragement to believe in myself when others chose to disregard me – Peter Hodgeson, Jonathan Stanley, Valerie

Lyon-Wall, Bryony, my key workers at Caldecott (they know who they are!), Rev Gaylor and KHAOS, to name a few. I would like to thank the Caldecott Foundation, for all its faults at the time of me growing up there, it still gave me the grounding and support I needed to make a go of it later in life.

Maggie Mulverhill deserves a special thanks for always choosing to see the best in me as do Hugh Pelham and Kevin Williams. The people who have opened up doors to me and taught me immensely – Mike Reid, Steve Power, Andrew Winton, Alex Hilton, Keesup Choe, Martin Evans, Dame Denise Platt, Ryan Robson and Stephen and Linda Sloss. And the people who gave me political inspiration and unfettered support – Hilton Dawson, Cameron Geddes, Bryan Osborne, Alan Thomas, Margaret Hodge MP, Tim Loughton MP and all my old ward colleagues from Goresbrook, Barking.

My journey would not have been completed had it not been the steadfast support of my friends. Rob (who was enormously helpful in early edits of this book), Stu, Gareth, Candy, Nat and Pete – we have shared our successes and our crises and I am a better man because of them. Thank you to my surrogate families, of which I have many, but in particular Nicole, Lucienne, Gareth and Sam who allowed me to be part of their life throughout my later childhood and to Stu's parents, Bonnie and Alan; they treat me like their son and I feel able to achieve more because of that (and thank you for allowing me to live with you while I finished this book late into the night with Patch by my side).

I thank the Publisher, Psychology News Press, and David Cohen, who delicately took me through the editing process, always aware of the sensitivities of both an author and someone sharing the most intimate parts of their life. Both me and my staff have enjoyed working with David immensely and every conversation has brought new knowledge and understanding to my mind.

A big thank you to my staff at Care Matters Partnership – Katie, Dean, Kate, Lizzie, Narmin, Cameron – and my business partner and friend Harvey Gallagher. Only through your dreams, passion and hard work are we beginning to make waves. And to Susanna Cheal OBE, my Chair, friend and mentor – who has supported me from day one of my professional career at the age of 19. Never has someone taught me so much and in such an empowering way.

Lastly a mention to all the children I grew up with who had some of the most harrowing and traumatic experiences. Thank you for sharing parts of your childhood with me; I will always remember where I came from and each and every one of you, your stories, your dreams, your pain – will remain forever with me.